P9-DHC-111

THE CORRESPONDENCE OF SHELBY FOOTE & WALKER PERCY

THE CORRESPONDENCE OF

SHELBY

FOOTE &

WALKER

PERCY

EDITED BY

JAY TOLSON

A DOUBLETAKE BOOK

PUBLISHED BY THE CENTER FOR DOCUMENTARY STUDIES

IN ASSOCIATION WITH W. W. NORTON & COMPANY

NEW YORK • LONDON

First published as a Norton paperback 1998
This book is composed in Sabon.
Manufacturing by Maple Vail
Book design by Bonnie Campbell
Typesetting by The Marathon Group, Inc.
Photo research by Julie Stovall
Cover photograph reprinted courtesy of Washington County Library System

The following letters by Walker Percy first appeared in other publications as
"Shakespeare Had It Easy" [October 19, 1973] in *The New Yorker* (June 24 &
July 1, 1996), and "How to Explain Some Heretofore Unexplainable Things"
[September 10, 1980] in *DoubleTake* magazine (Fall 1996).

Library of Congress Cataloging-in-Publication Data
Foote, Shelby.
The correspondence of Shelby Foote and Walker Percy / edited by Jay Tolson.
   p. cm.
"A DoubleTake book."
   1. Foote, Shelby—Correspondence. 2. Percy, Walker, date—Correspondence.
3. Novelists, American—20th century—Correspondence. 4. Southern States—
Intellectual life—20th century. 5. Historians—United States—Correspondence.
I. Percy, Walker, date. II. Tolson, Jay. III. Title.
PS3511.O348Z468   1996
96-22222
813'.54—dc20
ISBN 0-393-04031-3
ISBN 0-393-31768-4 PBK.

W. W. Norton & Company, Inc.
500 Fifth Avenue, New York, New York 10110
http://www.wwnorton.com
W. W. Norton & Company Ltd.
10 Coptic Street, London WC1A 1PU

1 2 3 4 5 6 7 8 9 0

DoubleTake Books & Magazine publish the works of writers and photographers who seek
to render the world as it is and as it might be, artists who recognize the power of narrative
to communicate, reveal, and transform. These publications have been made possible by the
generous support of the Lyndhurst Foundation.

DoubleTake
Center for Documentary Studies at Duke University
1317 West Pettigrew Street
Durham, North Carolina 27705
http://www.duke.edu/doubletake/

To order books, call W. W. Norton at 1-800-233-4830.

To subscribe to *DoubleTake* magazine, call 1-800-234-0981, extension 5600.

For Ben
a lesson in friendship

Contents

Introduction   1

Master to Apprentice   11

Adversities and New Directions   75

Recognition   117

The "Third Half" of Life   187

Last Things   281

THE CORRESPONDENCE OF SHELBY FOOTE *&* WALKER PERCY

Introduction

"This is a strange business," Walker Percy observed in a letter to his oldest friend, Shelby Foote, in early 1971. The business at hand was a novel, the earliest draft of what would become *Lancelot* (1977), and it was giving him a devil of a time. But the lament also hinted at something larger—at the peculiar workings of fate that had brought him, a would-be physician thwarted by tuberculosis, to the strange shoals of literary practice. Although Percy had already proved his mettle in three previous novels, including the National Book Award–winning *Moviegoer* (1961), the challenge of writing fiction seemed to grow greater with each successive book.

Percy knew Foote would understand without elaboration. Foote, too, had had his desperate moments with the craft. After writing five novels in fairly rapid order, he had come up against a block so formidable that he had abandoned fiction and turned to work on what he at first thought would be a short history of the Civil War. Twenty years and almost a million-and-a-half words later, Foote completed a three-volume narrative history that many critics immediately recognized as a modern classic.

Percy knew Foote would understand him for a more personal reason as well: the bond between them was intimate, almost fraternal. Though Percy had two brothers by blood and remained close to both of them throughout his life, Foote was his brother in art, his secret sharer, and with Foote, Percy knew, he could communicate in something close to shorthand.

"You, for example, know exactly what I am talking about," Percy joked in early 1979, "because you are a writer and because we have known each other forever—and because we are Southern?"

Not quite forever, but they had known each other since the summer of 1930, when Percy, then fourteen, came with his mother and two brothers to Greenville, Mississippi, to spend what they thought would be no more than a few weeks in the rambling three-story house of their cousin William Alexander Percy. A remarkable man in almost every respect—a lawyer and planter, a decorated World War I veteran, a poet and author of the incomparable memoir *Lanterns on the Levee*—Uncle Will, as the boys called him, would soon become more than their cousin and host. Indeed, after the death of their mother in a bizarre automobile accident in the spring of 1932, he would become their surrogate and adoptive father, and possibly the greatest single influence on their lives—and on Shelby Foote's life as well.

Shortly before his relatives arrived for their visit, Will Percy spotted Foote in the swimming pool at the Greenville Country Club. Foote, then thirteen, never forgot the moment: "He'd been playing golf—he was a dreadful golfer, but he liked to play occasionally in those days—[and] he came over and said, 'Some kinsmen of mine are coming here to spend the summer with me. There are three boys in the group and the two older boys are about your age. I hope you'll come over to the house often and help them enjoy themselves while they're here.'"

Foote didn't have to be asked twice. Uncle Will's house was possibly the most interesting house in Mississippi, if not the entire South. As well as sheltering Percy himself, it was a mandatory stop on the itinerary of poets, novelists, journalists, and any other notables touring the region. Anyone with a curious mind would have jumped at the chance to spend time in Will Percy's house, and Foote was a bright, bookish boy who had lost his father at the age of five and been raised—too indulgently, some Greenvillians thought—by his mother and his aunts. Will Percy, a connoisseur of intelligence, recognized the spark in young Foote and even thought he resembled the young Marcel Proust.

But there might have been a further reason for Percy's thinking that Foote would make a good companion for his "kinsmen": the shared experience of loss. The Percy boys, like Foote, had lost their father. It had happened the previous summer, when LeRoy Percy, a prominent attorney in Birmingham, Alabama, had taken his life after a long bout with depression. After the fatal shotgun blast in the attic, the boys and their mother, Martha Susan Percy, spent most of the following year in Athens, Georgia, in the house of Martha Susan's mother, until they were invited to visit Uncle Will.

Uncle Will's intuition about Foote and his young cousins proved sound. The friendship between Shelby and Walker took. Foote also became friends with the other two Percy brothers, Roy and Phin, respectively a year and three years younger than Walker, but there was something special about the friendship between Shelby and Walker. Not exactly loners, they were both unusually independent in their ways. More observers than participants, they were the kind who hang back in crowds, who look on rather than mingle (and, fittingly, Walker became the gossip columnist—"The Man in the Moon"—for his high school newspaper, *The Pica*). Readers, avid music fans, they even shared the same hobby: the building of model airplanes. Both were witty, prematurely cynical, irreverent, and generally attuned to each other's humor. Not that there weren't points of difference and conflict. Foote had a way of getting under Percy's skin—or just about anybody's, for that matter—but their natures were for the most part compatible and in some ways engagingly complementary. In what amounted to an almost too-perfect precursor of their aesthetic differences—Foote the art-for-art's-sake man, Percy the literary moralist—Foote preferred the kind of model airplanes that were built to be looked at, while Percy liked the ones that were built to fly.

Foote, born on November 17, 1916, was almost six months younger than Percy, who was born on May 28, 1916. A year behind Percy in Greenville High School at first, he fell back another year before graduating. Like Percy, he avoided sports and concentrated most of his extracurricular energy on the school newspaper, serving as its editor and leading it to first place in a national competition for overall excellence. Percy, after graduation, went on to the University of North Carolina, where he majored in chemistry, wrote essays and book reviews for the *Carolina Magazine*, and spent much of his time on the porch of the SAE fraternity house observing the passing scene. Foote set his sights on following Percy to Chapel Hill but almost lost the chance when the high school principal, much put out by Foote's insubordination and irreverence (he was caught reading Joyce's scandalous *Ulysses* in the newspaper room during PE period, among other acts of defiance), sent the university a scathing evaluation. Though rejected for admission, Foote showed up at the university registrar's office on opening day and argued his way in.

Foote's progress through college proved to be almost as irregular as the means by which he entered. Since earning a degree ranked low among his priorities, he more or less set his own curriculum, attending classes he liked—mainly literature and history—and staying away from those that bored him. The stacks of books in the Wilson Library provided his steadiest intellectual pleasure, and he also began to exercise his fledgling literary talent in stories that he contributed to the *Carolina Magazine*.

Percy and Foote stayed close friends during their two overlapping years, even though Foote was turned down by Percy's fraternity, SAE, because of his partly Jewish background. (Foote's maternal grandfather, a Vienna-born Jew, had come to America and made his way to the Delta, eventually marrying the daughter of a plantation owner for whom he worked as an accountant.) The two friends went on dates together, made the ritual trips to Durham in search of drink and women, and even journeyed to New York City during one of their semester breaks. Though Percy was heading in the direction of science and medicine, literature remained one of the friends' stronger bonds, and Foote never tired of recommending authors—Mann, Dostoyevsky, Faulkner, and, above all, Proust.

Percy required little pushing. He admired many of the same authors, with the notable exception of Proust, whom he considered a fussy snob. And much earlier than Foote, he discovered the perils of falling too much under the spell of Faulkner. Imitating Faulkner's all-too-distinctive prose style on his freshman English placement test, Percy had found himself assigned to the remedial section.

In the spring of 1937, at the end of Percy's four undergraduate years and Foote's two, the two Greenvillians again parted company, with Percy entering Columbia University's College of Physicians and Surgeons in New York and Foote returning to Greenville to take a series of odds jobs while working on a novel. In early 1939, he sent a draft of that novel—what would eventually be published as *Tournament*—to Alfred A. Knopf. Although the editors were impressed by his talent, they urged him to put the novel aside and work on something a little more marketable. Foote, however, was busy with other matters. Following Hitler's progress, he had enlisted in the National Guard, and soon his division, the 31st "Dixie" Division, was mobilized for national service.

As Foote trained to become an artillery officer, eventually being sent to Northern Ireland to prepare for the D-Day invasion, Percy made his way through medical school with minimal effort. (His classmates recall that he seemed to read more novels than medical textbooks.) But in another way, these were not easy years: the melancholia that had stalked his father and grandfather was beginning to haunt him as well, and three years of psychoanalysis, most of them with a female analyst, did little to allay the problem. To compound matters, his psychological uncertainties now seemed to merge with growing doubts about his fitness as a doctor.

It was a peculiar pass to have come to. Though Percy knew he was good at medicine—particularly pathology, his chosen specialty—he realized even before he began his internship at New York City's Bellevue Hospital that medicine was at best a "sloppy science." More disturbing, his once-boundless faith in science was beginning to crumble. The adolescent who had believed that science would one day explain everything—and, just as important, provide an answer to his own existential bafflement—was now beginning to see that it was a form of knowledge with distinct limitations.

How Percy would have fared in medicine no one can say, because halfway through his first year of internship, he and three other interns on the pathology rotation came down with pulmonary tuberculosis. As World War II got underway, Percy found himself a patient in Bellevue Hospital. Meanwhile, his brother Roy began flight training, while his other brother Phin, an Annapolis graduate, was only a stone's throw away, racing up and down the East River in PT boats, preparing for duty in the Pacific.

Soon Percy was monitoring the progress of the war from Trudeau Sanatorium in Saranac, New York, where he underwent the classic cure and spent most of his days on his back, reading books and listening to the radio. In 1944, he was back in New York City, teaching pathology at Columbia and unexpectedly reunited with Foote. Foote himself was far from happy about his premature return to the States: he had been discharged from the army on a silly technicality after driving a jeep slightly over the fifty-mile limit to visit his girlfriend, Tess Lavery, in Belfast. Robbed of his chance to be part of the invasion force, Foote worked briefly for the Associated Press, married his Irish fiancée (with Percy standing as best man), and then enlisted in the Marines in the hope of seeing combat before the war ended.

But Foote was disappointed in that hope as well. Slated for the Pacific after completing combat intelligence training, he made it only as far as the West Coast when the Japanese surrendered. Crestfallen, he returned to Greenville with his new bride and took a job at the local radio station while reworking parts of his unpublished novel into stories. Foote's renewed literary efforts eventually proved successful—he sold several pieces to the *Saturday Evening Post*—but his marriage fared less well. He and Tess Lavery divorced in 1946, but Foote at least had the consolation of friends, including Percy, who had returned to Greenville after a short sojourn in a TB sanatorium in Connecticut.

The relapse had left Percy with even graver doubts about his future in medicine. Living in the garage apartment behind Uncle Will's house, which Roy had inherited after Uncle Will's death in 1942, Percy reached a kind of dead end, emotionally and spiritually. He read, played with his young nephew, helped build a canoe, and dated various women, none seriously. In fact, the one woman he most wanted to see—Mary Bernice Townsend, whom he had met during the summer between medical school and his internship—was living elsewhere, attending Millsaps College in Jackson, Mississippi, and then moving to New Orleans to work for a physician. Mary Townsend—or "Bunt," as she was called—was the only woman Percy had ever felt truly at ease with, but his physical and psychological conditions did not bode well, and he feared making a commitment to another person when he was so uncertain about his own prospects.

Out of desperation as much as anything, Percy traveled west, accompanied by Foote on the journey, and tried to start a life in Santa Fe, New Mexico. But three months in the land of "pure possibility," where he interviewed for a couple of medical positions and spent most of his time riding a spirited quarterhorse named El Capitan, made him realize that there was no simple way of escaping the ghosts of the past, much less himself. In something close to a revelation, he decided to return to the South, marry Bunt (if she would take him), and then—most surprising of all to those who knew him—prepare to enter the Catholic Church. Thoughts of this last step had been on his mind for some time. In fact, when he mentioned it to Foote the day after they arrived in Santa Fe, Foote had warned him that his was "a mind in full intellectual retreat."

Percy followed through on all his resolutions, marrying Bunt on November 6, 1946, and entering the Catholic Church on December 13, 1947. Between those dates, the young couple lived for several months in Sewanee, Tennessee, and then returned to New Orleans, the site of their marriage, to receive instruction leading to provisional baptism. In Sewanee, Percy began to follow through on another resolution he had made out west: he started to write. The going was slow at first, but he stuck to it, supported in his labors by a generous inheritance from Uncle Will. Throughout his months in Sewanee and New Orleans the pages of a manuscript steadily mounted, while frequent visits from Foote kept Percy abreast of his friend's own literary progress, first with stories and then, in 1948, with the sale of a much-reworked *Tournament*.

Foote had other news, too, at the end of 1948: he had stepped up to the altar for a second time, taking Marguerite (Peggy) Dessommes of Memphis, Tennessee, to be his lawfully wedded wife. This marriage would last only four years, but those years would produce both a child—Margaret—and an outpouring of fiction, including, in addition to *Tournament* (1949), the novels *Follow Me Down* (1950), *Love in a Dry Season* (1951), and *Shiloh* (1952).

It was at the beginning of this period that Percy began saving his friend's letters, and it is easy to see why. The letters, almost without exception, are epistolary gems—detailed and carefully written, full of reflections on life and art, verging often on the didactic but never lacking in humor or irony or the playfulness of a mind just discovering its own powers. Responding to Percy's fledgling literary efforts, Foote felt free to counsel his friend on every aspect of the craft, from general suggestions about plot to detailed analyses of prose rhythm. The lessons Foote imparted were consistently those of High Modernism, and the pronouncements of Flaubert, Joyce, and Proust echo in many of his prescriptions. There were strong warnings in these early letters, too. Percy's religion and his moralizing tendencies were threatening to interfere with his development as an artist, Foote cautioned. Without care, he would end up writing "Sunday school tracts." There were also warnings about pernicious influences—particularly those of Caroline Gordon and Allen Tate. (Percy, to Foote's dismay, had asked Gordon to evaluate and criticize his first apprentice novel, *The Charterhouse*.)

Percy, of course, responded to these letters with his own, but Foote did not begin to save his friend's correspondence until 1970. Consequently, what we have until that year (with one exception, a 1967 letter from Percy) is more monologue than dialogue, a conversation in which the words of one interlocuter can only be inferred. Fortunately, Foote's prolific correspondence holds a fairly full mirror to the developments in Percy's life (a mirror whose cracks and insufficiencies I will attempt to compensate for in the notes). Reflected in these letters are intimate details about Percy's private and family struggles as well as his literary progress, which included not only two unpublished novels leading to his first published book, *The Moviegoer*, but also a steady stream of essays on subjects ranging from philosophy and linguistics to Southern culture and race relations.

When we are finally treated to the full dialogue beginning in 1970, we realize how lively the conversations had always been. Percy's letters are strikingly different from his friend's: generally shorter, they are more from the hip and far less composed. But what they lack in nineteenth-century leisureliness, texture, and composition, they more than make up for in trenchant, often self-lacerating wit and in quick revelations of character. Many of Percy's letters—perhaps most of them—are *cris de coeur* from a man who knew that the heart is an unreliable organ. But if Percy realized that the heart is whiny, demanding, easily chagrined, and prone to exaggeration, he also knew that it must be listened to, and his letters to Foote, apart from conveying the odd bits of news, were primarily a means of giving his heart a hearing. Making contact was their ultimate object, and the surprise is in how often they succeed.

In their own more elaborate way, Foote's letters aimed for the same goal—and the best proof of their success is the sixty-year friendship that they helped to sustain, despite geographical separation and the inevitable differences that can arise between even the best of friends. The great gift of these letters to us, the eavesdropping readers, is that we end them understanding these two men almost as well as they understood each other.

A few notes on the letters themselves: In almost all cases, except where fidelity would have led to confusion, I have let peculiarities of orthography and punctuation stand. They are essential to the style of the respective correspondents, and reflective of the moments in which they were written. I have tried not to intrude too busily with notes, intervening only when I thought most readers would be baffled by obscure or elliptical references. In addition to clarifying matters, many of the notes are intended to keep readers abreast of major developments in the writers' lives, particularly Percy's during the 1948–70 period.

With the exception of a few short notes and postcards, almost all of Percy's side of the correspondence is included in this volume. For reasons of space and balance, however, it was necessary to prune Foote's side, and even then, his letters still far outnumber Percy's. The complete correspondence of both writers is deposited in the Southern Historical Collection at the University of North Carolina at Chapel Hill.

The editor is grateful to Shelby Foote and Mary Bernice Percy, without whose assistance and cooperation this volume would have been impossible.

Roy Percy, Walker Percy, and Shelby Foote. *Courtesy of Washington County Library System.*

ONE

Master to Apprentice

May Day, 48

DEAR WALKER

I am glad to hear that Bunt is doing well and that you are acquiring a new home.[1] My first sight of the drawing (the one labeled "Before") was a shock: I recognized Brinkwood[2] immediately, but "Dear God," I thought, "theyve moved the chimney!"

The remodeling project looks good; it could be fun, too. But I'm thinking that house will sit there in all its pristine objectionableness—including the gingerbread trim—until old age collapses it, with you and Bunt inside warming your aged toes by the fire and turning the pages of an album containing pictures of the fifteen or twenty children you will have had by then.

Still no word on a single manuscript. Ive got the twitches and jumps

---

1. The house into which Walker and Bunt Percy and their newly adopted daughter Mary Pratt (b. July 25, 1947) moved in June 1948. It was located about four miles east of the center of Covington, Louisiana, then a town of about six thousand souls. Covington at this time was about an hour's drive from New Orleans.

2. A house in Sewanee, Tennessee, owned by William Alexander Percy (Walker's cousin and adoptive father) and Will Percy's friend and fellow Sewanee graduate Huger Jervey. Walker Percy and Bunt lived in Brinkwood for several months after they were married.

something awful, wondering what is cooking: it's been two months now. The current work goes slowly as a result of this nervousness. There is no telling how long it may continue, either: the Atlantic kept Shiloh four months before rejecting it—Lord knows what theyll do with the Fever Child,[3] which is infinitely more complex.

The current novel (Vortex)[4] has taken on implications I never dreamed of when I first conceived the plot—nothing less than the Fall of Man; entails a complete analysis of the sense of guilt in a man's soul, from all angles as well as from inside it. I hope I am not pitching it in too intense a key. The book is so closely knit (contrapuntal) that I am having to write it complete in first draft just to get it straight in my own mind. The story itself is simple and straightforward: it's the implications that give it its size.

First I'll tell you the frame. A tenant farmer from down on the Lake takes a girl to an island, lives alone with her in a deserted shack, abandoning his wife and three daughters. The only other people on the island are a fisherwoman and her deaf-and-dumb son. In the course of time (about two weeks) remorse sets in; he tells the girl he has to go back to his wife. She says no, and whats more if he goes she will follow him and tell his wife where he has been. So he drowns her in the lake and returns to his wife.

Three days later the fisherwoman finds the body: it came up with the concrete slabs he had wired to its neck: but she doesnt recognize her until the coroner takes a tiny anklet off its leg. They still dont know who the man was or where he had gone (he had given a false name). But Dummy, the fisherwoman's son, saw his name and address in the Bible the man brought with him; Dummy informs the sheriff, because he had fallen in love with the dead girl. The sheriff goes down to the lake and arrests him, brings him back to Bristol and locks him up.

He is tried in the September term; his lawyer proves insanity, and he gets life at Parchman.

Thats all there is to it. Basicly it is the story of Imogene Smothers and Floyd Myers, which came out in a trial held here in 1941. But wait.

---

3. "Child by Fever," first written as a short story, eventually appeared as part of *Jordan County* (1954).

4. The early working title of *Follow Me Down* (1950).

Here is the way I have cast it for my purposes:

I — I — the bailiff (trial scene)

2

3 — II — a news reporter (finding of body)

4 — III — the dummy (informing of sheriff)

5

6 — IV — the murderer (how he met & killed her)

7

8 — V — the murdered (life seen backward)

9

10 — VI — the murderer's wife (his background)

11

12 — VII — the fisherwoman (life on island)

13

14 — VIII — the lawyer (defense plea; man after crime)

15 — IX — the turnkey (jail scene)

Each of the Arabic numerals is a 7000-word Section; each of the Roman numerals is a narrator. . . . The first Section is a prolog, giving the story in small as it came out at the trial; the final Section sends him off the pen. Between these two Sections, the story is told from beginning to end. It gives me every chance to do the things I do best.

Many of the things that would require a great deal of explaining in a thirdperson narrative are explained by the characters themselves. For instance, why did the girl insist that she would follow him, when she must have known he would kill her for threatening it? This is told in her Section (8). What ails this man anyhow? The real answer doesnt come until his wife (in Sections 9, 10, 11) tells the story of his life. He himself (in Secs 5, 6, 7) has already told how he got involved, what his reactions were at the beginning and during the murder. The story, you see, has facets, like a diamond; has themes, like a piece of music; gives me room to really show what I can do, and yet makes for a peculiar kind of economy which I like. . . . The form makes it possible to heighten interest by the use of nine different styles — some straight narrative (Sections 2–3, for instance, are journalistic) as well as something resembling poetry (Section 8, a flashback as she goes down under the water, seeing the surface pale above her) and also some highly experimental writing (Section 4, by the deaf-and-dumb boy). Some are in the vernacular (1, 15 especially); some almost formal (13, 14: the lawyer); and some almost insane (5, 6, 7).

I can see, however, that all this will mean nothing to you. I look forward to telling you about it. I have finished the first five Sections in first-draft, and expect to complete the entire first draft by the end of summer. Then I will be able to see it whole; will be able to add and take away for the sake of total effect. God willing, I will finish it early next year.

Sorry I have no carbon of Child by Fever to send: Chambrun[5] has them both. Looking back on it now, I think even more highly of it than I did while I was writing it. It has faults: I know that: but the good things more than smother them, I think. Anyway, I did what I set out to do: which is all I ask of anything I write. I hope it is accepted, of course, and I believe it will be: but that has nothing to do with it, nothing at all. My time is coming: No writer ever developed without hard work and disappointment, and I am willing to have my share of both. I even realize I may never have anything else—there have been plenty of such artists, and some of them have been the very best.

If you are serious about wanting to write fiction you had better get to work. I honestly dont think it can be done without a background of four or five years of apprenticeship (probably more). Sit down with pen and paper and describe anything at all: do it again and again—either an object or an action—until you satisfy yourself. Then try telling a story that has a beginning, middle, and end. Then tear it up and do it over, and over, and over. Then try another one, and another one, and another one. Finally you may begin to feel like tackling something with strength to it (I hope you wont have felt up to any such thing before this, for if you have, youll have made a botch of it). . . . But the most heart-breaking thing about it is: the better you get, the harder youll have to work—because your standards will rise with your ability. I mentioned "work"—it's the wrong word: because if youre serious, the whole creative process is attended with pleasure in a form which very few people ever know. Putting two words together in a sequence that pleases you, really *pleases* you, brings a satisfaction which must be kin

---

5. Jacques Chambrun, Foote's literary agent.

to what a businessman feels when he manages a sharp transaction—something like that, but on a higher plane because the businessman must know that soon he will have spent the dollars he made; but those two words which the writer set together have produced an effect which will never die as long as men can read with understanding.

So much for execution. I cant even begin to speak of conception—it comes from God.

Give my best wishes, and Peggy's[6] too.

Shelby

2 July 48

DEAR WALKER

Chambrun sold Shiloh to Blue Book (!) for $500, after peddling it all over New York and having it admired but not accepted. I just got word this morning by telegraph.

Now I want to talk finances—something I can never do when we're face to face. I owe $300 to the bank, borrowed to complete payments on the car and go to New York and pay out small bills that accrued. I have to pay that by the first of September. That leaves $150 (the $50 agent fee being deducted). $50 will have to be held back for taxes, state and federal. That leaves $100. Now—I have felt that it would be wrong to pay you your $500 piecemeal: in a chunk it would really mean something to you, but sent $50 or $75 at a time it would dribble through your fingers, and when it was paid up youd feel more or less as if youd got nothing.

However, I think probably buying this house has strapped you. Youve been as backward as I have in discussing this debt. Tell me: do you want it in installments or do you want me to save up till I can send it to you in one piece, or do you really need it badly immediately—in which case I can sell the car. Let me know.

I'm writing my Bart book,[7] going strong. It's going to be good, good, good: really good! I'm getting $125 a month from Dial on contract.

_____

6. Marguerite Dessommes, Foote's second wife.

7. *Tournament* (1949), Foote's first novel, a version of which he wrote before World War II, and which he was now in the process of revising.

I'm going to give this letter time to reach you; then I'm going to phone and we'll talk it over.

Regards
Shelby

30 Jul 48
DEAR WALKER

Your letter on the Child came today. Both your objections are indeed valid. I intended Hector to be a cipher (which he is) but I intended him to be a tragic cipher (which he is not). And your second objection—too much blood and cunt—is even righter. However, behind that there is also an idea which did not come off. The idea was that this poor spook, who never accomplished anything, was nevertheless surrounded by blood and thunder. The two were intended to be contrapuntal, pointing each other up. I see now that I failed at both ends and resultantly in the middle too. But I still believe the conception was right. Execution, however: thats another matter.

I feel the writing went well: the individual scenes came off more or less effectively; the style suited the subject. But—like most writers, alas, and especially young ones—I tend to overwrite when I reach an analitical crisis. For instance, the high point in the book—the point at which it was connected with all life everywhere—was the three- or four-page description of Bristol in 1910 (telephones, movies, autos, etc). This made the story a tragedy, showing the essential franticness of modern life—or should have but didn't because I overwrote it: I hid behind fine words. Now doubtless I'll learn better, but it will take time.

I hope you realize there was no prurience or terribilita put in for the sake of shocking the bourgeois. It all had its purpose as part of the whole. Your objection to the drummer and the nightclerk as types is one I dont agree with all the way. Types can be useful. Naturally no man has that little to him, but in a book they can be used to point up the main characters. If you take away an author's right to be superficial at times, youll find he will pitch his narrative on too high a key; he'll be as precious as Pater or as long-winded as Wolfe. Flaubert's Homais (the chemist in Bovary, you remember) is an example of a successful type. Mind you, I think the "types" should be well done as such; I'm a long way from claiming that the drummer and the clerk measure up to Homais.

Anyway I'm learning all the time, and I learned as much from Child by Fever as I have from anything.

The Bart book, which I'm writing now, is as different as a book can be and yet be by the same writer. It has none of the horribleness that surrounded Hector, and Bart is far from a cipher. It's going well, very strong, and faster than anything Ive done. (I did 200 pages of first draft during this month that ends tomorrow—about twice my normal rate.) You read the early version a few years ago in NY; all I'm doing is rewriting that draft— of course with some scenes taken out and some others added. Essentially it's what you read rewritten, simplified so that the story comes out better. It's a good book in lots of ways, and if I do it justice, I think it may even be a fine book. However, thats something I'm no judge of, as I well know. I always think everything I do is a miracle of organization and exposition—at least while I'm writing it or typing it for the printer; later on it's a different matter. All art is an organization of experience, whatever the form, and in that sense all the arts are kin: what form an artist chooses to demonstrate his soul, to parade his intelligence, is accidental and even unimportant. Child by Fever, for instance, might have been a string quartet—and a damn bad one, too.

Peggy has gone up to Memphis to spend three weeks with her family and keep some dental appointments. I'm baching (put a t in that for me; otherwise I might say I'm mozarting, which as a matter of fact I am). Have you looked into the long-playing record idea I was telling you about?

Give my best to Bunt and the young one, and hurry up and get squared away down there. I want to come see you.

It's hot as blazes here: otherwise everything's fine.

Regards
Shelby

Greenville, 7 Oct 49
WALKER

Got back Tuesday from Virginia: enjoyed the trip very much. Thats a mighty pretty country this time of year. Sunday we drove to Fredericksburg, went over the battlefield—too leafy now to see it as it was, but very impressive indeed: I could do a job on that fight, but I'll stick to the Western theater: Vicksburg and Brice's Crossroads are on my list, as you know.

Phin[8] couldnt be better: has found a nery nice room and has made arrangements to eat (of all places) in the SAE house. He's having to work harder than ever before in his life: it's terribly hard, he says—almost as bad as medicine. He is really interested, and though he cant say for sure, he thinks he'll stay with it. A friend of your father's (Underwood, I believe) is up there and Phin goes over for dinner occasionally. He has been amazed to discover, for instance, that his father made a habit of speaking to a jury in the vernacular—used "aint" and so forth, when he drew that kind of jury. Also heard the tale of drinking the polluted water, which amused him as much.

It's a beautiful campus. I had never seen it before.

Ive received a few more reviews of the book and will send them to you as soon as they make a respectable batch. Theyve all been pro except the one you saw from the Indianapolis paper—the woman who was glad when Bart died so she could be quits with the book and me.

I know nothing of national sales except that the advance was 2054, which, as I told you, George said was "quite respectable for a first novel." Assuredly it's not going to make us rich. I'm going to be a poor boy all my days.

Did I hear aright? Did the Pope give some sort of decoration to William Randolph Hearst for "civic qualities, appreciation of spiritual values, devotion to humanity"?—My advice is, get out now; the ship is fixing to founder. However, I suppose youll say that all the nasty things Ive heard about Willy are Communist propaganda.

Anyhow, all's well.

Shelby

---

8. Billups Phinizy Percy (b. 1922), Walker's youngest brother and an Annapolis graduate, had retired from the Navy not long after the end of World War II. He was now enrolled in law school at the University of Virginia, the same law school his father had attended.

Greenville

19 Nov 49

DEAR WALKER

This is a wretched time for me, between books and waiting to hear from the publishers on a submitted MS. I sent it off ("Follow Me Down" I mean) a week ago, got a congratulatory answer from my agent—which of course means nothing; he is always encouraging—and now am biding my time till I hear from Dial. My monthly advances ran out last month and will not be resumed unless they accept the book (that was the arrangement), so of course I'm hard to live with along through here—poor Peggy. Fortunately I had a birthday this week, and among the gifts was a 10-dollar bill from my mother: that keeps me in cigarettes. As for my creditors (including, alas, the bank), if I can wait, so can they. God grant that all my troubles will always be financial: theyre the very best kind. Leroy[9] told me the other night youre waiting to hear the results on an important X-ray; which makes my troubles seem small indeed.

It's a strange life, idleness: I havent put pen to paper in a week. Ive been reading—background material on the Vicksburg Campaign, an intensive study of the Seven Days around Richmond, and Proust. Here is Proust on style: "Style is by no means an adornment as some people think, it is not even a question of technique, it is—like color for painters—a quality of vision, the revelation of the particular universe which each of us sees, and which is not seen by others." This is profoundly true. Later (and I think it is the basis for his great originality) he said: "As for style, I have tried to reject everything dictated by pure intelligence, to express my deep and authentic impressions, and to respect the natural movement of my thought." You do yourself great wrong not reading Proust. I still cannot understand your defection in that respect. For me he is the greatest, the very greatest, not excepting Dostoevsky.

I have gone into the Civil War reading quite seriously, drawing maps to follow the narrative and even going to the source material. This week, for the first time, I really understood Jackson's Valley campaign; and as a result,

---

9. After serving in the Army Air Corps during World War II, Leroy Pratt Percy Jr., the middle of the three Percy brothers, returned to Greenville, Mississippi, to manage his adoptive father's farm and other business interests.

I really began to understand Jackson himself. The Vicksburg thing is taking shape. However, I'm going to hold off for a few more years, till I'm good and ready. I know where I'm going, and I know how to get there, too.

When I took that previous sheet out of the typewriter I read it over, and I saw that the first paragraph might be considered a plea for money. It's no such thing. Freedom from money worries will come along with freedom from other things; partial freedom is no good, a negative sort of thing at best. Money trouble is never really serious; and, who knows? without it I might be much worse off. I mean that. Look at rich folks, lost and grieved by the wind; being without money wouldnt solve all their problems, of course, but it would solve a lot of them. As for myself, it gives me a chance to indulge in just the right amount of fret and self-pity. Besides, money with me leads to dissipation and sin—I'm a child where money is concerned, probably because Ive never really had any. If I had a thousand dollars today I would certainly act the fool, one way or another.

One more quote from Proust, which has nothing to do with the foregoing: "True literature reveals the still unknown part of the soul. It is more or less the saying of Pascal that I quote, wrongly, for I have no books here: 'A little knowledge separates [us] from God; much knowledge brings us back.' One should never be afraid to go too far, for the truth is beyond."—I suppose that ties in with what you called the Pascalian heresy. And that is what I find most regrettable about your going into the Church—you wouldnt dare go beyond. There is something terribly cowardly (at least spiritually) about the risks to which you wont expose your soul. Pushed, youll admit that doubt is a healthy thing, closely connected with faith; but you wont follow it. I believe that truth lies beyond and I'm willing to step into the mire of "The Almond Tree" and "Follow Me Down" because I know I'll find what I'm after, on the other side—beyond. You draw back. "A dirty story," you say (you said it of "The Almond Tree") and you draw back. I progressed beyond "The Almond Tree" to "Follow Me Down," and I'll progress beyond "Follow Me Down"—perhaps to a truth I'd never suspect if I'd stayed on your clean side of the mire. I seriously think that no good practicing Catholic can ever be a great artist; art is by definition a product of doubt; it has to be pursued. Dostoevsky had it to a degree beyond any I know: it seems even to have led him to tamper with little girls; it certainly led him to the conception of Ivan Karamazov and the Grand Inquisitor.

I said once I didnt think God would be hard on writers. We are the out-riders for the saints; we go beyond (where they wont go) and tell them what we've found. If we burn for that, we'll take pride in our burning, our pain; the triumph wont be God's.

All your dogma contradicts Proust's dictum: "Respect the natural move-ment of your thoughts." That is the secret of originality; it's so seldom done. And dont say it's simply Rousseau all over again—Proust is about as far removed from Rousseau as you are. Shakespeare's "To thine own self be true" is no less valid because he put it in the mouth of that old fool Polo-nius and had it addressed to a gadabout.

Of course with you it was simple. You rejected art. But how about those like myself, for whom rejection of art would be a rejection of life? You think God put us here as he put the devils? You think he gave us man's form and man's soul, and then gave us merely the choice between two things, sin or suicide? I say again, the triumph wont be God's, not even by God's own standards.

Much of this is a result of having been dammed up for a week—efflu-vium, youll say. Part of it (the more violent part) comes from anxiety and doubt. Nothing is sadder than a tour de force that doesnt quite come off, which perhaps is what "Follow Me Down" is. But I'm trying—not that I deserve any credit for that; I havent any choice.

I hope that X-ray[10] turns out good. My little fret is a mighty small thing alongside that.

Regards
Shelby

19 May 50

DEAR WALKER

I inclose the Indian story (tentatively titled "The Sacred Mound," which I dont much like). As you know, it is to be the final thing in my CHILD BY FEVER collection[11] which will include one short novel, two long stories, and four short stories—the whole making a book identical in length with

---

10. Percy was being checked for a recurrence of tuberculosis.
11. Published as *Jordan County: A Landscape in Narrative* (1954).

TOURNAMENT and FOLLOW ME DOWN: 100,000 words. I still have three of the short things to write; thus I'll spend my summer. I dont much like the short story as a "form"—there isnt room to spread out, and I'll be damned if I'll reflect the miseries of the world in a drop of water, as it were, which is the current manner in all the New Yorker, Atlantic, and even Partisan Review stories.

Whatever the merits of the present story (they dont really come through: I'm putting the thing up to cool for a month or so and then will return to it) you will be interested, I think, to see from it how facts alter fiction. For instance, you said that if the victim were a fat, older man, there would be yellow streaks; therefore the second trapper became fat and older. Also, you said the heart wouldnt "smoke" except in cold weather; I wanted it to smoke; therefore the sacrifice occurred during an autumn cold-snap. In both cases I had intended otherwise, but I changed to suit the facts. And, strangely enough, the story is better for the changes. Other things in it work likewise. It is a curious trade, similar to the poet's, who sometimes is led to conceiving his best lines because of the "tyranny of rime."

I'll welcome suggestions of any sort, no matter how small or big. You can refer to the text by page and line; I have the original of the carbon I'm sending. I plan to revise it thoroughly anyhow.

As to our discussion of the Thomistic views on esthetics and criteria, I'm swinging your way more all the time: particularly I agree with the things (most) you said in your last letter about pornagraphic effects distorting the overall construction: I think thats true. But I suppose, in the end, I'll go my way and wind up with a dart through my liver—alas.

Regards:

Shelby

6 July 50

DEAR WALKER

I am happy to report myself "with book."[12] I broke ground this morning. A tremendous undertaking, very different from my other two. This time the

---

12. Eventually published as *Love in a Dry Season* (1951).

hero is the Story: I'm trying what I can do with the old system of making the reader want to turn the page to see what happens next, though I approach the heart of the thing in a slow, ponderous manner. The first two-thirds of "The Enormous Eye," which I remember you liked, goes into it, along with about three times that amount of new material. I'm going to try to hold it down to 70,000 words—about two-thirds the length of my other two. It's third-person narrative, like Tournament in some respects; I'm going to break my heart over Amanda Barcroft. My possible title: "The Arms You Bear"—you know the Houseman poem: Be still, my soul, etc.

Started to phone you the other night. Ive gotten all heated up over the Korean fighting. I think Truman has done exactly right, except I wish it were more-so. Much as Ive sworn I'd never have anything more to do with the military, I'm perfectly willing to go right now. How are you feeling about the way it's going? MacArthur is the damndest creature I ever heard of, quite a combination of actor and hero; I'm glad we've got him.

What are the chances of coming down to see you around the end of the month or sooner?

Rgds:

Shelby

Greenville: Tuesday Aug. [1950]

DR WALKER

A review of FMD in the current New Yorker (combined with your reaction) convinces me that I am perhaps a very great writer; at least I am all things to all men—though in a sense it's also true that Ive fallen between two stools. Apparently they have no conception of a sense of guilt; apparently they dont admit the existence of sin. They admire Eustis because he "finds courage to take love (meaning tail) when it is offered." . . . The final two sentences are gratifying, however: "Except for an occasional ascent into rhetoric,* Mr Foote's writing is marvellously exact and positive. His attitude toward his people is respectful and human, as though he had thought about them a great deal and knew too much about them ever to take them for granted." The middle section, referred to above, is incredible: "Mr Foote, as well as most of the people in the book, seems anxious to explain away the elopement and the murder on the ground that Eustis is insane. This is too bad, because the strength and anguish of the story lie in the obvious fact that Eustis is a simple, disappointed, hard-working man who for a short time finds courage to take love when it is offered." Apparently my lawyer sold them a complete bill of goods.—A completely amoral publication.

If you could read all the reviews you would see why I say a writer can write only for himself, hoping that the time will come (after he is dead, alas) when some student will do a critical study that has value. Small hope, I assure you. Unless he becomes what you seem to prefer: Fulton Oursler[13] turned papist.

See you Thursday:
Shelby

*These seven words will be deleted in the ads. Of course.

Thursday [1950]

DEAR WALKER

I didnt at all mean for us to come down now or even soon; I couldnt if I was urged or threatened, for I am into the second part of the new novel, going great guns. I meant in late October or some such time when I reach a pausing-place and it is convenient to Bunt. We'll see.

Now I'm feeling good, partly because the writing goes well, but mostly I think because this completes a stage in my writing life. At the outset I promised myself three short novels in which to learn how to write; then three long novels, having learned; and finally three novels of undetermined length, experimental—all this in addition to things of slighter length, most of them tours de force such as SHILOH! and CHILD BY FEVER. Then as far as I'm concerned they can put me in the ground. TOURNAMENT and FOLLOW ME DOWN are the first two steps; THE ARMS YOU BEAR[14] will complete Phase One. Then Phase Two: which will begin with either the

---

13. A popular evangelist of the day.
14. *Love in a Dry Season* (1951).

Vicksburg book or a big modern novel—I keep saving that Vicksburg thing: if I dont look out, it will wind up in Phase Three, experimental, and no one will read it: I can see now how it would be—plotless, characterless: really wild, like a shellburst and as unintelligible. Did you see Hemingway's address to the reviewers, quoted in the Commonweal: "They say? What do they say? Let them say." Signed: Papa. Sometimes I almost like him.

Saw three shows in NY—Mike Todd's "Peep Show": lousy—I thought it was going to be burlesque but it wasnt anything; "The Cocktail Party," almost as bad, a terrible combination of shallowness and pretentiousness, much worse than I had realized by reading it and hearing it on records; and finally "The Member of the Wedding": superb! Just as good as good can be.* I never saw anything to beat Ethel Waters—all the warmth and friendliness in the world, right there on the stage—and the rest of the cast measured up to her. It was a fine evening; it made the waste of time spent at the others come out all right. I wish to God I could go back this winter; Louis Calhern is going to open in "Lear" and I'd get a shot at "Don Giovanni." It's a good thing I aint rich. The two things I want to see most in this world will be barely 1500 miles away; I'd throw writing to the winds.

So remember theres no haste at all in planning for us to get down to see you. Lets rock along and when and if you get squared away, let us know and we'll ride down.

Rgds:
Shelby

*The play didnt present a story: it presented a situation. And it presented it well. Youd like it very much.

Gville
10 Oct 50
DEAR WALKER

I'm glad you enjoyed the records but I dont want them back; keep them and I'll listen to them a few years from now.[15] I probably wont believe I

---

15. A 1946 recording of Foote, Percy, and Greenville friends reading from Shakespeare.

sounded like that. But I did; God knows I did. . . . Incidentally I think that particular stretch of writing is about the best narrative-sequence in the book. TOURNAMENT is really a gold mine for me: I'll be digging it for years. Yesterday a grandson of that sonbitch banker Tilden (the one who did old Wisten in) cropped up in my new book. He's not much like the old boy but every now and then you can see the kinship. In the first place he's a banker too—inherited it. He's the one gave Charley Drew a job in Bristol. Charley's a teller and the women are flocking to his window. He fascinates me as much as he does the women. Do you remember him? "In strong sunlight his eyebrows and lashes were invisible, which gave him a rather blank expression, like that of a face etched on a billiard ball, but in shadow they showed white and distinguished against his ruddy complexion. He had pale, light blue eyes and a prominent jaw and his hair was parted carefully

Roy Percy, Shelby Foote, and Walker Percy lounge on the lawn behind Uncle Will's house in the mid-1930s. *Courtesy of Washington County Library System.*

in the middle to show a line of scalp as neat and precise as if it had been run with a transit." I see him very clearly and catch all his movements as I write. He's not all bastard, though it's true he mostly is. . . . This book has really got *people* in it; they live and breathe; I know them intimately—much better, perhaps, than I indicate on paper: which is always a danger. I hope I indicate enough, however. You see, there are pitfalls in both directions: too much or too little—either can wreck a book.

I read the new Budd Schulberg book the other night: it will be out on the 30th. Lord, but I hated it. It's the fall of Scott Fitzgerald—a horrible thing to depict. It's cheap, shoddy in the worst way—like Wakeman, whom incidentally I remember you once praised: for which shame on you. The violence of my dislike is most probably based on my tremendous admiration for Fitzgerald; I think TENDER IS THE NIGHT is one of the best things of our time. And really this Schulberg book (called "The Disenchanted," which should give you some notion of what a crummy job it is) adds nothing to what F himself wrote in some superb articles collected posthumously in "The Crack-Up." Schulberg has done Zanuck, Carnera, and now Fitzgerald. Who is next on his list? And who does he think he is, sitting in judgment? And mind you, they are all his betters—even Carnera. Christ, even Zanuck.

Peg and Margaret[16] are still in Memphis: will be up there all month, apparently. I miss Margaret but I sure am getting some work done. Three pages a day (about 1000 words) like clockwork. This is the way a man ought to live—a writer, I mean. Any living you do for others means that much less for your work. . . . Isnt that a hell of a thing to say? Writers are people to stay away from, for this reason as well as for the fact that they have awkward characters. All the unpleasantness Ive ever seen came from unhappiness in one form or another, and writers are surely the unhappiest people on earth. Except of course when they are working, at which time there is of necessity no contact. Ergo: they are best avoided, as I said.

Thanks for the Waugh on Hemingway. I agree with much he says, especially about respect being due him; he's damned right.

I'm coming round to your way of thinking on the use of dreams. However, there is a particularly "Marlovian" dream in the thing I'm working on now. It's well done, though, and necessary to the plot. Incidentally, I wouldnt give up on Mitya's dream ("the babe! the babe!") for whole shelves of other great literature. But thats Dostoevsky and doesnt count. Generally speaking, youre right. . . . For example, Eustis' dream on the levee (wrestling with the angel that was Beulah) is honestly good; it's sound and effective within itself. His other dream, in the cafe (when Iverson appeared in nightshirt) was not—it's too pat, too bent to fit, too everything that can be wrong with fictional dreams. . . . So I dont abandon them; I will just tread softly.

Tell Bunt she has my sympathy. No cook: man, thats awful. If I was her

---

16. Margaret, Foote's daughter, was born on March 16, 1949.

I'd go back home till you found one. Thats what Peggy did, and mind you I had her a cook. Pus in her kidneys, she said. What she really wanted was to go into a schizophrenic huddle with herself while somebody minds the baby. I wouldnt put Peggy in a book for anything: too lurid.

Regds:

Shelby

Gville: 17 Oct 50

DEAR WALKER

These past two weeks have been hellacious: Ive never written so slowly, so tediously. A page a day, at a crawling rate: the fact that I know where I'm going doesn't help. You see, there is a change of pace at this stage of the novel; I planned it that way, to be effective; but I'm terribly afraid it will turn out merely boring—highly analytical, with a great deal of decor, including a whole raft of pages on the growth of Bristol, telling just how Charley Drew fit into the scheme of things. So far I have avoided pronouncing judgments; Ive tried to bring the reader to the point where he will be forced to pronounce them himself, and my fingers and brain ache with the labor. A writer pays a great price for objectivity. He cant just say: "He was really a scoundrel—yet not entirely so"; thats much too easy and doesnt give a fraction of the effect. It's as the newspaper motto says, "An inch of picture is worth a yard of text." I demonstrate, demonstrate, demonstrate!—both with action and description. And though I'm bolstered by the knowledge that the hard way is the best way, that doesnt always keep it from being tedious. All I can do is hope it wont be that way for the reader. (I dont mean because of the effect on sales. I mean when it is seen plain, by an outsider.) Fitzgerald once said that all really good writing is like swimming underwater, holding the breath. It's true. But it should be rapid and strong; otherwise it's apt to prove weak and jerky—as I'm afraid this is. Fortunately I have a plot that will bear a lot of lumber—I think. . . . If Mary Pratt ever looks like she wants to be a writer, hit her hard on the head with something heavy.

Have you read a really great work of fiction this season? I dont think anyone should let four months get by without reading at least one—Crime & Punishment, Jude the Obscure, The Cossacks, The Wings of the Dove, Measure for Measure, and so on: there must be at least 500 of them. If you read one every season (that you havent read before, I mean) it keeps you in touch and lends variety to your quality of vision ("a quality of vision" is what Proust calls Style). I spent a week recently reading Hawthorne, which I had never done before. I read The Scarlet Letter and The House of the Seven Gables. It was a mistake, a total loss—Ive never read such worthless junk. With the exception of Melville (though I'm no great Melville fan, for that matter) we had no really good writers before Mark Twain. . . . I made up for it, however, by reading Tender is the Night. Have you read any Fitzgerald besides The Great Gatsby? If you want I'll send you the Portable Fitzg: Tender is in it, along with Gatsby and half a dozen stories, including The Rich Boy. Youd enjoy it very much, I think. He's a real writer—the best example I know of a man who rose above his period; his tragedy (which he himself described in The Crack-Up) is the darkest of all. Let me send you the book if you havent read it.

London recording of Mozart's Abduction from the Seraglio is mighty fine—German as she ought to be sung: none of that Wagnerian beller and bloat. Whenever, if ever, I get down to see you, I'll bring it and play it for you. It's complete, three records. Nothing like as fine as Don Giovanni or Figaro, of course, but a real pleasure all the way through.

Regards to all. Be good.

Shelby

P.S. With regard to that "no good writer before Mark Twain" business—dont tell me Poe. As a writer of fiction Poe was no damn good except when he was imitating Defoe in The Narrative of A. G. Pym. Cooper I dont think youd even bring up. Washington Irving comes close to it; but he's the only one I can think of. . . . Dont misunderstand me though; we made up for it later. James, Fitzgerald, Hemingway, and Faulkner are right up there under Dostoevsky and Proust.

Sun: 29 Oct 50

DEAR WALKER

I had a good week, after the misery of the one before: got 2500 words of finished stuff through the mill—good, too, I believe. I'm approaching the midpoint of the book. It shapes up well, and will serve admirably to end my apprenticeship with. 2500 is about 1000 low, but I'm building it up gradually and the writing was highly analytical, with lots of thought behind it and much revision. When I hit the pure clear narrative stretch itll be like running downhill—hope I dont fall on my face. Writing is curious, the actual act of writing: you have to divide your self into two: one doing the writing, the other sitting back watching, riding herd on the words. The danger comes when one of the two halves tries to take over completely; thats what bad work comes from. You for instance (I think) have an overdeveloped "watcher" and thats the worst of all, for the fellow with the dominant first half (the scribbler) can at least work for the SatEvePost. But a man with an overdeveloped critical faculty cant even work for himself. He's comparable to a man with an anxiety neurosis, who cant even live.

No response on the offer to lend Fitzgerald's "Tender Is the Night"—I presume youve either read it or arent interested. If it's the second I'm ashamed of you. I tell you again, with all its grave faults it's one of the most interesting books of our time. It has one of the great themes: How a man lost his soul. It's quite long (400pp) and has a number of superficialities on its surface; but it has depths for the reader who will see them. And the writing itself is as clear as Tolstoy's—he's a better writer than Tolstoy, too; or do you see yet what I mean by that?

Rgds:

Shelby

Gville: 22 Nov 50

DEAR WALKER

It's much better than I had thought youd ever let it be.[17] If the rest is up to this—and more important, if the rest supplies the variety this chapter lacks (it's no fault here)—the book will be really good. I was most surprised

---

17. The first chapter from Percy's first apprentice novel, *The Charterhouse*, which he might have started working on as early as 1947. Part of it is set in a city resembling Birmingham, Alabama, and part in a mental institution with many striking resemblances to the University of the South and the surrounding community in Sewanee, Tennessee.

to see that you kept your sense of humor; I hadnt thought you could. That is the best sign possible.

What you have done stylistically is quite interesting. Youve crossed Wolfe with Kafka and brought forth this. (If you think this is a reproach, youre much mistaken. Faulkner crossed Conrad with Sherwood Anderson. Dostoevsky crossed Gogol with Dickens. Etc.) I think youre shaping up something effective which already is partly your own and later will be entirely so; the thing is to keep working.

I wont try to make an overall judgment: that wont be possible until I see it in relation to the other chapters: but I'll say that I'd been worried that it was going to dribble out toward the end—but it didnt: you brought it into focus wonderfully. A little thing like Gloria in the toilet bowl does wonders.

So without making any large criticism, I'll take just the little things, one by one:

p224: "the picture faded like a light-struck negative." Light-struck negatives dont fade; they come out sharper. Make it: "The picture grayed like a light-struck negative," which is not only accurate but sounds better too—though of course you wont admit it, having fixed the other in your mind.

p225: "An endless string of macaroni." Leave off the "of macaroni"—just let him be fed string. It is a mistake to tie your similes down too tight in most cases. Besides, it's an ugly picture—not the kind of ugliness that fits the predicament, either. I would leave the "eating" out entirely: make him a man compelled to unroll or reel-in an endless length of string.

p229: "What was he doing in this forlorn street in Ohio?" Here's a little lesson in style: to many "in's." Make it, "What was he doing in this forlorn Ohio street?"

p239: "She was still going to school. Doing graduate work." This is "cable-ese"—unforgivable in a writer except in rare cases for effect (as for instance when you used "The Thing"—thats OK). Avoid it, though: nobody is holding you down to ten words.

p250: "Whew. Let me come up for air." Thousands of girls have said it in the past; more thousands will say it in the future. But in a book it belongs to O'Hara.

It still needs some finetooth revision I think. For instance, look at your last paragraph reworked—not as I would write it, but as you should, keeping your style:

"He got sick as soon as he left her room. Now he sat submissively on the bathroom floor, waiting for the dreadful unease to localize in his stomach and erupt. The toilet was pink and at the bottom under water was the word Gloria. The whiskey came up; warm orange-tasting acid flooded his nostrils. He sat peacefully as if he were watching the spectacle from a distance, as if it were another person who was making the regular, almost musical whoops that echoed through the house."

You wont think thats better, but it is—in your own style. As for myself, much as I like it, I dont see like that at all: thats why all books are different.

Dont pay much attention to all this. Go on and write it. Then when you have finished you can look back. Right now, it's best to keep going. It's really good work; youre building something youll be able to depict with; youre learning how to make them listen—worry later about the fine points.

I enjoyed reading it, too, and look forward to seeing the finished job.

Shelby

Saturday: 25 Nov 50

DEAR WALKER

Here is a thing I meant to tell you concerning your writing. I hesitated to do so because I knew that an overdeveloped critical sense is a deathly thing. But I have decided it's important enough for you to be saddled with it from the outset. Prose rhythms. I think youre not paying much attention in that direction.

It's highly paradoxical and difficult to talk about. For one thing it must be unconscious; it must be developed until it comes naturally, unforced. But when you really work that field, the product is pure gold and a never-ending source of delight—it's one of the things that makes writing worth a grown man's time. For me at any rate, all writing is dead without it. When I complain that I find certain writers "unreadable" I mean that they have this lack. So I want to try to tell you a bit about it at the outset. Probably youve heard it before, but believe me, it's worth going into.

In English its basis is iambic pentameter. But thats only the basis: its beauty comes from the variations, the interpolation of short lines and the wrenching and crowding of meters. Sadly, it has to be learned by long hours of work. I think it's why most serious writers of prose begin by writing poetry; it's a necessary preparation. For good prose is poetry that has burst its seams; it never goes at a jogtrot.—I attach a page to show you what I mean. Ive taken a paragraph at random, which (believe me) was not at all written with any *conscious* striving after rhythm. It will show you what I mean, I hope.

Now read it.

Amy was aware of this, since it went on around her and colored all she saw. Then too there was this situation in her home, this invasion, this alienation not of affection, for there had been no affection from the start, but anyhow of attention; that was it, an alienation of attention. But her reaction was merely a vague dissatisfaction which took the form of increased languidness, which in turn—though there was no one to read it, not even herself—signaled a coming disturbance as plainly as a falling barometer warns of stormy weather. This, then, was the low-pressure lull, the vacuum that invites the wind, and she was at dead center.

    Amy was
    Aware of this, since it went on around her
    And colored all she saw. (PAUSE) Then too
    There was this situation in her home,
5   This invasion, this alienation not of affection,
    For there had been no affection from the start,
    But anyhow of attention; that was it,
    An alienation of attention. But
    Her reaction was merely a vague dissatisfaction
10 Which took the form of increased languidness,
    Which in turn (PAUSE)
    —Though there was no one to read it, not even herself—
    Signaled a coming disturbance as plainly as
    A falling barometer warns of stormy weather.
15 This, then, was the low-pressure lull, the vacuum
    That invites the wind, and she was at dead center.

Do you see? Dont curl your lip and call this "flute playing" or say that it has nothing to do with communication of meaning—it has everything to do with just that. The best test, incidentally, is reading aloud, and the best examples I know are in Shakespeare's late plays—The Winter's Tale or The Tempest are good examples. It's in the prose as well as the verse; as a matter of fact it shows up first in the prose of the middle-period plays: Henry IV and V are good examples, and Twelfth Night has many fine speeches in such prose.

Youre probably thinking that if you sat down to do such work the result would be terrible beyond belief. And youre right: for as I said at the outset, it has to come naturally. Youre probably thinking too that there is something decadent about all this—this is tinkering with words, not saying something. But youre wrong. It has been one of the chief concerns of all our best writers. With Flaubert, for instance, it amounted to a religion; he said he'd rather be shot like a dog than write a bad line. And mind you, he meant unrhythmical. Of course it can be worse than no rhythm at all—as in whole pages of Wolfe and Dickens, where they launch into bad blank verse.

However, overlook all this if you think the result will be paralysis. (It might well be.) I just wanted to make sure you are aware of what I think is one of the deepest obligations a writer owes his profession, unless he is satisfied to do no more than amuse or instruct on the surface.

I'm past the midpoint of the novel: past the point of greatest strain. It should go easier the rest of the way, downhill. Plot, plot, plot—I'll stand or fall by this one as far as plot goes; if the reader can limp through that long dry middle section, he'll have quite a lump in his gut by the time he gets done. He'll damn well know he's been in the presence of an artist.

Incidentally, if someone had been able to tell me at the outset all there is to be learned about writing, I'd probably have become an automobile salesman or a farmer. Thank God nobody did. It's really a compliment to your strength of character that I'm willing to risk telling you of the heartaches and sweats ahead. And as for your work in progress, go right ahead the way youre going—dont look back. But at the same time learn all you can while youre writing it. Theres always another until you get the old ax.

Regards:

Shelby

Fri: 1 Dec 50

DEAR WALKER

One reason I am tender of your sensibilities concerning your writing is the same as I'd be tender in speaking of your (or anyone else's) wife: I assume that they are about on par as far as anyone outside the ménage is concerned, and I'd as soon be gruff about one as the other. Do you see? But the other reason, apart from manners, is that I was favorably impressed. Not that I think anything will come of this book—it almost certainly wont get into print, for instance. But the faults are all correctible faults, and the virtues are virtues youd never acquire. You say youre fretting because nothing ever happens to this poor fellow. Man, thats a plot problem; and nothing is easier than plot—it's even much better not to be fooling with plot at this stage; you can be writing scenes for their own sakes, not for plot's sake.

However, the scenes should be *dramatic*, and I think you know what I mean by that after having put Gloria at the bottom of that toilet bowl; that was the nail the whole scene hung on, and you drove it home. Such effects come but God knows where they come from. One thing does alarm me, though: You say this poor bastard never finds the way out. Well and good. But I hope youre not going to miss presenting him with a *way* out. Here is a scene I think you could do:

Let him come upon a drunken evangelist (or maybe a crazy one) preaching on a street corner. Mockers are in the crowd, including street urchins. He is an unfrocked priest: someone in the crowd knows this and says so. But he preaches a wild crazy sermon that, behind the wildness, really shows your poor bastard the way. Of course he doesnt take it; it's just wild raving, he thinks. The sermon should be full of hell and brimstone; it should also give a peek at salvation. All this time the crowd is mocking; maybe they even throw things, I dont know. And the scene should end in defeat for the evangelist—he should be hustled off by the police, or maybe pass out. It could be good, given the gift to make it come alive; it certainly would point up your book. It would be valid, too: I think God might very well choose an unfrocked priest (one who's going to burn, himself) to show your boy the way. The irony would lie in his madness or drunkenness, in the fact that he is hooted, and in the fact that your protagonist, except for maybe a fleeting glimpse, doesn't understand at all.

It should be done with incisiveness; some nickname the urchins give him might sum up his appearance and character. He ought to be dirty and unkempt, with a suggestion of his former grace behind the dirt and muss—mad eyes that used to be soft, delicate hands now grimy, etc. The sermon of course I leave to you—there could be some real poetry in it, nearly opaque.

"Sentimental Education" comes by this same mail. It's Flaubert's handling of your theme: a young man in search of his soul—and he doesnt find it, either. I warn you, though: the first reading is merely a warm-up (at least it was for me); you dont see what the hell he's getting at until you can read it with the whole thing in your mind. Each of the characters has his fate, but it's not until you know that fate that the actions are understandable. It's one of the very great books. I hope youll read slow and retentively, always with the second reading in mind.

I spent ten years trying to find it. Applegate's finally located it for me. When you return it, wrap it as carefully as I have done; it's kind of flimsy and wont take rough handling.

Regards:
Shelby

22 Dec 50

DEAR WALKER

The check came yesterday afternoon. I accept it gladly; theres no such thing as tainted money—it's all just money; the taint is in the mind. And believe me it came at a time of dire need.

Something happened to me this week. I approached work sluggishly Monday morning and all of a sudden something took me by the hair: I had to hold back to keep from covering reams of paper with gouts of words. By yesterday afternoon (Thursday) I had produced 5000 of the best words I ever wrote: Amanda Barcroft finding her sister dead, and yearning for Charley to come take her away. It really went well: just the right balance between "inspiration" and objectivity. Unquestionably this is the best sustained writing Ive ever done (the whole book, I mean): it has a technical virtuosity that holds my interest—shifting point-of-view, intensive analysis, and a series of outrageous events that call for underwriting; characters who live in their own right, each with a contrasting personality, and not a "type" in the lot; counterpointed symbolism that can be taken or let alone, but which yet (I hope) gives the book a higher importance, places it in the stream of human experience—and all in all I feel very good about it. I am beginning to feel a part of what comes from being in the American tradition. The historical background (the 30s) pinpoints the plot, locates it in Time, and I hope is interesting on its own account.

It's not a book that will sell, any more than the others have been; but it will do what I most want it to do—it will add to my stature, my sense of "sureness" and will add possibly another couple of thousand readers who will remember my name and wait for my next book.

FMD, incidentally, is about to be published in England. I signed the contract last week. The publishers are excellent people: Hamish Hamilton. I'll get a 75£ advance and royalties the same as in this country. I may do what other American writers have done—Faulkner for instance:—get a reputation abroad before I do at home; in which case the American public become interested through a process kin to reflection; it will bounce back. What I most look forward to is being translated into the French, Proust's language.

Hope youre coming ahead with your book and above all I hope youre going to give your poor fellow a chance to turn down some offer of salvation. It's strange, in a way. I'm opposed to preaching in fiction; you sort of favor it. Yet when it comes to the actual work, I preach ten sermons to your one.

> Thou art not certain;
> For thy complexion shifts to strange affects,
> After the moon. . . . A breath thou art,
> Servile to all the skyey influences
> That do this habitation, where thou keep'st,
> Hourly afflict.
> Shakespeare

31 Dec 50

DEAR WALKER

Happy New Year—

I just finished a good day's work, approaching the two-thirds point of my novel: the end, that is, of Part Two. From here to the end is clearly in view: the problem will be to write from the heart rather than from the memory, to keep from amusing myself with doodles in the margin and psychological trickery of the kind that wins praise and admiration from intellectuals such as reviewers, unwelcome because you (the writer) know how cheaply they were attained. That is why, when you ask a painter to appraise one of his own paintings, he will most often point to a dark patch at one of the corners and say, "Thats a nice effect, up there," caring nothing for the brilliance of the brushwork in the center of the picture. In his mind, such brilliance is merely "literary," and therefore not as sincere, not so much from the heart.

However, as I said, Ive just finished a good day's work and I'm sitting here at my desk, about to get up for a bath and a ride down town. Ive been looking back through the typescript and maybe now I can tell you a little about what Ive tried to do. I can see it very plain.

The problem this time was the interweaving of three plots to a climax, thus demonstrating the synchronism of events—the narrative being divided into sections, so alternated as to stimulate and relieve (in turn) the mind of the reader. While the main interest, as in all my work, is based on Character, this time I have tried to utilize a highly complex plot, releasing the facts one at a time in a logical yet unexpected sequence. The hope is that the reader will want to keep turning the pages to find out what "happens." Always before, Ive given the plot in the first few pages, believing that *how* a thing happens is more interesting than *what* happens. (I still think so.) Yet strangely enough, this has turned out to be the most intensely analytical writing Ive ever done. The reason, I suppose, was because I wanted to hold my own interest (since I of course already knew what was going to happen); and while this probably interferes—on the first reading—with the very effect I was most anxious to achieve, I think it will make the book a better one when the reader takes it up for a second reading—which, incidentally, is what I always write for.

As for my purpose in writing, I think I can state that too. Some want to teach (or preach); some want to communicate sensation. I suppose I want a share in both of those. Yet I think I know at last what it is that I really want. I want to teach people how to *see*. I want to impart to them a "quality of vision" (Proust's definition of style). In 34 years I have trained myself through writing to look at the world a certain way, and I think that as a result I see a great deal more (both of beauty and *ugliness*)* than a person does who has not concerned himself with such. What I have learned can be communicated not by explanation but by exposition: if I tell you what I see, you see it too, and in the same way I see it, provided I have been able to choose the right words and released them in the proper psychological order. There is the problem: the tyranny of words. Alas, they are all we writers have to work with; to hope for something else is like a painter wanting to paint with sunlight instead of oils or watercolors. The main thing I thank God for is that I am an American and a Mississippian, where the words still have a freshness and a potential impact.

I'm gone downtown.

Shelby

*Here is where we part company, or used to anyhow. When you get to the pearly gates youll be asking God, "Why rattlesnakes?"

6 Jan 51

DEAR WALKER

I'm sending by this same mail a book I know youll enjoy: "The Day of the Locust." Real crazy and real good. Flaubert too. And by the way, did you read the "Education"?

Youre wrong about the possession of money and its effect on writers. My two favorite modern writers were both independant financially: James and Proust: and mind you, their financial independance was largely responsible for their doing what they wanted. It's the man himself: it's always the man himself. Even with those good ones who are supposed to have written for money (Dostoevsky is the best example), if it hadnt been money it would have been something. The urge itself is the only compulsion. If Dostoevsky had been rich as Croesus he'd have written to ease his gout or something. These Americans who "sell out to Hollywood or the slicks," they are handing the critics a bill of goods; the real truth is they are written out or in a bad mental rut. A good man is incorruptable as long as he is good, and for a very simple reason: All the money and tail and sunshine in the world (including California) arent worth the pleasure of doing good work, and every good writer knows this. If I ever "sell out" it will be because I cant work any more.

Did you say Cuba?

Shelby

Tuesday Jan. 1951

DEAR WALKER

I had a talk with Wm Faulkner yesterday afternoon. He was over here signing copies of "Notes on a Horsethief," which Kenneth & Ben & Hodding[18] are bringing out this month in a limited edition of 900. Any how, he said he liked my book (meaning FMD): "It's a good book," he said, and then looked at me rather piercingly and added: "Do better next time." I should have told him the plain truth: that I never do less than my best: but as it was, I just said I would and he said "Good." We got to talking about the Civil War and he said he wants to go up to Shiloh with me in the spring. He was very funny talking about the Nobel ceremonies, he in his split-tail coat among the notables. Said he was going to have the dress suit stuffed like a suit of armor and stand it out in the hall.

Wrote Saturday giving you somewhat limited hell about taking off for Cuba without having earned it with a solid spell of writing. But I think I forgot to put "Covington" on the letter. I remember the "Military Road" but I either forgot to put the rest on, or I had a thought-hiatus. Anyhow, have a good time.

I inclose a "Portrait of the Artist as a Bookend." It looks like a lineup photo—like those Roscoe Jeffcoat riffled through, trying to get the goods on Brother Jimson.[19]

Good sailing. Tell Papa H[20] hello.

Shelby.

19 March 51

Book going great guns after a two-day interruption of in-laws: Margaret was three yesterday and they came down.

I'm reading a book youd be very much interested in: "Revolt of the Rednecks—Mississippi Politics, 1876–1925." Contains a full account of

---

18. Kenneth Haxton, Ben Wasson, and Hodding Carter, three Greenvillians and friends of Foote, had their own small press—the Levee Press.

19. Two characters in Foote's novel *Follow Me Down* (1950).

20. Percy and his wife were going on a trip to Cuba, where in fact they saw Papa H (Ernest Hemingway) in a hotel bar.

the Vardaman-Percy race in 1911, along with an even fuller account of the alleged Bilbo bribing; was published last month by University of Kentucky Press. This is a library copy. I'll check it out and bring it down for you to look at when I come, if you want; or if you want a copy now I think Kenneth has one in stock which he'll send if you drop him a card. It's really a study of the Populist movement, its rise and decline, and though it could have been better, it's mighty good. The thesis (so far as I can tell 1/4th through it) is one that has interested me for some time: that even rascals like Bilbo can be devoted to the masses—whereas the others, the ones we have been raised to respect, the sincerely honorable men, are devoted to the vested interests (the railroads and the bankers, the planters and the money men in general), in a belief (false, I think, and he thinks too) that such interests are what make our country great. Except for such rare birds as Lincoln—who, at that, was foiled—our choice must lie between dishonesty and pridefulness or something like it. It comes at a time when I am wrestling with just that problem, but he hasnt the answer any more than I have. Of course there is another factor, perhaps a greater sin—the racial hatred such men as Bilbo use to whip up votes; but this man (the writer)[21] shows that this pitting of the rednecks against the negro was begun by the Bourbons after Reconstruction, in an attempt to claim that anyone who opposed the Democratic party was favoring a return to what we had under the Republicans. Then the Populists (whatever name they went under) turned around and used it too. Which of course makes it no less a sin. . . . Sometimes I think politics is too big a subject for my little pointy head.

Nembutol or no, Peggy wont bring Mgt. Last time she took the stuff was when we drove home something over a year ago, and she turned into an infantile Mr Hyde: squalled and bellered all the way home. Her forehead got two inches lower and her eyes turned small and beady—a real hellion.

At this rate I'll be done with the book by April 1st—certainly the first week in April. Soon after that I'll come down. I'm still trying to persuade Peggy but it's a losing battle.

---

21. Albert D. Kirwin.

Give me the dope on that granulation or primary-intention stuff—I'm really in the dark.

ta ta
Shelby

Sun: 22 Apr 51
DEAR WALKER

I put the corrected typescript into the mail last Tuesday and since then have been working at the plan for a big novel. The story is by no means clear as yet, but I have the subject, the characters, and the form; it will run about the length of my first three books all put together—five parts of 50,000 words each, Parts 1, 3 and 5 being a continuous story, Parts 2 and 4 being separate short novels designed to give the book historical and anthropological depth; 1-3-5 will be furiously paced, covering a short period, Dostoevskian; 2 and 4 will be biographies of persons already dead when the other story opens, and will be related to the other story only through minor characters; the contrast—emphasized through the interruptions—should be effective. All my books are one book anyhow, and this will dramatise the fact. The Delta is the hero and the book will be titled (or subtitled) "A Landscape With Figures." You see?

There is plenty of time to work it out, for I am going to NY in a week or so and then will come back and write a final draft of SHILOH, which I hope to persuade Dial to bring out in the spring of '52. The big one wont be finished for at least two years, if my past rate of composition is any guide. I should be at it seriously by early summer, God willing.

Be glad youve got your Book Find membership; Carson McCullers' collected novels and stories is the selection for May, including "The Ballad of the Sad Cafe" which you probably missed when it came out six years ago (or was it seven?). Very good for fantasy, which I ordinarily dont like.

I'll probably be in NY on May Day: I hope the Reds dont celebrate it by dropping the bomb on it. If they do, I hereby appoint you to see TAYB through the press—except of course there wont be any press to see it through. But you can drop by here, pick up my notes on Landscape, and write that too. Something ought to get you off your duff. The way to save your soul is lose it. If thats so I'll sure save mine.

No news—Margaret got through her maddog shots in good style.[22] I feel very good about everything.

Rgds:

Shelby

24 Apr 51

Youre in danger of making the same mistake about Lawrence so many of the pink tea set have made: calling him fascist. However, youll certainly be set straight when you come to the chapters about England during the war. DHL couldnt bear the very kind of authority Hitler & Co. represent. His real belief was set down in a letter (one youll agree with): "Men are less free than they imagine. The freest are perhaps least free. Men are free when they are obeying some deep inward voice of religious *belief*, when they belong to a living, organic, believing community, active in fulfilling some unfulfilled, perhaps unrealized, purpose. Men are freest when they are most unconscious of freedom. The shout is a rattling of chains, always was. . . ." In another place he said: "When man has nothing but his *will* to assert—even his good will—it is always bullying. Bolshevism is one sort of bullying, capitalism another." I am reading "The Plumed Serpent," his Mexican novel, next to the last thing he did (the last was Chatterly). In it he takes a swipe at the U.S.: "There are only two great diseases in the world today—Bolshevism and Americanism; and Americanism is the worst of the two, because Bolshevism only smashes your house or your business or your skull, but Americanism smashes your soul."

Of course, though, his great hate was Christ. He thought "spiritual love" was a profanation of our humanity. "The Man Who Died" is the damndest piece of blasphemy ever written.

In that short work he had Christ rise from the dead, wander off by himself until he meets a priestess of Isis, has intercourse with her, and repudiates all his teachings. Manhood is godhood—the phallic symbol replaces the Cross. . . . It is completely different from Nietzsche, for instance, who

---

22. Foote's daughter Margaret had received rabies shots after being nipped by a fox terrier, which subsequently disappeared.

was merely insanely jealous of Jesus. Lawrence really hated Him for all He stood for.

The best thing for you, I suppose, is not to follow him that far. He wrote ten novels:

The White Peacock (1911)
The Trespasser   Aaron's Rod (1922)
Sons & Lovers   The Lost Girl
The Rainbow   Kangaroo
Women in Love   The Plumed Serpent
Lady Chatterly's Lover.

"Aaron's Rod" marks the turning point. He very nearly dehumanized himself. I have read six of them and am reading the seventh. "Aaron's Rod" is a terrific book; youd be crazy about it. I can check it out of the library here for two weeks and send it to you if you want. Lawrence is strictly your meat as an artist if you can somehow keep from hating him in his final period. . . . If you want to keep on with him, let me know and I'll send you what I can. K. Haxton has them all, incidentally. Let me know.
Shelby

Thu: 26 Apr 51
The Dial editors like my book very much, they say, and are scheduling it for early fall. They also want to bring out SHILOH in April of '52. Which gives me everything I want. . . . I'm going up next week to talk finances (being broke) and then will come back here and write the final draft of Shiloh while completing the preliminary plan for the big novel, my two-year task. If I felt any better I'd bust. . . . I'm really very glad, too, in case I forgot to say so, that you liked the book. What I plan, if it's not inconvenient for Bunt and you, is for Peg and Margaret and me and a nurse to come down there for a week when I finish the Shiloh final draft—say late June or early July. Then I'll come back home and write my first big book; itll be as long as the first three put together, and the central figure will be the Delta itself: what a hero.

Want me to get you anything in NY?
Ta Ta.
Shelby

Friday: 11 May 51

Got back this afternoon—a good trip. Book will come out in September; publisher very happy. Changed title—now called THE DRY SEASON: much better, I think: expresses sterility of people as well as the 30s.

Browning comes by this same mail. Hope youll read it with pleasure, not only Bishop Blougram's Apology either.

Will write soon.

Shelby

16 May 51

Latest intelligence, Title department: LOVE IN A DRY SEASON. I was trying to think of a new title, couldnt think for hell, and came up with "Thoughts in a Dry Season"—then "Love in a Dry Season"—then "The Dry Season." I told George Joel (Dial) and he went crazy over Love etc. and has been bombarding me ever since, trying to persuade me to use it. So finally I said all right. As a matter of fact I think it's a good title. I'm considering using a sub-title too, making the whole thing read: "Love in a Dry Season; or, Who Put the Sand in the Vaseline?" However, I'll probably reject it on the grounds that prospective buyers might be misled into thinking it is a mystery.

Would very much like to come now, but Margaret is flower girl in some kind of function up in Memphis toward the end of the month. How would the second week in June be? Arriving, say, about the 7th? Roy says Phin will be here the 6th, will spend two weeks here before coming down to Covington. Would that avoid a jam? Coming the 7th, I mean.

All the best:

Shelby (OVER)

I am doing the final draft of SHILOH. I'll swear thats a good piece of work: it's a miracle to me how I did it. Incidentally, that one is yours—the dedication I mean. For one thing, you financed me through it. Maybe itll make a mint and get you back your money. Goerge Joel seems to think so—he's talking Book Clubs and so forth. Me, I dont think so.

S.

[May 1951]
Tuesday

I was glad to hear you say youve an idea for a new book.[23] But let me urge you this time to hold it to a novelette—of say 30,000 words, and by all means with a tightly knitted plot. And dont say you dont know any plots; everybody knows plots; whats more if thats your only excuse, I'll give you one of mine—Ive got about a hundred. The problem is *which*. All plots are good, correctly handled.

My point is that I think you need the discipline a tight plot demands. It supplies a need for concentration, holds your pen in line, and drives you ahead. Look at The Brothers Karamazov: tremendous narrative drive and strong enough to support any mass of theory he cared to pile on it. Of course I dont mean that pseudo-detective-story crap of Graham Greene's. I mean a real plot that doesnt depend on coincidence or happenstance. New Orleans is right in your back yard and it has everything: intellectuals, whores, priests, merchant seamen: you could make it boil and bubble. Use yourself, use me, use Bunt; fling us into that melee—something is bound to come of it.

But the main thing is for you to plot it carefully from beginning to end, making it fit a rigid time-scheme: Mardi Gras, for instance, with its climax and the following holy day. I hate to see you giving yourself so much rope. The moral is in a popular song: "You Cant Fuck Around With Love."

Dont worry about the end product resembling the original: it wont. Not even you yourself, for instance, suspected you were Duff Conway.

Draw up an outline and a calendar and do the character sketches before you ever begin writing. Here is a section from the Calendar I'm using now:*

1938
Munich—SEP—Florence dies; Drew runs.
conf   OCT

---

23. Percy's second unpublished novel, *The Gramercy Winner*, about a tuberculosis patient in an upstate New York sanatorium. The manuscript of this novel, unlike that of the first unpublished novel, survives. The original is in the Southern Historical Collection at the University of North Carolina at Chapel Hill.

1939

War—SEP—Drew-Amy in station wagon.

Major's 1st heart attack.

DEC—Suitor, Henry Stubblefield.

1940

Nazis   APR—Amanda rejects Henry's suit.

Cross—MAY—Death of Major Barcroft.

Meuse   Hullabaloo at Briartree.

You see what I mean? Then when you sit down to your desk you know where youre going and you know how youre going to get there.

Hope you dont object too much to this Dutch uncle attitude, but it frets me to see you down there going months at a time without working, and I think if youd tackle something tightly plotted youd stay with it. I'll be done with my book within six weeks (I think) and then I'll come down and we'll talk about it if youd like. Meantime work up something; we'll kick it around, make it coagulate, and put your nose to the grindstone. Man, thats living. Carlyle was right, providing a man has a choice. And God knows you have—though maybe thats the trouble.

Shelby

*This is a bigger canvas; yours, where Ive used years & months, would use months & days, or even days & hours.

22 May 51

All the time something. Sunday I had to drive Peggy up to Memphis for a funeral and Monday night when we got back there was a letter from Dial—some bird who sings dirty Dwight Fiskish songs in the Edison Hotel has the name Charley Drew; so he's not Charley now—he's Harley. I damn well wasnt going to change his last name: not after spending eight months of avoiding using the past tense of the verb "to draw." Harley Drew—I dont know; maybe it's better. It would be best to write books, pegging away till they were absolutely the best you could do, then put them away in a drawer.

I rewrote 72 pages of SHILOH last week; will do an equal amount this week; and therefore will be done with the whole by the 1st week of June. I will bring it with me (if we come) so you can give it a final going-over. Ive changed it very little, though this is the third draft. . . . In some ways it's the best thing Ive done. But I was certainly amazed to find the Dial people so excited about publishing it next April.

The British (Hamish Hamilton) edition of Follow Me Down will be out early this summer, and if it catches on, there will be another source of income. The Signet edition will be issued sometime during the last of June.

The weather here is very hot and very dry. Farmers screaming blue murder—as always. Really hot, though, especially out in the sun. I like it.

Roy and Sarah[24] and all the children are fine, enjoying the coolness of the country.

Heard a funny joke. General and Mrs MacArthur were sitting together somewhere and a band began to play The Star Spangled Banner. He took her hand and said, "Listen, darling, theyre playing our song."

Another. Moss Hart, the NY producer, is very conscious of being a well-known personality. He is supposed to have gone into a hotel in Atlantic City, approached a bell boy, and said: "Hello; I'm Moss Hart. Where's the men's room?"

Thus endeth the second lesson.

Rgds:

Shelby

24 May 51

No news. I just finished re-reading the letters of Keats: they amaze me more each time I read them. For instance this is his account of his writing habits:

"Whenever I find myself vaporish (he means while he is in the midst of writing) I rouse myself, wash and put on a clean shirt, brush my hair and clothes, tie my shoestrings neatly, and in fact adonize as if I were going out—then all clean and comfortable I sit back down to write. This I find the greatest relief."

No Bohemian, Keats.

---

24. Sarah Farish Percy, Roy Percy's wife.

Walker Percy and Shelby Foote, as they appeared in the 1936 University of
North Carolina yearbook. *Courtesy of North Carolina Collection, University of
North Carolina Library at Chapel Hill.*

The writing habits of writers interest me very much. Do you know anything about Trollope? On beginning a novel he used to prepare a diary divided into weeks, and allot to each week the number of pages necessary to complete the work by the date set. This number varied according to his other duties, from twenty to a hundred and twelve pages a week. After his retirement from the Post Office, he rose habitually at 5:30 and wrote continuously for three hours with his watch before him on the table, exacting from himself 250 words every quarter of an hour.

The strange thing is that, in his way (a lesser way, it's true) Trollope is as good as Keats. You should read him; you would like him; you just might like him best of all novelists—no ax to grind, just a story to tell, and plenty of time to tell it in.

The new novel has gone to the printers—after a change of title (two, in fact) and a change from Charley to Harley. I hope now I'm shed of it except for reading galleys and page-proofs. They are using that Third Man photograph down the back flap of the dustjacket, saving the verso for quotes on TMENT and FMD from reviews. Do you reckon I'm going to be a low-sale writer all my life? Tis a comsummation devoutly to be wisht. Dial believes that SHILOH is going to go like a house afire; they have some confidence in the new book too but not as much. Publishers are very strange people, past my understanding.

I want to know if youve let your novel completely Go. Whether you like it or not, I think it's very bad to abandon a piece of work. Shorten it if you want, but dont just drop it. And by all means go on to another. Shakespeare himself probably couldnt write if he laid off for six months; it's like musicians keeping their dexterity. But there's a better reason. Prayer may bring a man in touch with the angels; I dont know. But I do know that the closest to God I ever come is when I'm at my work. Otherwise I dont even feel that I'm part of creation; I'm like a rag. But then a spirit leaps and lifts me by the hair. (Browning.)

Shelby

22 Aug 51

DEAR WALKER

I'm having a great concerted go at the Greeks, whom I have read in volume but spottily up to now. In the past two weeks Ive read the ILIAD, the

ODYSSEY, about a dozen plays, Aristotle's POETICS (wonderful!), and am now settling down to what will be a through-the-winter job—a three-volume thing called PHAEDIA[25] by a German named Jaeger, a survey of Greek culture from archaic times through Plato. It's very good. I'll re-read the standard things (Thucidides, etc) as I come to them in the Phaedia. It's quite a program; I should have done it years ago. I'm plunged into Hesiod now: WORKS & DAYS.

Advance copies of DRY SEASON should reach me either the end of this week or early next week. When theyre at hand I want to come down and spend a few days with you. NO BO.[26] Your charity really runs out before you get to him, like Our Savior and the money lenders. From now on a simple "no" will suffice. But I'll keep asking. . . . I should be able to rip through some of the obscurer Greeks in your Loeb collection while I'm down there—meanwhile you can be briefing me on bonedeep prostate cancer; I want to draw up a calendar schedule for it—also the same on the freak lobectomy. I have a nice scene in mind: The old man in bed after the castration, pounding the floor with his knuckles, singing No Balls A-tall.

I'm still making jottings in the big ledger, notions for the background of the book. It will be called TWO GATES TO THE CITY, subtitled: A Landscape With Figures. The title comes from a passage in Odyssey XIX: "Stranger, dreams are tricksy things and hard to unravel. By no means all in them comes true for us. Twin are the gates to the impalpable land of dreams, these made from horn and those of ivory. Dreams that pass by the pale carven ivory are irony, cheats with a burden of vain hope: but every dream which comes to man through the gate of horn forecasts the future truth."

My young man (the third cousin) has a choice (industrialism or agrarianism, spiritualism or materialism, and so forth) and the making of this choice is the novel—all played of course against the background of his heritage. The Delta itself is the "hero": therefore the subtitle. . . . But we'll talk of this later. It's going to be quite a thing, God willing. Half Romantic, half Classical—another tie-in with the title.

Take keer:

Shelby

---

25. *Paideia: The Ideals of Greek Culture* (1939), by Werner Jaeger.
26. Bo was Foote's notoriously aggressive bulldog.

18 Sep 51

Back hard at work on the plan for the new big book. It goes gropingly but good; surely this is the one. I think I see the mission, one you have quarreled with from the beginning. A study of suffering: evil. Thus I free myself of obsession and thereby deliver whoever follows me. Not disciples (who wants disiciples?) but readers and the writers who come later. Part of this resolve was caused by my re-reading of The Rainbow; it gives off something really holy for a writer—a reaffirmation that the heart of man, the strength of the man-man and man-woman relationship, is subject enough for all writers for all time, and whatever adds to this is just for extra, truly needed but always merely extra; and no writer must ever forget it. You seem to think the thing not worth the risk, that in dealing with evil you soil your hands and soil your book. Shit! As far as I'm concerned even the man-God relationship comes under the category Extra—I'll deal with that and I'll deal with much else; but the hard core will always be what I *know*. Anything else is speculation, never more than interesting; I dont feel it. Blasphemy . . . Watch now; I'm on my way.

Shelby

7 Oct 51

The Lawrence book,[27] at long last, goes into this same mail; Peggy finally threw up her hands, about fifty pages from the end. I enjoyed it: more, however, for the factual information than for the "interpretation." An overdose of the so-called New Criticism has made me leary of all such conjectures; for though I read such stuff with great interest, I find it more interesting than valid. One thing I am certain of: it would be a great mistake for a writer consciously to go about writing a book the way most of these critics seem to think it's done. I am as serious a writer as ever existed, and my work has these effects they marvel over; yet they were achieved by intuition in the main—even when they seem most obvious. Symbolism for instance. I wrote a book (Dry Season) which is a technical exercise in the handling of dissimilar plots; at only one point in the book do these plots actually cross

---

27. *The Life and Works of D. H. Lawrence* (1951), by Harry T. Moore.

or come in contact; and when I wrote that scene I hung a stoplight over it, blinking alternate red and green. Now surely nothing could be more obvious than that—yet it was not until I looked back on it, actually in print, that I realized what I'd done. I dont mean by this that the effects are accidental or that the symbolism is entirely unconscious; I just mean that it frequently is, and that no critic can pretend to validity in such matters. I read them the way some people read detective stories—as exercises in ingenuity on the part of the critic. As such, theyre fun—and the more farfetched the more fun, up to the point of absurdity.

Not that Moore's book is that kind of thing. It isn't; it's really almost a model job, and as I said, I enjoyed it very much. I'm talking about the critical writings of such people as Richard Chase—the one who referred to Faulkner's "linear discreteness" and "holistic consciousness." (You see what I mean?) There is a priceless volume on Kafka ("The Frozen Sea") which reduces all his writing to a parade of Freudian symbols—literally. This week's New Yorker has a parody of such writings, an avante-garde dissection of *Black Beauty* wherein the critic takes sideswipes at an imaginary Marxian rival who has handled the book from *his* point of view. It's very funny, though not as funny as it could have been.

To get back to Lawrence, though: the work has impressed me enormously during this re-reading, especially in the quality you pointed out: his awareness of the tremendous mystery of man and his ability to communicate, without solving, that mystery. Stendhal was the first to do this (I'm surprised you werent bowled over by him) but the trouble is, he isnt a very good writer technically; it satisfies only the intellect, which isnt enough for me at any rate—it isnt enough even when it's skilfully done, as it was by Tolstoy (there I go, hacking at your man again): which is slicked-up Stendhal. But never mind that (and to get back to DHL): I must say, though, that the parts of Lawrence's work I like best are the graphic incidents, like the charivari in *The Rainbow*, or the letter-incident in the London club in *Women in Love*, or the England-in-wartime chapter in *Kangaroo*. It's strange, however, how very bad Lawrence could be when he wrote of actual all-out violence, as in the attack on Don Ramon's hacienda in *The Plumed Serpent*. I wonder if youve read his novelette "The Fox"; it's in the Portable—a marvelous thing: symbolism as it should be, wherein the symbols are graspable and apt and can be taken or let alone. . . . Here are DHL books I have that you havent read; if you want any of them let me know: Selected Poems, The Virgin & the Gypsy, The Lost Girl, Aaron's Rod, the Portable, The Man Who Died. Only the third and fourth of these are full-length novels.

Tell me, has your St Fiacre arrived? If it's damaged in any way send it back and I'll have it replaced; shipment's guaranteed. And tell me something of him. Is there any reason why he's holding a shovel?

Cold weather here and Margaret has picked up a virus. Hope I dont come down with it; I'm leaving the 17th, a Wednesday. Sorry you and Bunt arent going. Maybe next year.

Rgds:

Shelby

10 Oct 51

DEAR WALKER

Ive finished the final fine-tooth combing of *Shiloh*: I have it ready to take with me next week. The main purpose of my trip is an interview with an editor of LIFE magazine to try to interest him in doing a picture-&-text article on the battle; this is the 90th anniversary. It could be done either as a review of my book or as a separate article. George Joel (Dial president) says, however, that probably nothing can be arranged until they see galley proofs of the book, which wont be until six weeks or so after I deliver the typescript.

Yesterday I had an interesting experience: went to the courthouse for a public hearing before the governor, asking for a commutation for a man sentenced to be electrocuted the following night. About 600 people were there. There were two speakers, Gervys Lusk[28] & myself—a curious combination. It came off well; the governor granted the commutation, a thing he's never done before. I feel good about it, though I still consider myself a private man—meaning to hell with the public & their troubles except as they provide grist for my mill: which, incidentally, like the will of God, grinds exceedingly slow. I certainly will be glad to get back home & back to work—thats my life; thats *all* my life.

---

28. Gervys Lusk was a fellow Greenvillian.

Of course we're all "involved in mankind," but it seems to me we should be something more: "involved in God," youd call it. I think there is beginning to be an interesting emphasis on "meditation"—Ive even seen references to it lately in the press, not only in the religious columns, either. Lord knows it's true, a man ought to have some private hole—or tower—to crawl into. He'd damn well better have, what with the increasing complexity, the technocracy. Otherwise he'll either become a cog or a psychotic; I'm not sure which is worse.

The new, big book has come on decently. I have a ream of notes—they half fill a ledger—which I'll settle down & digest when I get back. It's going to be very good I think, experimental in both context & form, but valid in the best sense. Serious books all require the reader's interest & sympathy; the best of them compel it. This one will do just that. I feel very sure of it as far as *form* goes, for I have it completed in that respect. The emphasis will be on character. Action will be for the sake of delineating character; there will be no "fine" writing for its own sake; the whole thing will be inexorable, unavoidable, unrelenting—always with that precision which I hope has become characteristic of my style, my "quality of vision." It's what Ive been trying for, from TOURNAMENT through DRY SEASON, & I think Ive got it now, or I'm winning near: selective but myriad, giving at once an impression of economy & completeness; even the incidentals are important, else they wouldnt be there. You see I ask of a reader confidence & sympathy; thats why Ive kept my books short at the outset—I have to demonstrate my right to my demands, which really are presumptuous in a beginner. I didnt do all I wanted, by a long shot. But it's too late now; I'm not a beginner anymore. After SHILOH (which is a sort of spark thrown off in the process) comes the big one: TWO GATES TO THE CITY. We'll see. . . .

I wish youd go on & get yourself another boxer, now that youve found out how lovable they are. You might not believe it but another boxer will have all Mädchen's traits, especially if you get another female. I think it's a shame to have that fine Kentucky gate without a big dog to dash back & forth behind it. Not to speak of the security from prowlers.

Hope you can read the writing. I didn't feel up to plunking on the typewriter. Prenez garde:

Shelby

I'm reading volumes III & IV of Freeman's WASHINGTON. Very dry, & very good.

28 Oct 51

DEAR WALKER

The NY trip was a successful one, especially for Peggy; she literally had the time of her life. It's an outrage you havent taken Bunt—I can say it now that Peggy has accompanied me on the fifth of five trips. She really did enjoy herself. For her the highlight of the visit was seeing Brenda Frazier in the Stork Club; but I also took her through the Metropolitan and the Frick and one night to a concert of Mozart quartets by the Juilliard Quartet.

Big hopes for SHILOH, they say—both as regards the critics and sales. Hope so.

One feature of my trip was a speech to a creative writing class at your alma mater, Columbia. I talked for an hour and could have gone on for two more; I was under the obligation to refute much that had been told them by the previous week's speaker, Norman Mailer. I enjoyed doing it, too. Charles Rolo was the teacher and he said it was the best job in his experience. I certainly appear to be gifted—to me, I mean.

DRY SEASON appears to have been a terrible blow to those who considered themselves my "discoverers." It seems they thought (judging from FMD) that I was going to save American literature with a quality too long missing, namely compassion. Then here I come with this thing in which I took the characters apart with a sort of fiendish pleasure in their squirmings under the knife. Or so it seemed to these few admirers. . . . They vary 180 degrees from you, in other words. To them there was something highly moral about FMD, lacking in DRY SEASON. I see what they mean, of course, but it means nothing to me, absolutely nothing. It's death to pay the slightest attention to them on even the smallest matter. The Herald-Tribune reviewer (from Ohama, Neb. of all places) went into a tirade about what a shame it was that a young man with my gifts was unable to see anything in American life but "maggots." I suspect I'll fall between the two stools of Protestantism and Catholicism every time. If I listened to them I'd write like, say, Robert Nathan; if I listened to you I'd write like Graham Greene. I dont know which is worse. It's much better up here, above the conflict.

Come on up, I'd say—except of course youve lost my most precious possession: invincible ignorance.

Dial wouldnt do what I wanted on SHILOH. I wanted it to be a $2 book. They say it wouldnt sell. It's to be a $3 book, with larger type. I reckon they know best.

This is mighty spotty. I'll sit down and write a sensible letter sooner or later. We're all fine and hope you all are too.

Shelby

31 Oct 51

DEAR WALKER

Ive just read Greene's "The End of the Affair." Curious: at once banal and morose, matter-of-fact yet pretentious; an unhappy, cheap book. And yet it would have been a fine book if it had been written by a true unbeliever. Good writers are not wise men, nor men with faith; good writing proceeds from doubt. It was Dostoevsky's doubt that made him great—Ivan is a portrait of his doubt, as Mitya is a portrait of his lust. Faith kills art. To have sure faith in anything but the efficacy of art is a sin against art, and the artist pays a terrible price for such sins—immediate and future too.

When you come right down to it, Greene is about as unperceptive as the "I" of the novel, except the pretentiousness might fool you from time to time. I liked the end best, the part that follows the woman's death. Most of the rest is truly bad. For instance, page 27: beginning, "What a summer it was . . ." on halfway through page 28: "Had he learned the gesture from her?" It's contrived and weak—pretentious.

Turnell's[29] article on the Catholic novel was interesting. I think I know what the trouble is, though I'm not sure. Given a gifted man, why should he need to write about doubt? Thats what all the religious novels Ive seen are about; they seem to think nothing else is interesting. To me thats a cheap, commercial notion. There should be some really positive writing—doubt need not even be considered. Let him write of faith as coolly, as detachedly as Maupassant wrote of sex. Then I think youd have a true religious novel.

---

29. Martin Turnell; the article appeared in *Commonweal*.

But I guess it will never be done; even the would-be writers take doubt as their subject. I had no reservations in reading of the miracles, any of the four or five in the book; I did not think it weakened the book at all; rather I think it was the one good section of the book, except that now, looking back, it seems to me that Greene was throwing them in as a clincher, like the last ten pages of one of his "entertainments." He cant get that stuff out of his quill; he never will; the confessional helps very little in art. You sin and then you learn to live with your sin and if possible sin no more, but that sin can never be undone; there is no one you can go to, no box to kneel in. It's more like the Old Testament than the New.

I have learned something these past few years, however. All religions except the Catholic and the Jewish are absolute junk. I went to church Sunday; they were dedicating a window to my uncle—the bishop preached. The whole affair (not the dedication: the service) made me want to stand up and call them fools. There was Johnny Kirk, chief vestryman, and a lot of exMethodists wanting to capture the carriage trade, and Ben Wasson enjoying the beauty of the language and the proximity of Alou Haycraft. There wasnt the slightest touch of sanctity; they werent even lukewarm. The blasphemer is ten times closer to God than theyll ever be.

Ive begun my book. It's going to be a great book; I feel ten inches taller than Shakespeare.

Shelby

8 Nov 51

DEAR WALKER

Our difference of opinion over the purpose of the novel is one of degree; for while I certainly agree with you that "words exist to communicate meanings," we dont at all agree as to the nature of meaning. You seem to think the novelist is some exalted kind of pamphleteer, and whats more you seem to think that his "meaning" is preferably derived from some standard body of thought his mind has discovered and accepted as a duty to pass on to others—seeking converts to his discovery. As a matter of fact, as I have said before, the best novelists have all been doubters; their only firm conviction, the only one that is never shaken, is that absolute devotion and belief in the sanctity of art which results in further seeking, not a sense of having found. That part of any writer's book which says "Look: here Ive found the answer" is always the weakest. The search is always better done; the discovery is invariably a letdown. Dont tell me you have swallowed that hokum about the writer being a Wise Man. As a matter of fact he is stupid to an amazing degree about the things that people value; he has a bloc that stops him short of acceptance, that makes him examine what others accept; he can be fascinated by the shape of his own hand, watching it by lamplight hold the pen; for him "understanding" is merely description—that is enough. Your wise-man says "There is my hand; all right; lets get on to important things. How about the relation of God to man?" But the artist, I believe, concentrating on the hand itself, without even a thought of God, comes closer to finding the meaning simply by observing how the hand, held between his eye and the lamp, becomes semi-transparent, showing the skeleton hand beneath.

Or if thats not plain, let me state it plainer. I think the novelist's principal task is the communication of sensation. If he does this, and does it right, he has rescued something from time and chaos. It can be done in just two words if they are words that come together with a shock and strike the reader as memorable, drive themselves, thus juxtaposed, like a two-spiked nail into his brain: "blue night": then Blue and Night can be elaborated on for five hundred words. Call it feeding oneself if you want, but I know it's more. It's an act of devotion beyond prayer—which, incidentally, comes at least as close to "fondling oneself" as any tracing of words on paper—or at least it's prayer with art; he's praying, too. As far as that goes, I'll bet Anatole France's juggler (who juggled for Our Lady because that was all he had to offer) found grace in Her sight. And if She laughed, watching him: "Look how well he does it; isnt it clever?" that too was to his credit and made his offering all the more acceptable.

One of the things I have most admired the Catholic religion for is its unwillingness to compromise and its essentially realistic outlook. But the Catholic intellectuals seem to destroy all this. Here we've been better than five hundred years (since the Divine Comedy—which, incidentally, is as much a spiteful paying-off of personal animosity as it is "Catholic") without a single devoted Catholic writer producing one big lasting thing in the field of poetry or fiction; and yet, mind you, these intellectuals insist that the advantage lies with writers with an orthodox background to fall back on; it

gives them a scale of reference, they say. It ought to be true; it ought to—
but look at the result. Graham Greene, or a bare handful of minor poets
like Hopkins. . . . Thou shalt have no other gods before you, is a dictum of
art; and whoever departs from this is penalized to the degree of his departure. (Dont point to Dostoevsky, that sin-eaten man; he hated your pope
like poison. I agree with Carr that when D's psychology is as outdated as his
theology, then indeed we'll be able to see his greatness, though it's also true
that he was so great that whoever wants to can concentrate on a single facet
and be struck with the terrific power of the whole, like the point of a spear
with the weight of the shaft behind it.) (Incidentally, when I spoke of "outdated" in that parenthesis I didnt mean untrue; I meant unshared by the
reading public and by those (like me) who, I believe, appreciate his greatness best.)

What you need, and need badly, is a really intensive study of Proust—
Dostoevsky's only rival. Ive said this to you so often it seems silly to keep on
saying it. I know too it seems to do no good. All youve read is SWANN'S
WAY, which is almost purely objective and serves merely to introduce you
to Proust's world. The landscape lies beyond that introduction and the subject is a great one: the discovery of a hidden vocation. Art hunted him down
like the hound of heaven and found him in the end.

All this is a bit on the manic too I reckon, but now I'm settling down for
my two-year job. In conception at any rate it's the greatest thing since Aes-
culus' Orestia (which, by the way, youve neglected too; why dont you get
some reading done?). I have a suggestion. Billy & Robert are having a
birthday on the 17th; Sarah and little Roy are putting on a marionette
show, "The Frog Prince," which Mary Pratt would enjoy enormously. You
three come up. It's been a long time now and it's high time.

Daniel[30] is still in Knoxville; it's just that he has a good friend who is an
editor at Knopf. This friend put him up to it. I'm quite a catch nowadays it
seems; Rinehart and Random are at it too, but it doesnt mean a thing. Part
of it is because of FOLLOW ME DOWN which has quite a flock of admirers among bookmen and talk is beginning to get around about SHILOH
(which incidentally Random refused in the old days, because "women read-

---

30. Robert Daniel, a professor of English and lifelong friend of Foote's and
Percy's.

ers constitute about 75% of the bookbuying public"); it doesnt mean a bloody thing; they scent the buck along with a whiff of Class, and that always sets them wild, especially after some small publisher has absorbed the early losses or at any rate taken the risks which would have been losses except for the subsidization by Signet.

Well, here's been a great to-do, and mind you I didnt say half that I intended. Are you there?

Rgds:

Shelby

10 Nov 51

Began book:[31] here's opening sentence.

"Three years ago they took it off; but up till then, since back beyond the memory of any man now living, there was a midnight train out of Memphis, south one hundred and fifty miles to Bristol; the Cannonball they called it, in inverse ratio to the compliment implied, for the trip was scheduled at just under seven hours and even so the thing was always late, stopping at every station along the line, backing onto spur-tracks to reach others, and panting on sidings—not so much from impatience as from age—while faster trains ran past without even a hoot."

Thus youre prepared for an introduction to my hero: the Delta. The book opens with a trainride, as do The Idiot, The Magic Mountain, and Of Time and the River.

I am supposed to be writing from the vantage point of 1953. The next sentence begins: "Five years ago . . ." which sets the date of the narrative: 1948.

Shelby

17 Nov 51

We're so far apart on the matter that anything we say only serves to emphasize the distance; the words sound faint, as if across a valley, a valley that I suppose should be called Unbelief, or Belief. This latest remark, that

---

31. Foote's intended magnum opus, *Two Gates to the City*.

the characters in a novel must be "redeemable" or else theyre uninteresting, proves conclusively (though I understand your point and sympathize with it, too) the invalidity of your position. Youre taking a part for the whole. . . . Why, man, there are plenty of other basic things as important. For instance, the most interesting book Ive read in the past year was "Geraldine Bradshaw"; the most *un*interesting was "The End of the Affair"; and while I happen to be prejudiced against Greene (I find his style mechanical) I'm willing to concede that he and Willingham are about equal as far as being gifted goes. Then why (for me) was the latter's book so much better? The answer is simple: vitality.

The most unredeemable character in all literature is also one of the most interesting: Don Juan. (Youll claim that thats what makes him interesting: being the reverse of everything positive. Balls!) Mozart's version of Don Juan—Don Giovanni—is a magnificent conception, vital, masculine, never ridiculous, and all this mind you without a single great aria: pure vitality and intentness of purpose.

But never mind.

My cold is better; I'm back at work on the book and it goes well in spite of all the cruel interruptions of sickness and a wife who wont get out of bed in the morning and inlaws who come calling. After Xmas I'm going to shave my head and grow a beard and growl like a bear at anyone who comes near me, including Margaret. A year's solid labor and I'll've written one of the big ones: Ive got my subject and my form—it's just a question of sitting down to it now.

Today I'm thirty-five. Why didnt you tell me it was like this? After all, youve been 35 for some months now. In my case, though, it's different: I dont look it.

Didacticism is death to the creative urge; a story had better be told for its own sake. Then, but only then, it will bear the burden of whatever the writer wants to load it with. Nobody knew it better than my boy Dostoevsky; Mitya and Ivan are certainly redeemable but youve overemphasized its importance outside The Brothers—you think the only tragedy is the spurning of redemption, and your mistake comes with that "only." The best way to tell a story is to tell the truth as you feel it: leave the reader to find what he wants therein—and if youve told it fully and truly, it will all be there. Leave psychology to the psychologists, theology to the theologians, and never put the cart before the horse. The novel will bear all kinds of strain; you can wrench the time-sequence and gain from the effect, you can throw out grammar, leave the book without beginning middle or end, you can do any number of such things and gain from the effect. But the instant you make it something besides a novel FIRST, youre going to wind up with nothing. . . . I think the real difference is, I'm talking about novels and youre talking about Protestant sunday-school tracts; old John Calvin is breathing down your neck.

Shelby

29 Nov 51

I'll vow and declare it's going mighty good! The manuscript is stacking up apace, solid good thick analytical stuff which I'll pick up as I come to it in the start-to-finish writing of the book, which should be something like assembling something shipped directly from the factory; all I need is a few cotter pins and a couple of tubes of glue (Duco cement).

Galley proofs are due next week on SHILOH—for which George Joel (Dial) is still singing hymns of praise and claims the critics are already in a flurry. I'm in like Flynn, he says. Now watch everything go haywire. I predict it with a confidence born of selfknowledge.

Hemingway's right: it isnt good to talk about a book until youve written it. But I declare I feel awful good about this one, and I wish I had a chance to tell you all the various developments since I saw you last. It's going to read like a disassembled jigsaw puzzle until the reading has been completed; then everything falls into place as clearly as if I'd told it chronologically, but with ten times the effectiveness because (as in fact) the past is always strained through the present. The subtitle explains much: "A Landscape with Figures." Incidentally, if I were a Catholic this would be a fine Catholic novel, for the immediate situation is a choice on the part of one of the main characters; which way shall he go? Therefore: TWO GATES TO THE CITY. All the same, the city's the City of God.

Will you be there on that great getting-up morning?

Shelby

Walker Percy, an undergraduate at UNC (left leg thrust forward), waits in line for the 3:30 show at the Carolina Theater in Chapel Hill. *Courtesy of North Carolina Collection, University of North Carolina Library at Chapel Hill.*

30 Nov 51

Work still goes good, which means I'm still on the crest of a manic wave. The work is all that really matters; I think I could smile at the clap if my work was going good. If not—why, the very ants seem to have been put on earth just to devil me; my paranoia comes down.

Letter from Calder Willingham yesterday. I wrote to him last week, telling him (somewhat fatuously) that I thought he and I were the only writers under 50 worth our salt. (He more or less agreed.) I said, different as we are, our work was vital and had a deeper seriousness than what the flits are doing, yet him the critics call Naturalistic, and me they largely ignore. He said: "Well, as for naturalism, I used to worry about all that but had to lay it aside. They can call me whatever they want to, I dont give a damn, or if I do, to hell with it."

He is living in New York City, but says: "Ive thought of going back to Rome, Georgia—do you like it in Mississippi? I dont think I would like it in Rome, not that I like it in New York, this is no civilized place to live."

Sounds lost and wind-grieved. I suspect he hasnt gotten that Bradshaw girl out of his mind, whatever her name really was—a thing like that can age a man before his time. Anyhow, he's not thirty yet; thats one thing he can be thankful for, except it never occurs to you till you *are*.

The Dial people still seem hepped over SHILOH: theyre really going to get behind it and push. I dont know: I'll believe it when I see it. A thing like that could fall flat on it's face. Me, I'm an island, entire in itself. . . . Theyre still talking Book Club—baloney! Ive never put much faith in Fortune. But if she ever takes me by the hand, I'll give her a thundering jump that will electrify the very marrow of her bones.

Gott mit uns!

Shelby

6 Dec 51

We are essentially in agreement as to Willingham et al, and Faulkner too; I blush for the latter every time he opens his mouth, but fortunately he seldom does—I think as a matter of fact he's terribly afraid of snubs and sneers; after all, he's had twenty years of being called the corncob man. He ought to have said, early in his career, like Willingham: "I dont give a damn—or if I do, to hell with it." That contains much that I like best about W's work: it expresses the point of view he'd like to have, and then qualifies it with truth, or anyhow the truth with some brashness. . . . I know I'm right in staying home, but some folks *cant* stay home and it's quite true that once youve left you cant go back. Look at you, even. It takes a war; that you *can* come home from, and with your appreciation heightened.

Terrific burst of creativeness! To date, after six months of futzing round, I have 9/22nds of TWO GATES in first draft, 260-odd pages. Mid 53 is the wind-up date. I'll make it, too, God willing. . . . The best thing about being a writer is you know youre going to get nothing but the finger and therefore no bad luck is quite as bad as it is with most people. There are other compensations, too: an inner satisfaction that only comes from the relationship of a man with himself, an occasional handsome woman (strictly windfalls, though, without denoument: that is best), and the knowledge that you did your work on your own, undependant on catering to the public. I can see you sneering at Item Two in that list. You were never wronger. Didn't they tell you at the outset, man's a beast?

Little Margaret had her tonsils and adenoids out Monday: came through fine and now is on the mend. The tonsils werent so bad anyhow; it was the adenoids—they were really bad. She was spitting mad, however, when she woke up hurting. They had told her it was going to be a lark. I'm afraid, though, she's been infected with the literary virus: the first coherent thing she said when she came from under the ether was, "Wipe my tears." Sounds like Louisa Mae Alcott—I was tempted to disown her. . . . They are up in Memphis: I keep in touch by telephone, and am getting a prodigious amount of work done.

I'm doing almost no reading, just a dab of the Greeks every night. Translation is a big drawback, though, and I'm certainly not going to learn that frightful-looking stuff at this late date. Small latin and less greek was good enough for Shakespeare and it's good enough for me. . . . Speaking of Shakespeare, I composed my epitaph last week. Here tis:

HIC JACET

SHELBY FOOTE.

OF ALL WHO EVER LIVED UPON THIS EARTH

HE LOVED THREE:

SHAKESPEARE, MOZART, AND HIMSELF

ALTHOUGH NOT NECESSARILY IN THAT ORDER

Shelby

8 Dec 2

DEMAND THAT YOU RETRACT THE STATEMENT THAT (AND I QUOTE) "SHILOH IS EXACTLY THE KIND OF THING THEY (THE BOOK-OF-THE-MONTH-CLUB PEOPLE) WANT."

WHAT KIND OF A THING IS THAT TO SAY TO A SO-CALLED FRIEND OF YOURS?

UP YOUR LEG!

S. Foote

Dec. 1951

Sunday

Youre right I'm in the miseries, but youre a little off on why. I havent seen a single panning review on DRY SEASON; in fact youve seen all the reviews Ive seen—and thats the trouble. It seems to have been launched like a brick and to have sunk as fast. My three old friends, the ones who have been kindest to me in the past—The New Yorker, Herald-Tribune, and Time Magazine—gave it the complete go-by. I'm in the doldrums consequently.

No matter, however. I'm off for NY Wednesday with the typescript of SHILOH—thats the good thing about all this: there's always another one. Some day when the tank goes dry I'll take the easiest way of all and walk west till my hat floats.

Peggy is going with me; she finally talked me into it after having said, one month ago, wild horses couldnt drag her. Man, you cant tell about women, Mr Merton, no way in the world.

Rgds:

Shelby

11 Dec 51

I approve entirely of your idea; Paris is the place, too. We could set up quite a menage, a sort of duplex, sharing the kitchen and parlor-diningroom; Mary Pratt and Margaret could be together, with one nurse for the two, while Peggy and Bunt were off marketing and culture-soaking—I mean I think it would really be fine; and I'll bet it wouldnt cost a cent more than we're living on right now. I could even put everything in storage and save house rent; we'd have one car over there instead of two—it would work out fine all the way round, I'm positive. Besides, Ive intended to do it all along. The question is WHEN: when would be the time to take the break? Certainly not until I finish Two Gates (mid53, is the schedule). Then would be the proper time psychologically. Money isnt the problem, no big one anyhow—I'll get a Guggenheim, or just live on royalties plus an advance on the work-in-progress; I really could. I think we ought to count on it; there is plenty of time, barring war—and if war comes, it will mean an end to all plans whatever, so what the hell. I say definitely Yes; we'll do it. Summer after next we'll pack and take off: Mid53. Check. That would be the year before the children start to school, and therefore doubly perfect; we'd come back in time for them to start school in the fall of '54. They'd be six.

One reason I approve of the notion so thoroughly is that I want to spread out a bit: not for subject matter, not my essential subject matter anyhow, but for a sort of broadening of outlook, a sense of Europe. I only got a taste of it, but even so, I tell you man, it's something.

I think you have resolved our argument on Art; I think youre right—but the New Criticism is mighty sorry ground to draw a truce on. A bunch of clowns, I'll swear. I tell you what writing needs, and badly. It absolutely needs a sense of Place. A book like The Sun Also Rises (I'm deliberately taking the best of the lot) is a goddam total loss in every way except for entertainment and psychological observation. What the novel needs is a sense of proceeding from generations of knowledge. This may come from my being Southern, I guess it does, but I know that good work has a sense of permanence. I dont mean the Family novel, certainly not in the old sense; but there does have to be a family and a past, or else the book is like a free-flying balloon being carried whichever way the wind blows. This, or something like it, is what I'm trying to get away from—Two Gates is going to be planted solid as a rock. Not a bloody damned Incident, for God sake: rather a permanent thing that it took eighty years to live. The time is the present: yes, it must be: but all the past is behind it, you know it's there.

Statement in last week's NYTimes Bk Rev quotes John S Harmon of the Great Books Foundation in ref Dry Season: "Shelby Foote is no ordinary novelist. This book places him as one of our major writers." You see? Theyll come along one by one, slowly but surely, and believe me it's better that way. Everything's going to be all right; youll see. All I need is longevity.

Shelby

Greenville:
New Yr's Eve [1951]
I just finished reading page-proofs of SHILOH and I'll give you my considered opinion. This one does it: I'm among the American writers of all time—got there on the fourth book, which surely is soon enough, and at the age of thirty-five, which surely is late enough. Still, I dont regret that five-year chunk the war took out of my life. . . . Of course I'm perfectly prepared for its nonrecognition; it may sink without a ripple—though I dont see how it's possible. Still, I KNOW what Ive done, and I know what I'm going to do. Jesus, I'm lucky. Mind you, it's a many-faceted talent, too. Here in the middle of my main anthropological Jordan County examination Ive tossed off something in the Stendhal-Tolstoy-Crane tradition, and I honestly think it stacks up with those others. All I want is time—another thirty years. Think I'll go have an electro-cardiagram to find if it's possible. Then under that nice cool grass and let posterity take care of the rest. Life is a wonderful thing, believe me: a Godgiven wonderful thing.

Or so I say now. Next month I'll be tearing my hair, messing up reams of paper with unsightly inkblots and cursing God for having put me on this clod of a planet. Ooooo!—like a dog baying the moon.

Got the dust-jacket too, and I like it. A wartime engraving of a battle scene, printed in blue and gray. Also the engraver did a good job on my three-color map; it will be used as endpapers. The book itself will be bound in black, with gold lettering. Youll like it I think.

Tell Bunt I thank her for the phrase "brunt end of the stick" though I quoted her without acknowledgment. Also I thank you for having called my attention to the fellow with his balls jumping through the front of his jacket, an acrobatic figure to say the least.

All's well on the delta front and I wish you and yours a happy new year.

Shelby

TWO

Adversities and New Directions

5 Jan 52

Sorry Phin lost his shirt, but next time he bets on something let me know so I can get some money down vice versa. He is unquestionably the most snake-bit man I know.

There is no news from New York concerning SHILOH, only a sort of thunderous silence; I think the pot is simmering, though. All I am waiting for now is advance copies; they should be along in about a month or six wks. That bookclub talk is pure malarky, though I think "Life" may do a feature on it; they are trying to convince them now, and it shouldnt take much doing—in fact I may go up myself and turn the trick, in early spring: a quick flying visit, then return.

You dont understand about this work-in-progress. It's no straight Geneological novel, except perhaps in the sense that, say, THE SOUND & THE FURY is. It's a current conflict illuminated by a heritage of a particular endemic, historical nature—away and by far the most serious thing Ive undertaken. I'm scared to death at just the prospect; it could be one of the worst books ever written, and it's going to take two years to whip into shape. So far I have exactly 19/44ths of it written in 1st draft. But thats nothing: even when I have 44/44ths of it in first draft I'll only just be ready to start work, because itll have to be re-written and put together and re-re-written. A monster of a thing.

VICKSBURG will come in time; 5 yrs from now wont be too late, or even much more. That one is on ice. BRICE'S XROADS too. Just let me run the show; I know where I'm going and I'm going to get there, too. Or if I dont it wont be for lack of trying, and the trying is the main thing, at least in some ways. Anyhow I wont stand still, and if I were to do the Vicksburg thing now, it would have too many overtones of SHILOH. Just sit still and dont rock the boat. Or as they used to say in the joke, Who's fucking this goat?

I'm in the process of tapering off on a two-week holiday devoted to drinking, dancing and staying out late. I fell in love, too, and it's wonderful, but never mind all that. . . . To tell you the truth, I feel like hell and I'm confused and God knows what will come of all this. The only thing I'm dead sure about is writing. The writing is all right; the writing's fine. They dont make the creature that can touch it except incidentally, and incidentally doesnt matter; "incidentally" is material for more writing. Except sometimes I feel like a damned gristmill and I grind exceedingly small.

Regards to all. Stand by.

Shelby

Gville: 24 Jan 52

DEAR WALKER

This is probably utter foolishness but Saturday I am driving up to Memphis and catching the night plane for N.Y. and for the past two days Ive been having the damndest presentiment of death; I think I'm going to be killed somewhere along the line. The reason I'm writing is, I havent told anyone and of course wont tell anyone but you (who wont get this till after I have left and am safe or dead). I just wanted to tell someone and then we can laugh about it or you can set it down as a manifestation. If I knew a Hail Mary I'd surely say one; pray *for* me.

Regards:

Shelby

10 Feb 52

I have every line H James ever wrote: suggest you drive up here and I'll lend you the whole five-foot shelf to take home with you on the back seat of your car. . . . The inclosed bibliography is one I made some years ago; hope you can read it—the novels are marked with stars; dont overlook a single one of them, and I advise that you read them in the order they were written. Or if you dont want to read them all, anyhow read at least the following:

THE AMERICAN	THE AWKWARD AGE
✓THE PORTRAIT OF A LADY	✓THE WINGS OF THE DOVE
THE BOSTONIANS	✓THE AMBASSADORS
THE TRAGIC MUSE	THE GOLDEN BOWL
WHAT MAZIE KNEW	

Or if not all those, then anyhow the three with checkmarks by them. THE WINGS* is my favorite American book, but for Lord's sake dont try to read it without reading some of his earlier things first—I started it three times before I managed to finish it, and still didnt like it. Then I went back and read up to it, and emerged with my present high opinion of it.

At least as interesting as his novels are his notebooks; I have them too. But they dont make sense unless youve read the books themselves. The same thing goes for his introductions to the NY edition**—absolutely the most valuable collection of criticism in literature: for a writer, I mean. . . . Man, you better watch what youre doing. You get on a James jag youll be on it quite a while. I stayed on it three years, single-mindedly, and it not only took all my time, it kept me bankrupt because most of his books never reached a second edition and I had to pay premium prices. It's much better now, though, and of course youre welcome to mine. Three of them you gave me, anyhow.

Why dont you start listening to me in the first place? In 1947 I did everything but throw a full nelson on you to get you to read James. . . . Next thing I know, youll be wanting to know if I can tell you anything about a French writer named Proust.

SHILOH arrives this week.

Shelby

"Henry James: The Major Phase" by Mattheison (Oxford) is a fine book on J's last period. I also have a collection of essays by various critics, "The Question of H James"—it's good, too. Come on up.

*1952
**1946, I think.

12 Feb 52

DEAR WALKER

Hope you got SHILOH and were pleased with the dedication. I'll expect
you to dedicate *your* fourth book to me.[1]

I am sending by this same mail a little book that I consider an excellent
introduction to H James; it's one of the American Writers Series. The selection from the works is no better than ordinary (except the essay on the Art
of Fiction, which I urge you to read first; it's an early thing and makes,
itself, an excellent introduction to the mind of James); but the front matter—bibliography and a critical essay covering his life as a writer—are
very good, just what you want to start on.

But you must be prepared for one thing. James was the most Godless
man who ever lived; God apparently had absolutely no share in his life. Yet
curiously, his one concern was Good and Evil. Isnt it odd that this never
brought him to God, or at least to feel a need for God? It never did.

I also inclose a skeleton outline of my work-in-progress, which is
absolutely the most stupendous book since The Brothers. The subsections
faintly checked already exist in a fairly finished draft: Ride Out and Child
by Fever youve read already.

Shelby

TWO GATES TO THE CITY
—A Landscape With Figures—
(200,000 words or 150,000)

ONE: THE RETURN: EARLY SPRING.

1. a. Paul arrives on Cannonball; also Alice.
    b. Met by Ben and Wiley, drives to house.
    c. Katy meets them, goes to the hospital.
2. a. Lundy and Katy; he asks for the pistol.
    ✓b. Grandfather's biography: the last-born.
    c. Katy returning home meets Wiley, Alice.
3. a. Wiley the young businessman, his plans.
    b. Interviews: Ben & Alice, Paul & Alice.
    c. Funeral; Katy to hospital with pistol.

---

1. Percy's fourth novel, *Lancelot*, is dedicated to Foote.

TWO: RIDE OUT: 1910–1939.

4.✓a. Prolog. Boyhood, reform school, home.

   ✓b. Mansion House, showboat, NO, NY—TB.

   ✓c. Chance & Julia: the shooting. Epilog.

THREE: THE VORTEX: LATE SUMMER.

5. a. Gfather unsuicide; Katy acts as nurse.

   b. Wiley after legacy—Wiley & Alice.

   c. Ben's problem as to Alice; her reaction.

6. a. Paul and his work—the two gates.

  ✓b. G'grandfather's biography: Lieut Lundy.

   c. Paul & Wiley: statement of the problem.

7. a. Events leading up to the club dance.

   b. Dance at country club: Walpurgis night.

   c. Climax of dance; death of grandfather.

FOUR: CHILD BY FEVER: 1878–1911

8.✓a. Prolog. The Wingates: birth of Hector.

  ✓b. His boyhood; a sketch of early Bristol.

  ✓c. Youth—the death of the grandmother.

9.✓a. Marriage to Ella—sketch of background.

  ✓b. Death of son; infidelity; he forms plot.

  ✓c. Ella and drummer: a hotel asphyxiation.

10.✓a. Her funeral; Bristol as it was in 1910.

  ✓b. The "biography"; return of the dead wife.

  ✓c. Ghost leads Hector to the attic. Epilog.

FIVE: THE ENVOY: FALL & WINTER

11. a. Grandfather's funeral; then transition.

   b. Ben & Alice; Wiley; rivalry to a head.

   c. Rivalry resolution; Paul on Cannonball.

16 Feb 52

Glad you got SHILOH, and thanks for the letter. I know exactly what you mean, "isolate the elusive ingredient that makes this book go, and hold to it." It's wise advice—professionally. The thing you dont understand (but will when you work harder and come to it yourself) is the artist's terrific affinity for the difficult, the thing he *cannot* do. In his eyes the most important thing is development, a sense of pushing ahead in each thing he undertakes. Without that sense, that feeling, he cannot undertake a piece of work—that is what communicates the excitement, that is what enables him to "break through the shell of indifference and pessimism every time he takes up the pen." It's one of the saddest things about writing; as Eliot says, "One has only learnt to get the better of words for the thing one no longer has to say, or the way in which one is no longer disposed to say it. And so each venture is a new beginning, a raid on the inarticulate with shabby equipment always deteriorating in the general mess of imprecision of feeling." That is from the second of the Four Quartets and I have quoted it to you before. It's profoundly true. Without the excitement this communicates, writing is simply not worth a grown man's time.

Another fact is that in the final analysis you can learn absolutely nothing from another—I mean another person, as a person. (That is why I scream against the Tates.)[2] You can by example; you can learn from the great writers themselves, as I'm sure youve already started learning from James. But anything else is a waste of spirit, a marking-time. No one—NO one—should ever monkey with a writer's manuscript. All it does is short-circuit the line of his talent, and absolutely no good can come of it. These articulate people who can put their finger on the trouble, and tell why, are archfiends incarnate. My perversity and unkindness toward the Tates, however, is based on something in addition. I think they are to be avoided as you would avoid something contagious, for the simple reason that they have smothered their talent in the very way I'm warning against. They know this very well and (at least in their subconscious) they are busy as bees trying to see that it happens to others. . . . I give no man credit or even admiration for liking the things I like in literature; the things I like are to me so obviously superior that it certainly doesnt surprise me to find them

---

2. Caroline Gordon and her husband Allen Tate both read and criticized Percy's first apprentice novel, *The Charterhouse*. Gordon wrote an extensive critique of the novel and tried her best to drum up interest among book editors she knew. Though her efforts failed, she remained close to Percy and followed his later successes with great pride. (She had offered similar critical services to another southern Catholic writer, Flannery O'Connor.)

appreciated even by fools. Whats more I dont admit that you "tried your best to read Proust." If you had, youd have finished him. Anyone but a cretin is bound to admit that Proust is our greatest modern writer, provided he reads with even a minimum of receptivity. In Proust's case it's not even necessary to take the personality of the reader into consideration, for he was so various-minded that the appeal is there for absolutely anyone. . . . For you to speak against Proust to me is as if I were to run down St Francis (or, better, St Augustine) to you.

And while I'm at it there's something else I'd better explain to you— forgive me if I make like God Almighty. You talk a good deal of your "laziness." Rot! I'm the laziest man I know: always have been, always will be. It has nothing to do with writing. Writing, when a man is dedicated to it, has such an overpowering pull that the laziest man in the would couldnt keep from doing it. Your terrible reluctance comes from guilt at having reached thirty-five without dedicating yourself to at least the point of studying what you now recognize to be your vocation—you want to write but you havent developed the ability to do it. The only way to learn to write is to write as many hours a day as your hand and brain will let you. It is an instrument that must be forged in the fire of labor. You discover things one by one, and you only learn by doing.

For instance: Do you want to write the greatest book ever written? Very well: here's the theme, neatly arranged for a 3-part novel. "1) Know thyself; 2) Suffering brings knowledge; 3) Death, after suffering, is victory." There. Do you want to try it? . . . No—and I dont either. I'm not enough of a writer yet, and no man ever was. But I am learning with every book I write, and someday I may believe I am great enough to try it (I wont be; but I may believe it). I said I was against advising writers, but I'll give you one piece of advice worth all the others put together: Never lie to yourself. When you come right down to it, thats the only *rule* a writer needs.

The reason I speak with such assurance and denial of contradiction is that you are in my world now, the world of art—we've left Jesus and the saints. I can say with Lawrence, "Being a novelist, I consider myself superior to the saint, the scientist, the philosopher and the poet. The novel is the one bright book of life." That isnt blasphemy; we've come into another world, and blasphemy exists back in the world we came out of. . . . I have every day a sense of growing strength. I have forged this instrument and it's a good one—not so much for what it is as for my knowledge of what it can be; it is basically the right one. I know I have what cant be gotten except from within—vitality. Poor as my first four books may be, they all have that; a lesser writer would have made five novels out of each of them. . . . Stand by: I'll tell you true—I am going to be one of the greatest writers who ever lived. Or if I'm not, it wont be from a lack of knowing the requirements and it wont be because I lied to myself, ever.

Regards:

Shelby

Come get these Jameses; I'll tell you a few more things good for your soul.

Monday: 18 Feb 52

Yesterday's letter as I remember it was far too snappish and dogmatic. Let me elaborate a bit. As for perversity and uncharitableness, I think you ought to understand that my attitude toward what I was condemning is at least comparable to what Christ Himself felt toward the moneychangers. And let me elaborate on that; here is my point: I think a writer's mistakes are infinitely more interesting than any editor's "corrections" (and mind you, a critic is only an editor-once-removed)—I think no one can have the view of the book the writer himself has, the CREATIVE view, the containing of the force that brought it into being. It sometimes happens that certain scenes have no evident function; the critic says, Take this out. But these very scenes work in some way to bring out the total effect, heighten the contiguous scenes, and give the whole book its peculiar individuality. Yet any smart editor would have cut them—I'm not talking about a dummy, I mean really *smart*: the speed of the book would be picked up, the reading would go better, it would have "drive." But dont you see? it wouldnt be the same book; above all, it wouldnt be the writer's book. And God knows what effect this would have on that same writer's following work. A man must learn from his mistakes (even granting he was wrong)—from MAKING them, not from being saved from them.

I'll go still further. A good writer *never* makes a mistake in a basic sense: not when he is writing of things that matter to him—and when he is not doing that, no amount of editing can correct it; the fault will be so intrinsic that *no* amount of editing can correct it. All the editor can do is make it "readable" (for Godsake!) or artistically "interesting" (for Godsake!). . . . Dont you see?

I am talking about something that I think is the most important thing in the world. I think really you must not take this wrong tack at the start. For God's sake, Walker, do not listen to anyone who would try in any way to tell you how to shape a book; above all, dont listen to anyone who would tell you how to REshape a book. . . . Now I may be wrong: maybe they didnt tell you any such thing; maybe they just wrote in general terms about what you should do about preparing for your future writing of *other* books. Thats all right, especially as for recommending reading you should do— but the other is pure poison, of a kind that is unremovable, malignant.

(Here I wound up even more snappish & dogmatic.)

I think each book has its own problems. All a writer can do is tackle it on its own terms, see it the clearest he can, and then sail in. Each is a voyage beset by shoals. If he fails, he fails and thats most miserable . . . but there is a great resource left—there will be other books and other problems; life is long and the individual facets of Art are fleeting, except of course in the long view: which no writer ever takes, being a peculiar sort of fool, & therefore wise.

Part of this difference between us proceeds from a basic difference of approach. You, I think, believe that you have something to TELL people, and youd appreciate any help from anywhere that you thought would enable you to TELL them this thing more effectively; also you have a sort of modesty. I'm different on both counts. I dont want to TELL anybody anything; I want to SHOW them—I believe that is the only way to tell them; I want to communicate a view of the world; I think thats true wisdom. So that our difference springs from the fact that you think my end-endeavor is merely a stop on the way and you are willing to jump over it, take the word of others as to how to accomplish it—you want to get by it as swiftly and effectively as possible. . . . Youre so wrong. Youll come before long to see that I am right; wisdom is frequently just an ability to see that you passed the really important point somewhere back down the line—as in this case. DONT PASS IT; STOP AND SEE WHAT I'M TRY-ING TO EXPLAIN. If you let anyone fiddle with your way of seeing— fiddle deliberately, I mean: not by example but by pointing out—youll nick this instrument beyond repair; youll wind up with nothing but regrets.

Let me illustrate. Take any really great piece of work; take the Ode to a Nightingale. What is he telling?—namely, that this bird sang in longgone times and all men are connected by such sensations; that youth is difficult because it is all feeling and no wisdom. It's a good thought, certainly. But what did he TELL you?—only that, and not nearly so clearly as I state it. . . . But now go back and read the Ode. Wherein lies its greatness? Certainly not in what the poem TELLS you. Dont you see? . . . Now imagine Keats getting help from Leigh Hunt (or whoever—and mind you, Leigh Hunt was quite a fellow in his day, though now we know better)—imagine Hunt reading the first draft and saying, "You dont have quite the pitch in this stanza. "Deceiving elf"—thats a villainous pair of words; you need something stronger at this point," and so forth. . . . And dont think, because youre not the writer Keats was, that you can accept lower standards; you cant; you are obliged to think your every page is another Nightingale— thats one of the gambits of the game; and if you play by other rules, youre not a writer, youre a journalist or (for Godsake!) a teller of parables for imbeciles. . . . Also dont object on grounds that Keats was writing POETRY. The rules are no different, not now that the novel has come of age; it's a dedicated calling. You criticised me once for writing for "angels"—and so I do. The dirty minds, the slow wits, the critics with their pickbrain tendencies: these people must be ignored in the creative process. Nothing but ruin can come of even considering them. A man must write for himself, and then he must accept the penalties—including the possibility of damnation. Youve got to put it all on the line; anything less than *all* is hedging and your work is weakened at the wellspring, hopelessly flawed, shot through with rot. Not to mention the sapping of vitality; thats what hurts.

Now take SHILOH, which you say you like. It doesnt TELL anybody a damned thing. Can you for one minute think I should have let anyone on the big green earth step between me and the paper to guide my pen? . . . Or the others, for that matter. FOLLOW ME DOWN, which you dont like (and youre so wrong): Do you think I should listen to your talk about being ashamed I wrote it? Certainly not, for the fact is it contains a whole new world of good and evil, seething with them, and it was a step along the way in developing a style. TOURNAMENT, too—which contains errors in judgment on every page, errors the damndest fool critic on earth could correct: Do you think I, as a writer, would have benefitted from having these corrections made before the book went into print? Certainly not. DRY SEASON, which is little more than an exercise in the manipulation of plot (or plots) covered by a certain brilliance of style, is a book they say I shouldnt have done at all. Balls! . . . Dont you see? The only thing is to pay no attention to anyone at all.

Except me, of course. But I'm wise; I dont hand out specific advice; I just rare back and beller, and that cant do any harm beyond tickling your risibilities perhaps.

Believe me:
Shelby

[March 1952]
Monday
DEAR WALKER

I'm being dragged through hell by the heels but I hope I'll win through in the end. I know what suffering means at any rate, and now I dont want any more of it. My hair is turning gray; I doubt if youd even know me on the street.

The coming success of SHILOH is going to be a great help, I hope. Or if it's not, to hell with it. I may never write another line. Funny, though, I havent wanted a drink in two days.

I'll get through this somehow and I'll let you know when I do. Meantime I cannot explain and I ask your forbearance. I'll see you when I can.

Regards:
Shelby

Sunday 9 Mar 52
DEAR WALKER

I came on here from Harrisburg: will have been here a week tomorrow afternoon. I'm doing about as well as youd expect, plus being pleased to discover that SHILOH is going to get a good critical reception; the critics Ive met seem genuinely impressed with the book as an original & *good* piece of work—which it damned well is, of course; I dont credit them with any great perspicacity, for seeing it, & really have no more use for them than I ever did.

The divorce[3] went through Thursday. I'm going back home the end of this week, leaving Wednesday or Thursday, probably, & will get in touch with you soon afterward.

Regards:

Shelby

Sunday: 23 Mar 52

DEAR WALKER

Ive spent the past week reading—this by way of getting back to work, which I shall do this week thats coming up. Ive been reading Keats and Lawrence, a strange pair youd say, yet they compliment each other and were indeed much alike in many ways. For one thing, they both had genius and there is always a certain kinship in that. Knopf has just published "The Later Writings of D.H.L." Included in it is one of the finest short things Ive ever read: "Reflections on the Death of a Porcupine," written out in Santa Fe; youd be crazy about it, the first half at least—also another thing from the same volume of essays, "Love Was Once a Little Boy." A strange thing happened to him that seems to happen to many of the best writers—they attain a real measure of wisdom in the short period just before they die or stop writing. It happened to Keats; it happened even to Fitzgerald, a much lesser man. Listen to Lawrence in his late wisdom: "Collapse, as often as not, is the result of persisting in an old attitude towards some important relationship, which, in the course of time, has changed its nature." And: "Hate is not the opposite of love. The real opposite of love is individuality. You cant worship love and individuality in the same breath. Love is a mutual relationship, like a flame between wax and air. If either wax or air insists on getting its own way, or getting its own back too much, the flame goes out and the unison disappears. At the same time, if one yields itself up to the other entirely, there is a guttering mess. You have to balance love and individuality, and actually sacrifice a portion of each. . . ."

---

3. From his second wife, Marguerite Dessommes.

Thats what I call wisdom, and it is brought to bear (as true wisdom nearly always is) on what seems trivial at first sight—this, however, is, I think, because the profundity of its truth makes it appear almost axiomatic; it's what I admire so much in that Rebecca West book "The Meaning of Treason."

However, it was Keats I started talking about and there is something I want to quote to you from a letter of late 1818; he was 21 and had finished "Endymion" that year. It is in line with what I was yelling about in the letters I was writing before I took off into the night three weeks ago. Listen to him: of "Endymion":

"It is as good as I had power to make it—by myself. Had I been nervous about its being a perfect piece, and with that view asked advice, and trembled over every page, it would not have been written; for it is not in my nature to fumble—I will write independantly, *without Judgment*. I may write independently, *and with Judgment*, hereafter. The Genius of Poetry must work out its own salvation in a man. It cannot be matured by law and precept, but by sensation and watchfulness in itself. That which is creative must create itself. In Endymion I leaped headlong into the sea, and thereby have become better acquainted with the Soundings, the quicksands and the rocks, than if I had stayed upon the green shore, and piped a silly pipe, and took tea and comfortable advice. I was never afraid of failure, for I would rather fail than not be among the greatest. . . ."

You wouldnt listen to me; will you listen to Keats? He's saying the same thing I said, a thing we both (Keats and I) absolutely know.

I am settling down, still with a mountain of woe upon my head, but I have learned a great deal in this past month. Dostoevsky was absolutely right about suffering: I always knew it—but this was the first real suffering of my life. I lost fifteen pounds and came out all gaunt and hollow-eyed, but I would not swap what I got from it for a month of romping in the greenest meadows. I touched absolute bottom; then I came back up. Man, it's dark down there!

It must be near-bout MP's[4] birthday. Margaret had one last week. Tell her I said Happy Birthday when it comes. Also give my best to Bunt. I wish

---

4. Mary Pratt, Percy's oldest daughter.

I could get down there but I'm still whipped and I have to get to work else I might never. I hope I'm not flogging a dead horse.

Shelby

Wed: 9 Apr 52

Great God: I (of all people) had forgotten the enormous, puncturable vanity of writers! What was behind my attack (for attack it was, most certainly) should have been clear for you to see—I merely hated to see you taking what was essentially the amateur's attitude to writing; that was what you were doing, and I thought it wrong and wicked. To turn to others is the first mark of the dilettante who has finally managed to produce something of his own. My unkindness was flattery, if youd but see it as it was intended; what I was saying was that you were no dilettante and shouldnt act like one. . . . I was delighted that the Tates liked your novel—I thought that went without saying. Of course you felt good about their saying they saw so much promise in your book: I'd feel good too if they said such about a book of mine. But I wouldnt take a scrap of "advice" about a particular MS either from them or from anyone; that was the point I was trying to make. You hit me where I'd been doing some hard thinking. A man must make his mistakes to profit from them. I didnt like your apparent eagerness to cock your ear in their critical direction. Critics are for readers and have nothing whatsoever to say to a writer; the instant he gives what they say any serious attention he is lost—as lost as they are, and believe me they are the two most lost writers I know. Cant you see the absolute truth of this? It is a thing I know right down to the lining of my stomach. All that so-called "begrudgment" was merely an attempt to steer you off those shoals (they *are* shoals; and you appeared to be heading for them full-speed-ahead).

I am so much opposed to this (this heading for those shoals) that I flung aside all consideration of rejoicing over the good feeling they sent you with their high opinion; I concentrated entirely on warning you of what I know is ruin. Believe me, the only thing a writer can ever regret is those occasions when he followed anything but the prompting of his own heart and intellect; and mind you, this applies to the smallest particular. Silence, exile, and cunning: Joyce was right.

Writing does not preclude friendship, but it certainly limits it—limits its being widespread, I mean. A writer can have few friends, but that makes those he has all the more valuable. Do you know how many real friends I have? Two, at most. However, for all I know, thats more than the majority of people have. I'm beginning to think friendship is a pile of crap. But I'm in bad shape anyhow: I'm in the way of working up an anxiety neurosis—it's much worse than you can possibly imagine. I havent written one line in more than a month, and for all I know, I'm utterly through, both as a person and a writer. Suicide is much in my mind and I may come to it yet. I am truly in love for the first time in my life and I am being kept from the woman I love. Waiting to see how it comes out is what makes me hold on. If it falls through, I am going on an extended rip; I'm going to stay falling-down-drunk until it either brings me through or lets me take the other way. Whiskey has never meant much to me, but maybe thats because Ive never given it a fair chance.

SHILOH has gotten good reviews but nothing like the prominent attention I thought it would. I should have known better. Who gives a damn about a battle in that war? The only thing to do is build a solid body of work that *demands* attention through its honesty and variety. I'll do that if I come through this hooraw, and if not, to hell with it. . . . For the first time in my life writing is not the most important thing in the world, not even when I lean above a sheet of paper; and if I cant feel that when I write, I just wont write—it's that simple.

Dont talk to me about "peace." This is no problem to be solved by anything but the working of events. Meantime I'm like a man flayed alive and I cant seem to learn to live with it. But I want you to understand one thing. God and Jesus are completely outside this; I wouldnt speak to either of them if I passed Him on the street. I got enough fret without those Two. Or Freud either. Or any of the happiness boys.

You go on, do what you think is best about your work. I'm no one to advise. For all I know, you might do your best work writing a novel according to an outline someone sent you. It probably wouldnt be worth a damn but if it would be the best you could do, then thats the main thing. . . . Youve been a pretty coldblooded sort of fellow all your life. "Live alone and at peace" indeed! "Alone" and "at peace" dont go together where I'm concerned, not now. There comes a day when all the minutes we've lived add up to misery—so it is with me. You go ahead.

Shelby

Shelby Foote in Greenville, Mississippi, 1951. *Photograph by Bern Keating.*

23 Apr 52

I'm much better, Walker, really very much better. Next week I'm taking off on a short trip and then I'm coming home and get hard at work; it's what I want to do and now I can. . . . Youre wrong about what is going on; this is the end of a search. But I know you wont believe it until you see it, and of course you are right not to believe it until you see it—youve had every provocation. But I'm no "professional": far from it. . . . What I face now is at least a year's wait with everything hanging in the balance. It wont be easy, but I have a measure of real confidence and I'm going to turn to my work with a singleness of purpose I never had before. I learned this through suffering, the most acute suffering I'd ever suspected the world could hold for a man. What you saw in my letters was merely the exuberance; there were far worse periods of absolute misery, silent as the tomb, right down there on the bottom of despair. I'll tell you about it when I see you, probably in late May or June when hot weather is upon us and Ive reached a convenient stopping place after resuming my novel. It's going to be a good one, I can tell. I have a tremendous bundle of notes, a lot of scenes sketched fairly fully, and a firm grasp on the various characters. It's going to go like a house afire once I get past the prime inertia. Are you back at yours? My attack on you these past two months showed a sad lack of respect. You go ahead any way you want; everyone has to do it his own way and it's folly to argue Art or method.

Rgds:

Shelby

P.S. *SHILOH* went into a second printing one week after publication. Total so far = 8000 copies.

Greenville: 7 May 52

DEAR WALKER

I'm back; returned in good frame of mind but the restlessness is coming down on me again—I'd thought it wouldnt. Jesus! . . . I'd wanted to get down to see you and Bunt but it's no go—I'm going off in mid-June and

will be gone through September. 35 is the hardest age of all. Do you remember how it was?

Peggy and Margaret moved to Memphis yesterday, for good. There went my child and now I'll see her maybe three or four times a year; the court gave me what they ingeniously call "reasonable visitation." The move was for the best, though Peggy's people had to threaten to cut her off to make her move; it will be best for Peggy and whatever's best for Peggy is by reflection best for Margaret. Thats how it goes; the moving finger writes, etc.

I'll keep in touch occasionally but what I mainly need is for this blasted year to be done with. A hell of a year.

Shelby

(SHILOH goes into third printing soon. I dont care.)

Thursday 15 May 52

DEAR WALKER

Things go from bad to worse; I'm still not working—not a writer, not much of a human being, not anything. And the worst thing about it is there's a good deal of quivering self-pity involved, along with the anxiety and hostility (anxiety always involves hostility). I always thought that ugly, and now I think it even more-so. So it goes.

James Jones (HERE TO ETERNITY) came through and spent three days with me last week. I'm still trying to recover from it—the excesses it involved. But I like him very much.

There is this awful problem. I'm the kind of writer who must think nothing is as important as the words he is putting on paper; if he doesnt think that he cant write a line. As long as this other thing hangs in the balance it has to come first. Result: no writing. It's just that simple, and the only cure is the death of love, which unfortunately isnt equipped with an off-on switch. Love itself is fine and would be an enormous help, but love denied is hell. Thats the trouble. . . . Sooner or later I'm going to wake up some dawn and come driving down to see you. I'll tell you all about it, to your disgust. Stand by.

Rgds:
Shelby

26 Dec 52

Thanks very much for the wonderful picture book; Ive been looking at it all afternoon. I have only two objections: first, there arent enough naked women; and second, it's so big I dont know where to put it. There's nothing much I can do about the first, but as for the second I think Ive found a solution. I'm going to build some legs for it and use it as a coffee table. . . .

Man, Christmas really hit me wrong. I am utterly and completely flat broke. Which is why you and Bunt got nothing for Noel. However Ive sent up a flare-signal to New York and should be solvent before long; meantime I'll be looking around for a New Year's gift.

Tomorrow I'm going up to Memphis after Margaret. She'll be here for a couple of weeks. I certainly missed her Christmas. A hell of a Christmas; I dont care if it never comes again.

I'm not doing so good. Still cant write. Maybe I wont care in a couple more months or years—however long. I dont care. One thing nice about it is, if I'm not a writer I'm not anything; so if I ever really decide I'm done with it I can really let go. I'm done with it for now, all right. 1952 was pure nightmare, and here comes 1953. Peace be with us.

Got me a new girl, very smooth number down Vicksburg way, but I cant afford the gasoline to go see her. It will keep; thats one article thats strickly nonperishable, never a shortage, either; the good Lord knew what He was doing when He contrived that job. Thank Him for me; I'm not on speaking-terms.

Happy New Year:
Shelby

Monday [1953]

O.K. I agree; Christians aint artists; let it go. But that 9th chapter of St John is mighty fine. It's true, my position is indeed akin to that of the Pharisees': "It is because you protest, 'We can see clearly,' that you cannot be rid of your guilt." Yes.

No news from this direction, only heat and lots of that.

I'm not doing so good. Terrible in fact. Much oppressed. Maybe I'll get back on the manic kick again; I dont know. Useless feeling. Lonely. Loneliness is an artist's strength; thats where everything comes from and he knows it even though he hates it; thats why he wont surrender it. But I am finding it intolerable—which indicates how much less an artist I am nowadays. . . . It's singularly unproductive, too: no sense of gain from the disorientation, no feeling that I'll emerge a wiser man, no nothing. . . . No outlet. I dont know. Meantime I'm getting through by wishing each day would pass as fast as possible. Cant sustain a mood or even a desire. Work by fits and starts, and only a little of even that. All it's giving me is a bit of insight into a crackup such as Fitzg's, which isn't really profitable except as a pathological curiosity—and I'm beginning to understand that the pathological isnt really interesting. Healthiness is far more interesting.

So maybe I *am* learning something after all; but it's negative—or to be strictly accurate: negative-negative.

Whats worse, I lost my skill when I lost my concern, my intensity. Do you understand that? . . . Whatever I wrote would be very bad and I know it—I mean the word-order and -choice, let alone what I chose to say, to write about. . . . I'm not even marking-time. Anxiety (combined, as it always is, with indecision and a measure of hostility), the inability to choose or act, is a hell beyond anything I suspected. Formerly I could tell myself it was just a nervous reaction to a situation that harrowed me. Now it's something far worse. It's not a reaction; it's a condition. All the drive is gone except what comes in fitful flickers and wont stay. Without it I can never be anything but a very minor writer, even by "adjustment." I have nothing but contempt for myself in the shape I'm in; no sympathy, very little understanding, even. I still have my honesty, however. I wont accept peace if I have to get it by adopting solutions I know are false; I wont lie to myself or allow others to do so. I wont take hokum from either the soul-warmers or the head-shrinkers, the Happiness boys of either ilk.

Destroy this—not later: now.

S.

697 Arkansas

Memphis, Tenn

10 Dec 53

DEAR WALKER

I am now a native of Memphis:[5] have taken an apartment (half of a duplex) on the bluff overlooking the Mississippi—a beautiful spot, in niggertown—& for the first time in my life am truly a bachelor. It's strange; I dont like the cooking & the loneliness, but I'll learn. . . . I finished my book, JORDAN COUNTY: will do the final typescript by the end of the year. Dial plans on April publication date.

The past week has been hectic—moving furniture, etc. But now I'm getting settled at last. Next week I'll be back at work—the sovran remedy for all ills, the absorber for all the shocks that flesh is heir to.

Regards all round—

Shelby

697 Arkansas

19 Feb 54

DEAR WALKER

Our letters crossed in the mail. I havent had such good news in years—news that youve finished another book,[6] I mean, and have discovered a new ability to read poetry. I believe in very few hard-and-fast rules, especially as applied to writing, but one thing I believe I know for sure. Being blocked

---

5. Foote had moved to Memphis, the home of his ex-wife Peggy, in order to be closer to his daughter Margaret.

6. Percy would have no more success in getting *The Gramercy Winner* published than he did with *The Charterhouse*, despite Caroline Gordon's best efforts in his behalf. His lack of success with the second novel turned Percy away from fiction for several years. Devoting his attention to philosophical and linguistic matters, he published his first essay, "Symbol as Need," in the Autumn 1954 issue of the philosophical journal *Thought*. He also started work on a book-length project, *Symbol and Existence*, which, though never published, would provide material for a number of essays that did make their way into print. Percy also began to write about social, cultural, and political issues for such periodicals as *Commonweal* and *America*.

off from the beauty of, say, Keats' ode "To Autumn" (from whatever causes) would indicate an absolute inability to deal with words in any satisfactory way. That poem is an excellent example of what I mean when I speak of what I find best in art. It makes no slightest attempt, except overtly, to tell anyone anything; it only demonstrates a way of looking at the world ("style"); it is indeed pure art, has no theory to advance (except of course Keats' central theme that truth is beauty and beauty truth), and by never trying to preach does in fact do the most effective preaching of all—the kind done by music and great painting: Beethoven and Vermeer, for example.

Philosophy is the core of all the arts; without it, none of them is anything. But to my mind it must be so much a part of the man that he uses it only as an expression of his being. Therefore, for a writer, his study of philosophy will avail him nothing until he has assimilated it into his being—until it literally affects profoundly (I would add, unconsciously) his way of viewing the world. The philosophy must be submerged, used naturally as it proceeds from character; having been assimilated it has therefore been "forgotten," and having been "forgotten" it has become truly a part of the man. A book like BOVARY, which is characterized by never "explaining" anything, may be the kind of book that teaches us most. He had a very rudimentary philosophy, and in fact hardly more psychology, but he had those two saving things, a good eye and a marvelous style. If a man will give all they are enough, and what he builds will never fall or even fade. The truths they set forth are universal, impervious to time.

But there's the catch. We could all be great writers, perhaps, except that we know the cost; and few are willing to pay it. No wonder. For the cost is nothing less than laying down our lives: "Except a grain of wheat fall to the ground . . . If it die not. . . ." (I do not mention the risk of the soul, for I believe in fact that this is the one way of saving it.) Many of us are willing to go half way, some few even three quarters of the way; but there are few who go all the way—Shakespeare, Mozart, and maybe Proust, who (all three) put all that they were into their work; anything else was for extra. They were great men, and must have been charming; but the charm did not really matter and they knew it; basically they gave up love, friendship, even God, because they knew these things were less than art. (To my mind, Faulkner's best claim to belonging to their company is the fact that he hardly exists outside his work—though the worst of him is frivolous, even careless; also I doubt the extent of his suffering, or anyhow his willingness to suffer (witness the Hollywood trips, which he turned to during his dry periods instead of staying home and sweating blood, though he must have known exactly how much suffering had to teach him, provided he would undergo the pain).) It's a rather embarrassing thing to speak of, but I know it well at last. I have never learned the slightest truth from happiness. As for the above, I know it so well that I know I am approaching that renunciation—the crisis you say Kierkegaard speaks of. In the past month I have drawn much closer to it; I may be on the brink, though I wont know until I'm actually over the lip. During this time I have been outlining a tortuous novel, absolutely black and savage, with all the horrors of a nightmare; I intend to work my way through it to greatness. For the past two months, also, Ive done a great deal of drinking good whiskey and fucking beautiful women, but the one is about as unsatisfactory as the other, except at the time. Unfortunately, too, the law of diminishing utility obtains. Too much is almost as bad as none at all—like money—unless you have a genius for handling it, which I certainly have not.

Whiskey I handle the best of the three; in college, you remember, I would throw up and pass out—now, at a certain stage, I quit; which is just as good, and infinitely easier on the constitution. Women I'm no good with, except in the sack; the reason, I suspect, is that I have no real respect for them and they know it—except when Love enters the picture, when the reverse is true: I respect them too much, and they naturally resent having to measure up to all those expectations. Money is even worse: I know nothing about it at all, though thank God I'm not extravagant with what I havent got; I have no itch for things I cant afford. Food, rent, gasoline: these are about the limits of my desire. They do come high, though, as I'm discovering to my sorrow now that I'm trying to live alone. Right now, on the 19th, I dont know how I'm going to pay next month's rent. As for food, I can live on bread and peanut butter and coffee. Gasoline I get on credit.

I dont know how you feel about it but if youre willing I'd like to read the recent novel. I should have advance copies of JORDAN COUNTY by late March and of course will send you one as soon as possible. I wish there were some way you and Bunt could come up for a visit, if only to see the bluff above the river. But I know it's a long drive, plus the fact that Bunt is probably partridge-plump[7] by now. I'm glad to hear that Phin and Jaye[8] get on so well; good Lord it's wonderful when two people find each other, hook atoms, balance frets, whatever. It's not for me but I love to see it when it happens.

Take care. Stay in touch. Write when it's fitting—the work, I mean.

Regards:

Shelby

1955

697 Ark: 31 JAN

DEAR WALKER

Forgive delay: Ive spent all this time deciphering your letter. Had no trouble at all deciphering the check: for which much thanks: it came like rain on parched grass. But when wouldnt it? . . . Work[9] goes slow and well, particularly on little-known events, like Roanoke Island, whose neglect I cannot understand, now that I know how important they were. Loss of that island, for instance, lost the Confederacy the whole NC coast, both Pamlico and Albemarle Sounds and Norfolk to the north. Also it began the career of Ambrose Burnside—so perhaps it was a Southern gain after all, collectable at Fredericksburg. The whole thing is wonderfully human: poor damned forked-radish man, subject to all the skyey influences. In that furnace (the War) they were shown up, every one, for what they were.

Marvelous that youve got a lot on the river![10] Ive been here two years now, and I feel the river is part of me. Last week we had snow, and there it was, running chocolate brown between glistening white banks.

---

7. She was pregnant with their second daughter, Ann Boyd, who was born on July 11, 1954. Shortly after Ann's birth, the Percys discovered that she was deaf.

8. Walker's brother Phin had married Jaye Dobbs, the stepdaughter of Alan Rinehart, a cofounder of *Time*, on August 13, 1953.

9. Making no headway with his novel, *Two Gates to the City*, Foote had accepted a proposal by Bennett Cerf at Random House to write a short history of the Civil War. Quickly seeing that he couldn't keep it short, Foote proposed a multivolume narrative history. Cerf accepted, and Foote was now hard at work on the first volume.

10. The Percys had bought a new house, closer to town.

About money. Mainly I'm hoping for a renewal of the Guggenheim, though thats a long-shot. There is a deal in progress, too. A West Coast producer wants me to come to NY in mid-February at his expense, to talk about doing the story-line on a Civil War movie: I can work at home, he says, but he wants to talk about it. I said yes I'd talk, at his expense, but wanted no part of California. My agent is dealing with him. Nothing may come of it. Those people are all crazy, them and their funny money. Like counterfeit.

So there's that: Guggenheim and Hollywood. All I want is to work at my book, a great wide sea of words with a redoubled necessity for precision. If I dont watch it every instant, it bolts off with me, degenerates into detail, conversation and discussion. Every item is worth pages and pages: just finished a hundred on the opening maneuvers in the West: Grant and Sidney Johnston. What Ive done so far is about one-fourth again longer than FOLLOW ME DOWN, and I havent even got to Shiloh, the first big battle. 1st Manassas and Ft Donelson, Wilson's Creek and Ball's Bluff, Belmont and Logan's X-road, Ive done, along with events leading up to them & Sumter. So far, R E Lee is a failure: failed in W Va, failed again on the South Atlantic coast: Granny Lee, they call him, The King of Spades. Forrest is an interprising Lt-Col. McClellan and Joe Johnston are top dogs.

Soon as can be, I want you to see what Ive done so far. Next time you go to St Louis,[11] plan on stopping by here for two days. I want you to see my house, too, a hundred feet above the water. I'll come down there when I can. The NY trip (if it comes off) delays it until next time I can take a break. But I do want you to read what Ive done so far. I think it would revive your interest in the war, and I want you to see how I'm going about it.

No news otherwise. I'm living a hermit's life. My girl's in Florida and I dont want any other. Whiskey bores me. Movies are no damned good. The War is all. I feel fine about it.

Regards to your ladies and to that cushion-shaped Joey.[12] Bo is fine.

Shelby

---

11. The Percys had gone to St. Louis to look into a school for the deaf for their daughter Ann Boyd; in the end they decided against the school and, with Foote's help, found a remarkable itinerant teacher, Dorris Mirrielees.

12. The Percys' dog, a black cocker spaniel.

697 Arkansas

Memphis: 18 Feb [1955]

DEAR WALKER

Just got back last night from New York. Went up to talk to some movie people[13] about doing the story-line for a film based on a Civil War incident; I agreed to do it provided I could work here and not in California; they said all right, and I will. It's not a heap of money—$3750 in all, and none of it payable except in stages of completion: $500 on submission of outline, $2250 on acceptance of complete script, and $1000 on beginning shooting—but it will be welcome as food and rent money for the coming year if I can do it. I reckon I can. They seem like good people and apparently want to do a decent film. We'll see.

I also went by Random House, who are happy to know the work is going well. I am not asking them for any more money beyond the original advance, which is what I lived on all last year. . . . Too, I went by the Guggenheim office for a personal appearance, in hopes it would help my application for renewal of the fellowship. They were nice, and perhaps it will go through, though Ive heard it's hard to get renewals. . . . Anyhow I got all that done and now I'm back home, where I'm glad to be.

Are you making another St Louis trip soon? Remember I'm counting on your staying in Memphis overnight. I want you to see where I live and how the work is going.

I'm going down home next week, Tuesday or Wednesday, to spend a couple of days with Margaret and Mother. I havent seen them since Christmas.

Just finished writing an account of the Roanoke Island campaign. Quite a thing. I'm sorry I never got over to Hatteras or New Bern: sounds like a miracle of a place, on Pamlico and Albemarle Sounds. It made interesting writing, too.

All the best, all round:

Shelby

---

13. Stanley Kubrick was one of the "movie people" Foote talked to. Though Foote did produce a script, the film was never made.

Sat 1955

Glad you liked St Louis. You ought to study its history; must be fabulous. Your German ought to come in handy if it's anything like what it was during the War.

Here is the woman's name and address:

Miss Doris I. Mirrielees
5048 N.E. 19th Avenue
Pompano Beach, Florida

I got it from Dr John Shea Jr; he thinks she hung the moon.

No news outside my work, which goes dreadful slow. One goddam battle after another. I'm learning one hell of a lot of geography anyway.

Rgds all round:
Shelby

I take it hard you didnt spend the day here, seeing my living-place. Next time, see you do.

Memphis: 13 Apr 55

DEAR WALKER

Hope youre fine. I am; have been working hard and steady—about 80,000 words into the thing, approximately one-fifth, and going strong. I think maybe I'm writing a great book; but thats nothing: I always think so. Yesterday I fought (and won) the Battle of Belmont, winding up military operations for '61. When I polish off the Trent Affair I'll be set for A S Johnston and '62, leading up to Shiloh, which I can write in my sleep. . . . I would enjoy talking the war with you, though it could be you wouldnt enjoy listening. Dont underrate it as a thing that can claim a man's whole waking mind for years on end. For one thing, it's teaching me to love my country—especially the South, but all the rest as well. I'm learning so many things: geography, for instance. I never saw this country before now—the rivers and mountains, the watersheds and valleys.

I'm on tenterhooks right now, expecting to hear from the Guggenheim people whether I'll be financial or unfinancial this coming year. The announcement comes soon after April 15th; I dont know just how soon. It's crazy, I know, to expect it; but I do—I always do. When I hear I havent, I'll be cast way way down. I want to visit battlefields, for one thing—as well as eat and pay alimony and rent. I'll let you know posthaste if I win. If not, I'll get around to letting you know that too. Random is solid behind me, thank God. I ought to know better than expect favors from civilians who sit on boards. But I do.

I want to know what youre doing. Has all that activity merged into a book? Are the things youre doing all part of what will be a whole?

Little Margaret gets more beautiful every day. Sweet natured, too—and smart in school: something I never was, if youll remember. "Teach him to deny himself," Lee said.

I wish somehow youd been up here to see where I'm living. It's perfect for work: three rooms in line like boxcars, the middle one being where I sleep and work, with a desk I invented from a flush-face door to make a 6-ft 8-in workspace. I like Memphis and look back on Gville with something kin to horror, though I know I'll feel the tug again. If the book makes me living-money I want a year in Europe when it's done—mostly Rome.

First time I feel Ive earned it I want to come down and see you for a week. Say late summer, God willing.

Give regards to Bunt. Is white-chinned Joey still around? Bo's thriving—sleek and handsome and lovable as ever, a great chaser of mallards and dumb gray geese. He thinks the world and all of me, and I of him.

Regards; but give me some word of yourself.
Shelby

697 Arkansas
Memphis: 10 May 1955
DEAR WALKER

Good news: I got my Guggenheim renewed—which means rent, eating-money, and alimony for the coming year. . . . I'm halfway through the film-script (THE DOWN SLOPE is the title) and expect to have it finished by the middle of next month. I like it: think it will be a good movie: but will be glad to get back to my book. Signet is having me edit a short selection of

Civil War fiction (less than 100,000 words in all); a simple task I'm glad to undertake. I plan to use a bit from C. Gordon's NONE SHALL LOOK BACK, and maybe A. Tate's "Ode to the Confed Dead." Also selections from RED BADGE, SHILOH, ANDERSONVILLE, GONE WITH THE WIND, and Ambrose Bierce, and a wonderful short sketch by Fitzgerald called "The Night Before Chancellorsville" about a trainload of Yankee whores who got sidetracked by the fighting; all theyd come there for was business, and it turned out to be a battle.

I'm still hoping you and Bunt will come through here before too long. Any plans? . . . I'd misunderstood you on St Louis: thought you already had a lot and were planning on building. Just what do you plan, and how soon? Isnt it high time you jarred loose? Thats always painful; but exhilirating, too.

Has your reading and study included an examination of the Greeks? Ive been reading Greek tragedy, along with the lyric poets and much critical study of it. Oh man! . . . I still cant read philosophy, though; not even Plato. The historians are a different matter. Thucydides is pure pleasure. . . . Aeschylus is my particular favorite: I put the ORESTEIA (Agamemnon, The Libation Bearers, the Eumenides) with Lear and Don Giovanni and Isaiah.

Roy got elected president of the Delta Council—big thing.[14] He is doing a fine job (I hear) of counteracting the Citizens Council: not by open warfare, but by using his influence with friends of his who otherwise would be taken in. It's a serious thing down there, no easy thing to meet effectively, and I for one am proud of the way he has met it. God bless the rare bird who is in a position to act and does. Senator Percy's fight against the Ku Klux was a small skirmish compared with what Roy has before him, I'm afraid. It's worse than you may know down there. So far, except for individual idiots, Mississippi has remained decent—most likely, alas, because she hadnt had any real call for concerted indecency, like Georgia and Alabama.

Give me what news you can of yourself, and pass on my regards to your household of women.

Shelby

---

14. Walker's brother's efforts to frustrate the segregationist strategies of the Citizens Council reminded Foote of the struggle against the Ku Klux Klan carried out by Walker and Roy's great-uncle (and Will Percy's father), Senator LeRoy Percy.

8 Nov 55

DEAR WALKER

Thats good news youre going to retry Proust; youll be the gainer. What you say of the artist's looking for truth within himself is true, insofar as it points out the dangers. It is indeed a malignant heritage. But that is the condition of the tournament; he has no other place to go—no other valid place. God is (or may be) there; but He wont answer, not even in the silence of the night. . . . My other favorite modern writer, Keats, was just such an artist as you proclaim—in Endymion, St Agnes, even in the Odes; but in the end he looked within (the second Hyperion) and it helped to kill him (as much, I think, as Fanny Brawne); he turned back, as from an abyss—and wrote his greatest incidental poem: "To Autumn." . . . Yet there's no other place to go for the man who would be more than a story-teller. Look what happened to Tolstoy, another who wouldnt go there. He wound up writing fairy tales, frightened of what he had seen glimmering at the end of the road down which "Anna Karenina" had been taking him: Levin saw it and Leo got frightened and turned back. . . . The past fifteen years of my life have been spent discovering that practically 100% of the things told me as indisputably true—the so-called eternal verities—are false. I should think the problem would be even more dreadful for a philosopher, who would be forced by honesty to deny much of what his church, for example, had taught him was true, and to support what he had been told was blasphemy. What if honest thinking brought you to agree with the Manicheans?—I cant spell it but I remember I found their concept most attractive.

You use the word "refusal" in too special a sense. Surely a refusal to accept as truth anything not tested on one's own hide is not so much a "refusal" as a refusal to accept as truth whatever does not come at secondhand—no matter Whose that Hand might be. . . . Strangely enough, the Proustian inner discoveries led him to a more Christian outlook than you might imagine. The Montjouvain incident concerning Vinteuil's daughter (Swann's Way, p204ff) is an example of what I mean. He concludes: "Perhaps she would not have thought of wickedness as a state so rare, so abnormal, so exotic . . . had she been able to distinguish in herself, as in all her fellow-men and women, that indifference to the sufferings which they cause which, whatever names else be given it, is the one true, terrible, and lasting form of cruelty." It is by no means mere love of paradox that brings out the following: "'Sadists' of Mlle Vinteuil's sort are creatures so purely senti-mental, so virtuous by nature, that even sensual pleasure appears to them as something bad, a privilege reserved for the wicked. And when they allow themselves for a moment to enjoy it they endeavor to impersonate, to assume all the outward appearance of wicked people, for themselves and their partners in guilt, so as to gain the momentary illusion of having escaped beyond the control of their own gentle and scrupulous natures into the inhuman world of pleasure." I think perhaps this is something priests know well, having learned it in the Confessional.

I could never read Dante with enough attention to appreciate his great-ness. What stays with me are his tremendous figures; I can never forget, for instance, the man with the lantern strapped to his back, stumbling up a stony path in darkness so as to light the way for those who follow; or the gluttons under the fall of stinking snow; or the sensualists who have lost their sense of touch. Even though I read him down to the footnotes, I brought nothing away except those figures—whereas with Proust, what I brought away was a vision of the world, a way of looking at it which I had never suspected until I read him. He too is a celebrant of being—no one more so.

Wonderful that Miss Mirrielees is coming to spend some time with you. I can well believe that there might be more to such a person than to all the doctors in the world. It isnt true that we shouldnt question God's judgment; we learn from just such questioning how marvelous this world is—and how marvelous God is, who gave it and gave us the mind to question with. What kind of a God would it be who resented questions and even doubt? I can see that He might even send us troubles, enormous ones, for just the purpose of bringing us to doubt—and reaffirm our faith through doubt. Death of a loved one nearly always does that; and yet there is nothing that brings a man to God more surely than the loss of one he loves. I remember even such a scamp as Howard Dyer turned to God when he lost his little boy—though of course he turned away again as soon as the pain let up. Tragedy brings us what it brought Mitya Karamazov: "There underground we'll sing hymns to God!" But he only said it after he came through doubt—and, being Mitya, he would soon be back in doubt again. . . . What can we know of Anne's life? I can see that it may be a thing of beauty beyond anything possible to you or me. Surely, too—if half of what they

Walker and Bunt Percy at Brinkwood shortly after their marriage in the fall of 1946. *Courtesy of Mary Bernice Townsend Percy.*

tell us is true—she has a better claim on Christ's love than the rest of us put together. . . . Right now, through a study of one of the world's most horrible wars, I am coming to an understanding of the beauty of goodness—not for me; I cant attain it; but as a power in the world brought to bear by men like Lee and Grant—& Forrest. Grant's simplicity is his goodness, Forrest's strength, and Lee's purity and devotion to duty. Any other period of history would have served I reckon, but this three-year (or whatever) period is doing for me what similar "retirements" have done for many: Dostoevsky's Siberia, Grant's Galena, Lincoln's Eighth Circuit, Davis' Briarfield—Proust's cork-lined room.

I wish you every possible fraction of the pleasure I have gotten from the reading youre about to undertake.

As ever,
Shelby

697 Arkansas
Memphis: 30 Jun 56
DEAR WALKER

Finished the filmscript this week and am going down home tomorrow for a visit. It has the makings of a great movie, but what they do with it is their affair. There's no nonsense to it, a true picture of the war in its last stages, off in the Valley, after it turned bitter—hanging and retaliation, and the effect this sort of thing had on the men engaged: hangers and hangees. I like it. Of course I hope they do a good job. But after all it's not my craft or even concern. Stanley Kubrick is the director; the only authentic genius to hit Hollywood since Orson Wells, they say. I believe it. He'll do a good job if anyone will.

The main thing is I'm happy to be back at my History. Ive been having a great read at the Greeks—especially Homer and Aeschylus, who seem to me infinitely superior to the rest (except maybe Pindar, whom I like almost as well). The Illiad is the great model for any war book, history or novel, and how I could have read it so unprofitably years ago is something I'll never understand. Maybe it's the translation. The Lattimore (University of Chicago Press) is a miracle in all respects. He translated all three of the above.

I hope youre thriving. It's wrong, not having seen each other all this time. Ive continued gaining weight: weigh 170 now. I'll look like Uncle Hughie within ten years. Thats all right with me—long as I keep my handsome head of hair. I'm in love, too; what I call love, anyhow. (We all operate within our limits, especially me.) I went without that warmth a long time. It's scarcely living. Never again. Now I see beauty everywhere—a sunset or a flower, a birdsong or the pressure of a hand; I even smile instead of scowl at people, though I'm still convinced that there's no good in them.

No news. I just wanted you to know I'm thriving. Let me know the same of you. And give my regards to your brood. Come through here when you can.

As ever:
Shelby

697 Arkansas
Memphis: 8 Aug 56
DEAR WALKER

Hope you enjoyed Pt Clear.[15] Had a card from Robert,[16] who pronounced it idyllic—or rather the reverse in the best sense. Love that lap of luxury. Whats wrong with this world is there isnt more of it all round.

I cannot return your Commonweal;[17] I gave it to Faulkner to read, knowing he'd be interested. . . . Something you said in there interests me very much: that the Negro and the Poor White (or whatever he's best called) are drawing closer under the present pressure. I think it's true, and I would

---

15. Point Clear, Alabama, on Mobile Bay.

16. Robert Daniel, professor, critic, and friend of Percy and Foote.

17. The July 6, 1956, issue of *Commonweal*, in which appeared Percy's article "Stoicism in the South," a critique of the code of noblesse oblige in race relations and a call upon white Christians to live up to the principles of their faith in dealings with black Americans.

like to see it demonstrated. Long is a sport; as Huey's brother he doesnt really count. But Folsom of your native Alabama and Coleman of your adopted Mississippi are good examples of governors who are not rabid segregationists. I suppose the real test will come when they go up for reelection on their records, but it does seem to me that both (especially Coleman) were elected over opponents who tried baiting the poor-whites with the nigger threat. I know this was true in Mississippi, where my cousin Fielding Wright, among others, was defeated in such a campaign. Do you know a book by a mid-West professor called "The Revolt of the Red-Necks"? It traces the development of the Populist movement—Vardaman et al—and tells how their supposed nigger-baiting was foisted on them in the first place by the post-Reconstruction bourbons. The thing is being repeated. I know nothing of the Cit Council membership, but it seems to me to be largely recruited from the upper middle class; certainly the ones I know are from it, and they seem to be the leaders. Their claim is that they have taken the lead to offset violence, which is shit-talk; all they mean is that they are forming the organization; then when violence comes (if it comes) some of them will step aside and watch with horror while the red-neck element starts shooting. . . . You are absolutely right, of course, in seeing Christianity as the answer. Plato's cardinal virtues were prudence, courage, temperance, and justice; and to these the Church added faith, hope, and charity—thus producing the seven cardinal virtues, four "natural" and three "theological." We are going to need all seven in this thing, God knows, and it cannot be indicated too often. It seems to me the new alliance (which isnt really new at all) is worth all the study you can give it.

I inclose the opening five pages of my history, to show you something of the method. The battle scenes are lit by a strange, lurid light, and the long analytical sections (analytical in a new sense; not explanation, but demonstration—the problems are not so much analyzed as just shown, together with their effect on the men who tried to solve them, principally Lincoln and Davis). I have never enjoyed writing so much as I do this writing. It goes dreadful slow; sometimes I feel like I'm trying to bail out the Mississippi with a teacup; but I like it, I like it.

Regards and best wishes all round. Let me hear. Hear?
Shelby

Memphis

6 Oct 56

DEAR WALKER

Silence was occasioned by two-week honeymoon (Va NY NC); then a prolonged spell of housecleaning (it needed it badly); both are over now and I can breathe and write.

Wife's name's Gwyn;[18] she's 26 and quite handsome. Memphis girl. Was married to a young doctor[19] here and had two children, which she gave up to come with me—keeping, of course, what the court poetically calls "reasonable visitation." Big thing. Cant very well be told of in a letter anyhow. Youd have to know her, and us together, before you could very well do anything but suspect and disapprove. It's all right. . . . I cannot function outside the married state, no matter how much I'm galled inside it. (Nothing special about that. I think it's true of most people: women as well as men.)

Do send me a copy of Partisan Review[20] when you get hold of a copy you can spare for a while. I'll return it. That goes for anything else of yours you could spare me reading-time on.

I have a plan, a longrange one, if you and Bunt approve. Ive got about six months' hard work ahead of me, winding up the first of three Civil War volumes. When Ive done it, I'd like to come down with Gwyn for a three or four week stay in the guest house, doing the final typescript. We'd do our own cooking and everything, maybe even inviting you over for an occasional sandwich. (Gwyn's an excellent cook.) We could work all day and talk all night. I think it's a great shame we've been apart so much these past three-four years. Friendship is so rare a thing, it should never be neglected beyond necessity. That way we could make up in part for much of the being apart. . . . I think youll be interested in the War, no matter how unlikely it seems to you just now. (Incidentally, I think in your writing youve overrated the Old South about as much as Mr Will. Those

---

18. Gwyn Rainer became Foote's third wife.

19. Dr. John Shea Jr., the physician who had recommended Miss Mirrielees to the Percys.

20. "The Man on the Train: Three Existential Modes" appeared in the Fall 1956 issue of *Partisan Review*. An important essay, it contains much of the philosophical foundation of *The Moviegoer*.

virtues were more admired than lived by—and, at that, more lived by than believed in.)

I wonder if Joey is still among the living. Bo is fine, but showing a bit of middleaged spread, like his master. Do you, like Joey, have a tuft of white in your beard yet? And is the hair worn off your rump? Have you progressed as far as he in monomania, pursuing some ideological ball? Bo is still rambunctious, spry and handsome, and loveable as ever; like his master.

No real other news. I'm back at work and liking it, bedeviled a bit by odd jobs Ive taken on to earn a living, but mainly content and hard-working.

Regards to all your ladies:

Shelby

697 Arkansas
Memphis: 29 Nov 56
DEAR WALKER

Forgive the lapse, the long hiatus. All thats happened to me is I have been engaged in the hardest, or at least the most tedious, occupation of my writing life. That doesnt mean I dont enjoy it; I do indeed. What I have to do is learn everything possible from all possible sources about a certain phase or campaign, then digest it so that it's clear in my own mind, then reproduce it even clearer than it has been to me until I actually began writing about it. (The right words will invariably do that, if theyre arranged so as to bring out the essential meaning and drama. Drama *is* meaning, just as character is action, provided it is clear.) Just now I'm on something I think would interest you: the New Mexico campaign, a wild and little known action, fought for control of a few thirsty rivers, with ownership of California in the offing. Christ, what a lost opportunity! Davis saw it, too; but he couldnt do more than he did. You just cant whip 23,000,000 people with 9,000,000—especially when nearly half of the latter number are slaves. . . . The further I go in my studies, the more amazed I am. What a war! Everything we are or will be goes right back to that period. It decided for once and for all which way we were going, and we've gone. Just in the past two months Ive watched us disintegrate into an ineffectual murmur of platitudes. We'll even vote with the Communists if only they are "right."

And mind you, this comes at a time when we could really break those bastards. What kind of a friend is it who only stands by you when you're "right," who wont commit himself in your defense except in the form of massive attacks—mass murder? We're building up for genocide beyond anything the Russians ever contemplated; not on purpose, but through stupidity and a lack of moral fiber. I dont blame Eisenhower; I think he's exactly what we deserve; I think he expresses us at the present we've reached, sorry as it is. And I think thats why we (or at least you) voted for him, knowing just what he would do. A man of peace. . . . Just eighteen years ago we learned what devotion to peace at any price would bring, and here we're off on that track again—with less excuse. Instead of getting tough now, when I know the Russians would turn back, we're going to get tough later, when they damned well cant turn back. Then will come the Bomb, on us and on them. Oof!

Enough of that. . . .

I dont know when Ive enjoyed anything more than I enjoyed your Partisan Review article. What encouraged me most about it was your seeing an answer in art (openly expressed) as well as in Jesus (only implied, and hardly that). Yes! All that matters in writing is the quality of the writing itself, the dedication of the writer. That in itself convinces, provided he has talent, which very many do. He falls short to the extent that he lacks dedication, to the extent that he is unwilling to give himself completely. Only when he gives himself completely will the reader follow suit. Otherwise the blind are leading the blind, the disinterested the disinterested; writer and reader are alienated alike. Yes! I dont mean, I hardly need say, that the barbaric yawp is best, that the style itself is best unrestrained. I believe almost the opposite, in fact. I'm talking about the extent of dedication, of devotion, of application to the material. When Mark Twain remembered boyhood, he did it with a hot clear eye and nothing blurred his vision; for him the river ran true as true, and he told it as he saw it. We are good or bad according to the extent with which we can do likewise, about anything— including the Civil War. You never get fake when you are truly concerned. Hemingway is never fake until his interest wanders and he starts thinking on a tangent. What matters is concern.

Sent you a book yesterday—the Iliad, in the Richmond Lattimore translation: a miracle of a book. I urge you to give it a week of your life. This is writing as it should be. I never knew how really good war-writing could be until I read this translation. Put it up on the shelf; then take it down some time when youve got a week to spare. Youll be amazed and delighted. As for instance:

"The Trojans came down on them in a pack, and Hektor led them.
As when at the outpouring place of a rain-glutted river
the huge surf of the sea roars against the current, outjutting
beaches thunder aloud to the backwash of the salt water,
with such a bellow the Trojans came on, but now the Achaians
stood fast about the son of Menoitios, in a single courage
and fenced beneath their bronze-armoured shields, while the son of Kronos
drifted across the glitter of their helmets a deepening
mist. . . ." (XVII, 262–70)

You see?

Well, I'm working. Thats all. The main thing I hope is Gwyn and I will get the chance to come down there to see you and Bunt in the spring. I have no plans otherwise; will be right here working. It goes slow, but it goes well.

I'm glad youre seeing yourself in print. That has a value nothing can approach — if only the negative one of understanding how empty it can be in some respects. Not that the basic pleasure ever lessens. Isnt it odd, the attractiveness of type and paper and ink, bodying thoughts and descriptions? Isnt it odd how much the sight can teach us about writing? Commas really look like commas in print.

Regards all round:
Shelby

Memphis
16 Apr 57
DEAR WALKER
Enjoyed the War[21] piece very much, and would have answered sooner except Ive been in a state of shock over your retention of the first-draft

---

21. "The American War" appeared in the March 27, 1957, issue of *Commonweal*.

exclamation-point after SHILOH. Also the misspelling of Brice's Cross-roads. We buffs cant stand little things like that; sets our teeth on edge. Facts, man; facts!

Early May sounds fine. We'll make it or I'll bust a leg trying. Right now I'm into the Shiloh campaign. Soon as I finish it we'll come down—as soon after May 3 as possible; probably immediately after: the 4th, if that will fit in. . . . Would you and Bunt be interested in a ride down to see that country below New Orleans—Ft St Phillip and Ft Jackson? There's a road on the west bank of the river. I want to see them by way of preparation for writing about the taking of New Orleans in late April, 1862. Farragut's a bird. He went forward on Good Friday and had the city under his guns within ten days. A bandy fellow: 61, and used to stand on his head every birthday to see if he was still as young as he used to be—and always was.

You better sharpen up your reading eye. I'm bringing all Ive done on the book to date, and dont intend to leave till youve read it all and talked it over with me. Remembering Proust, I can see thats risking a long visit, if not permanent residence. Nobody has seen a line of it except an editor at Random House, and I want to find out if it is as clear as I think it is—if you agree that dulness lends solidity, a sense of difficulty, without which it would be untrue. The idea is to strike fire, prodding the reader much as combat quickened the pulses of the people at the time. Youll see.

No news. I'm just working. I like it fine and cant imagine any other life. When it's good it's very very good and when it's bad it's horrid.

Regards:
Shelby

Memphis
30 Dec 57
DEAR WALKER
Thanks for the Jellyroll; he's my favorite of them all, and I'd never heard a one of these songs before. It is amazing how clear they are. Also I like them early like this—ragtime.

Christmas, humbug. It broke up a long stretch of work. Now I'm getting back at it, hoping to re-hit my stride after a six-day warmup. . . . Off through Kentucky with Bragg and into Maryland with Lee. 250 more pages and I'll have Volume One ready for the printer. It's a long war, but enormously rewarding.

Let me hear from you. Roy says you found a house in N.O.[22]—sounds like the one you wanted, but had thought youd lost. Is that so? Tell me what youre doing. Are you settled there for the winter? Whereabouts? Working? Eating well? I'm doing all those things at the same old stand.

Regards and thanks to Bunt and the children, from Gwyn too. Happy New Year!

Shelby

---

22. Percy purchased the New Orleans house in the summer of 1957 so that the family could spend part of the week in the city, where Ann was having regular sessions with an audiologist. It was in this house that Percy began to write *The Moviegoer*.

THREE

Recognition

507 Yates Road

Memphis: 15 May 60

DEAR WALKER

First off, I want you to know how very much I like the dozen opening pages you sent.[1] It has a fine tone and carries right along; I wished hard for more. In spots it came home to me harder than anything Ive read in a long time—the idiotic logic of the bit on Holden and the litterbugs, for instance, and the unsentimental reaction of the 8-year-old who was relieved to find that all he had to do was be a soldier; the cellophane-wrapped girl on the bus, the newlyweds, the soured theater manager. All came through just fine. I think they will to everyone. In fact I'm somewhat alarmed at the notion of rewriting. Dont ever accept an editor's judgment on anything that has to do with literary matters. Believe me, they know less than anyone along those lines. . . . I'd use both titles: Carnival in Gentilly, the Confessions of a Moviegoer. I'm curious, though, about the length. It seems to me it should either be quite short, say 50- or 60,000 words, or quite long, 200,000 even. Which is it?

About the other, the need for recognition, I dont agree at all. I certainly know the ache for it is real enough, but it's nothing more than a weakness.

---

1. Pages from an early draft of *The Moviegoer*.

For one thing, it does absolutely nothing to improve the work, and in fact is far more likely to damage it, being extraneous. For another, it can end in nothing but dissatisfaction, if for no other reason than that there can never be enough recognition. Freud said we write (or paint or compose) for three basic reasons: desire for fame, money, and the love of women. I think it's true, but it only shows how puny we are. The true reason is too far back even for Freud to know about. Plato is much better on the question, though he had no real respect for artists at all. . . . The point I would make is that the feeling of dropping manuscripts into the abyss is inescapable. You can never, never be "understood" even by one reader; if one likes you, it's always for the unwelcome reasons. (His own, that is; not yours—as you must know from your study of "the Interpersonal Process.") You are wrong, too, about the pessimism. I assure you, you are better known than you think. We all are. There are people all across this land who think I am the very best living writer America has, including Hemingway and Faulkner. If you knew them you'd find some who think the same of you. It's nothing: absolutely nothing. The only satisfaction is in the work itself—the writing and rewriting, the little things no one will ever see but you yourself. You know that already, but you dont seem able to admit that it's enough. I assure you it is. It's not only enough for personal satisfaction; it's enough to warrant daily prayers of thanksgiving to God that all this came your way and not some yuk in the adjoining hospital bassinet. A writer who works honestly outranks all the creatures on this earth; even, I think, the painters and composers, because nowadays they are whipping a dead horse. Who was ever really basically happier than Henry James, even when he was bemoaning his lot? The pessimism I think is nothing more than our way of unwinding, or reaching down to get a firmer footing on melancholy, which we seem to need. I only take it seriously when I'm in the throes of it, which I seldom am.

If you go with Knopf we'll be having the same publisher. Cerf bought out Alfred A. a couple of weeks ago. Theyre in the process of a merger, Knopf to continue under its imprint but to be administered by Random. The gain for the latter will mainly be limited to a batch of European Nobel Prizewinners; Knopf was always weakest in native writers, expecially young ones, of which he had only one, Frederick Beuchner. Apparently he never really thought well of a writer until he had won some kind of international prize.

So he wound up with a list dominated by Robert Nathan and James Cain, an unholy pair of bedfellows if ever there was one, similar only in badness. Mainly to his credit is the fact that he published the handsomest books in the country—which, as you know, is quite a recommendation in my eyes.

I'm working hard and I think well. Ive made the rather amazing discovery that Grant was a son-of-a-bitch of the first water—basically, that is; which doesnt rob him of his fascination by any means. The best definition of him and his character was given by a friend who called him "only a plain business man of the republic," intending it as a compliment. . . . In a sense, the whole first two-thirds of my book (vols I and II, that is) is a preparation for the meeting of Grant and Lee in the Wilderness and southward: Lee, the representative of the best of the Cavalier tradition, and Grant, the representative of almost the worst of the Puritan tradition, which took over the country about that time (that was what the War was really about, I sometimes think) and has brought us to where we are, playing second leader to Kruschev because we put the dollar above life itself. . . . What I'm on now is not the siege of Vicksburg but the preparatory maneuvers in the slews and bayous, in the course of which Grant tried seven separate ways to take the city, only to have all seven fail. Then, on the eighth, he found the key and took it. It makes a wonderfully dramatic story and I'm giving it all I have. Gettysburg is an interlude, a desperate cast of the dice, when Lee crapped out.

Speaking of fame and recognition, I went over to Vanderbilt last month (after a great deal of pressure brought to bear by a professor there) and gave a two-hour reading from my work. It was quite an experience in a way. There were about 150 people, and I had the fantastic experience of seeing their hearts wrung in person by a sketch from JORDAN COUNTY called "The Freedom Kick." There wasnt a dry seat in the house when I got through. Then I read "A Marriage Portion," which convulsed them in laughter and embarassment. It was quite a thing—meaning, as I said before, absolutely nothing, but giving me a better notion than I ever had before of the power of the printed word, the stringency of art. Dont ever underrate it. Sometimes when you have 15 minutes to spare, take down JORDAN and read through "The Freedom Kick"; youll see what I mean, I think. . . . The present ten-year excursion into factual reporting is giving me all kind of new insights. When I come out on the other side, God willing,

I'm going to do some new and vigorous work. What I keep wishing for you is that you could invent a powerful framework on which to perform your stylistic dance, one that would hold up under all kinds of kicks—Dostoyevsky's POSSESSED is an example of what I mean: some crime or movement or catastrophe to put a skeleton into the flesh. There is a new novel you ought to get as soon as possible: Wm Styron's SET THIS HOUSE ON FIRE. It's due out in June, and I think youll like it. It's a long one and the first half is only a bit better than so-so, but the second half is wonderful. If you like I'll send you my copy. Let me know if you want it.

Thanks again for the opening pages. I enjoyed and admired them, and I look forward to seeing more.

All the best,

Shelby

507 Yates Road

Memphis: 7 Aug 60

DEAR WALKER

I read the book yesterday afternoon and evening, straight through, with only a short break for supper. I was feeling good, having just wound up a block of work I'd been going strong on for ten days or so—Longstreet southside, the Siege of Suffolk, a dull and very satisfactory task; I enjoy such stretches enormously; they give me something to surmount, if you see what I mean. Anyhow I was feeling good and I read the book, straight through as I said, and then I felt still better. It's a real good book. Partly this is because youre working from a point of view well beyond anything youve ever shown before. I take it as the best of all possible signs; a sort of breakthrough of the spirit. The genesis I guess was in the Man on a Train piece. But whenever it came it came just fine. I take it, now, you are ready for whatever it is you want to do. And I dont think for a minute you are anything like ready to give up fiction, as you said. This is more in the nature of a beginning; I think you must think so, too.

What impressed me most, among the more concrete things I mean, is the real sense of place. It was so well done that I see in it what will carry you ahead and not permit quitting. I wouldnt want any more of it here; it's just right; but I would like a great deal more of it in future work. That's a real feeling of New Orleans and its suburbs. Any place at all will serve but this serves magnificently.

I did as you said: read pencil-in-hand, and marked away whenever I took the notion—as youll see when the typescript gets back to you. (I'm sending it back tomorrow, Monday, so you should get it Wednesday or Thursday.) None of the markings really matters. All I found I didnt like were two short passages—flaws, I thought, but slight ones; you might not agree at all, and probably wont. . . . One thing I did think wrong, but it's so big you cant possibly do anything about it. The last third gets so caught up in the story itself and the excitement of the big change of scene, so self-involved, that it changes in tone as well. For one thing, your hero is no longer a real movie-goer except that he remembers Rory from time to time. Then in the confrontation scene with Aunt Emily, where he accepts the guilt she over-shovels at him, all this is redeemed—he isnt and never was a movie-goer. (I must say, though, I was startled at Mr Will's[2] transmutation. It was just such a scene as youd have faced if youd been caught cheating at algebra or dipping into the milkman's pennies.)

One of my minor delights, incidentally, was discovering that you finally got around to Arabia Deserta. My God, the wonder the paperback people have accomplished. And all these years you had the marvelous two volume original on the shelf in Greenville.

I'm a writer myself and I know there's nothing you can tell them, especially when you like their work. Otherwise maybe it's easy; I dont know. All I can say is I like it fine and I hope you keep on working in this very vein. I enjoyed it from start to finish and always with a sense of wonder. I congratulate you.

Rgds:
Shelby

---

2. William Alexander Percy, Walker's cousin and adoptive father, is in many respects the model for Aunt Emily in *The Moviegoer*.

14 Sep 60

Kauffman's[3] right: Cutrers were not in SUDDENLY LAST SUMMER—
they're in ORPHEUS . . . DESCENDING, which was called something else
in the movie with Brando & Magnianni.

I dont think there's anything wrong in keeping the name, though—not if
you really want it.

S.

507 Yates Road
Memphis: 8 Sep 60

DEAR WALKER

I couldnt be more pleased at the acceptance of your novel, though I had
had no doubt about it ever since I read the opening pages. What I hope
now is that youll come off the notion that you dont want to go on with
the work. The novel is just what Lawrence called it, "the one bright book
of life." All the points youll ever want to make can be made more effectively there than anywhere else; not only so far as reaching the greatest
number of people goes (to hell with that anyhow) but also so far as concerns your own personal satisfaction. Exposition is infinitely superior to
verbal persuasion.

By the end of the month I expect to have killed Stonewall Jackson dead
as a mackerel; which makes an excellent stopping-place before I tackle the
complexities of the Vicksburg Campaign. Gwyn and I are going to ride
down home and to Vicksburg for a few days. From there, God willing and
cash willing, we plan to go on to New Orleans. At that point we hope that
you will either drive over to see us or we will drive over to see you—I personally incline toward the latter, as quieter. In my old age I prefer calmness.
This, at 43. God knows what I'll prefer when I reach your age. Perhaps a
counteraction will have set in, not exactly senility, but hot flashes and all
that sort of thing, including a scabrous itch for nymphets. Are you holding
your own?

———

3. Stanley Kauffmann, Percy's first editor at Knopf, the publisher of *The Moviegoer*.

No news. It's all been one black blot of work for me for the past three months. Ive been subject to three-second fainting fits and mysterious sorenesses, giddiness and shooting pains in the upper left arm—frightening! I never minded dying young, and always thought I would; but there's something ignominious, even sordid, about dying middle-aged. Help me, doctor.

Respy yr obdt svt:

Shelby

507 Yates

Memphis: 12 Dec 60

DEAR WALKER

I approve highly of your notion of getting hard to work on Book II before Book I comes out. I had II *finished* before I came out, and I learned later (after I met some writers) how right I had been to do so. A freeze does set in, they tell me—the hardest of all freezes, especially if it has been a critical success. . . . So by all means stay hard at work. The science-fiction fantasy sounds fine to me. I even thought of an alternate title: The Strap Hangers (no hyphen).

As for proofs, what I meant by saying you should get off in a hotel room was a notion Ive had for a long time but have never put into practice, that a book can be better reviewed critically in entirely different circumstances and surroundings from those in which it was written. As for me, Ive never done much to proofs—just hunt for typographical errors; but Ive often thought I did wrong not to take another full whack at the whole thing. Different writers work different ways. The cost to the author depends entirely on the number of manhours involved in resetting; you pay for all over a certain amount, provided it was a good job of typesetting in the first place, which it almost always is. . . . I would certainly think twice or more before inserting a phrase that would call for resetting the whole paragraph, for that would cost precisely the same as revising it entirely. It's strictly, as I said, a matter of manhours.

Gwyn and I have a project. We're considering buying Mount Holly, the 32-room ancestral mansion on Lake Washington. It's 105 years old this month, a noble pile. My people moved out 50 years ago, so it would be a return of the native. How say you to this notion? You approve? Of course that $900-a-month figure would go completely out of the window, but what the hell; there's just this life and one more.

Wish I could read proofs with you.

Rgds,

Shelby

507 Yates Road

Memphis 13 Aug 63

Delighted to hear youre hard at it.[4] How many hours you work a day is nothing; what matters is that youre at it. I always assume whatever we do is right for us, and I know for a fact that some of the best things Ive done have been the result of delays—happy things that came to me because I waited: not because I wanted time to think or anything like that, but just because I waited for no reason at all except apparent laziness. I always remember Keats: "Poetry has to work out its own salvation in a man," and that if it didnt come as naturally as the leaves on a tree it had better not come at all. Which is not by any means to say it isnt hard work. It sure by God is, as anyone who ever tried it knows. I once had the nerve to tell a doctor here that I thought perhaps I had worked as hard to learn my craft as he had worked to learn his. Jesus, you could have heard him laughing clear on the other side of town—the idiot.

I'm pleased, too, to find you getting at the nub of the thing: what a novel really is. It's shape, a method of releasing experience, of relating words to life. How you tell it is everything, and every page is a new experience, a new endeavor to lick what cant be licked. You always come back to that: the realization that the craft is what makes it worth a grown man's time. Most people think mistakenly that writers are people who have something to tell them. Nothing I think could be wronger. If I knew what I wanted to say I wouldnt write at all. What for? Why do it, if you already know the answers? Writing is the search for the answers, and the answer is in the form, the method of telling, the exploration of self, which is our only clew

---

4. Percy was hard at work on what would eventually be entitled *The Last Gentleman* (1966).

to reality. This doesn't rule out the importance of the story and the people in it—not by any means. I think the superiority of southern writers lies in our driving interest in just those two things, the story and the people. But they are very much a part of the form; without them, the book is formless; they nail it down, they pin it to the earth, they support whatever burden it has to carry.

Keep the Chancellorsville galleys, or give them to someone you think they might encourage to go out and buy the book. Publication date is November 18: one day past my 47th birthday. How does it feel to be 47? Now that you know, I mean.

My boy Huger[5] is a buster, a dynamo. If I could hook him up to the power lines he'd keep Memphis in electricity for a year. I never really knew what a little boy was like, before. Man, theyre something! Funny combination of sturdiness and cowardice. Like men.

Gwyn and I are completely serious about building down at Gulf Shores. We'll be going there next month for a search for a lot and we already have a very hot architect at work on sketches. I want to reach out for more of life—not people, really (to hell with people I still say), but the beach and the Gulf and maybe fishing; the sea's edge appeals to me as a notion, the glassy expanse opening out and the salt wind coming off it in the winter. I feel death all in the air in Memphis, and I'm beginning to hate the one thing I really ever loved—the South. No, thats wrong: not hate—despise. Mostly I despise the leaders, the pussy-faced politicians, soft-talking instruments of real evil; killers of the dream, that woman called them, and she's right. Good Lord, when I think what we could have been, the heritage we perverted!—the misspent courage, the hardcore independence, the way a rich man always had to call a poor man Mister, the niggers who stood up for a century under what would have crumpled the rest of us in a month, the women who never lost the knowledge that their job was to be women. All that; and now we trust it to the keeping of Ross Barnett! . . . I want to go live by the Gulf.

Rgds,
Shelby

---

5. Huger Lee Foote II was born on November 13, 1961.

3020 Homewood

Memphis 38128

10 Jan 66

DEAR WALKER

As I said on the phone, God bless us all, it's very very good; much better I think than Moviegoer, especially the plotting and the writing itself. It gets seriouser as it goes, tightens up just fine, and doesnt break at all in two. That was what I feared, partly because you took so long and partly because you did extensive revision, which might have made it a couple of books in one; but didnt.

I dont know that I'd use the quotes at the outset. The one from Kierkegaard (sp) is o.k. because of brevity, but the second is all too explicit in a work so utterly implicit. I dont much like quotes anyhow; they remind me of crutches—or, worse, those Algebra books with the answers printed in. It doesnt need propping up at all, which this long quote seems to me to do. If quotes such as this must be used, I think they ought to be worked into the body of the work; no great task. All a character has to do is flip open a book or find one already flipped—he doesnt even need to read it. Or some other character (Sutter?) can quote it incidentally. Sounds also as if you werent really sure of being taken seriously, and sought thus to increase the specific gravity which someone (who?) might think it lacks.

I enjoyed the immortalization of Lige.[6] You got him good, especially playing cards. Do keep hold of him and bring him back sometime, at length. He's worth it.

Incidentally, I was wishing there had been some reference at or near the end to the telescope. It worried me he might have lost it—such an elegant thing as that in its leather case. He frets for a moment; then it disappears, or anyhow isnt mentioned.

Gwyn read first two chapters last night, with enormous enjoyment. She'll finish it today and tonight, and I'll mail it back tomorrow. I can tell you now she likes it very much, better than the first, which she liked very much too.

———

6. Elijah Collier had worked for the Percys first in Birmingham, Alabama, and then followed Mrs. Percy and her sons to Greenville, Mississippi, where he had been employed by William Alexander Percy.

I feel wonderfully encouraged on all kinds of counts. For one thing, it makes me want to get back to novels; something not many nowadays do. Meantime I'm up Red River with Banks—a wierd Kafkaesque experience, only matched by coming down from Little Rock with Steele, which I'm also doing now. Both got their asses knocked off Pope-style.

Congratulations. Quit that case of the stares and bust on into Three. And give us a couple of subplots, countercurrents, resolutions. What felicity!

Regards,
Shelby

17 Jan 67

DEAR WALKER

No news: except perhaps that I have undertaken, by way of earning a little living-money, a series of twenty lectures to students here at Memphis State, on a variety of subjects from Chaucer through T.S.Eliot. Eight down, a dozen to go. I rather enjoy them, truth to tell, but feel guilty at the frittering of time and effort—which last is all too similar to the effort that goes into the only thing that really matters. All the same, there is the delusion of doing good, of being to them what such things (few as they were) were to me; of tipping the scale, however little, in the direction in which they are encouraged very little.

What I'm writing for is to reurge you to come up here on a visit—you and Bunt and M.P. too if she likes. There's plenty of room, and it somehow seems all wrong for you to have no mental notion of how I'm living and what I'm doing with myself. What I wish is that you could come up to spend not a night or two but several days loafing around doing nothing. There's no hurry. Wait till February if you like. But I think it's wrong not even to be planning. (I glanced above and saw I left out Ann. She'd be the best of all company for Hugs, and by far the most welcome of you all. By all means Ann.) Flying's best, just forty or fifty minutes by jet; unless you have a hankering for six or seven hours on the road, which is a special kind of pleasure when the weather is right. . . . Anyhow I want you to start considering it seriously and get on up here. It's been too long already.

Gwyn said Bunt said Mary Pratt had a beau who set your teeth on edge.

I find that funny. Man, you better get braced for the shock. John Kennedy himself could rise from the grave and not be good enough for her in your eyes. What you want is the boy next door, although you know damned well it's highly unlikely. More likely Washington State, or Nome Alaska. . . . I can see you now, sitting there in that empty nest with a bald eagle scowl on your face.

No news, as I said. I just wrote to urge you to be turning your mind in this direction before you settle down to work and never come.

All best, as always:

Shelby

I noticed we're both in the new *Who's Who*. Nice going.

Sunday [January or February 1967][7]

DEAR SHELBY:

Your Chaucer-Eliot series at MSU very good deal. You neednt feel you are frittering away time—or merely "doing good"—for some time I've wanted for purely selfish reasons to hit upon some such deal with students, but haven't done so yet. Sometimes get the feeling of eating own tale, living in vacuum etc.

Am somewhat relieved to learn that yall didnt send Olde World Globe which was somewhat out of character, though it is indeed a handsome globe, being a new globe but cleverly antiqued to resemble an old parchment globe, with continents being distorted etc. It remains to be determined who did send it.

Yes, we very much want to come up and dig your situation, not presently having a clear notion exactly how you are inserting yourself into this world. Things continue fairly hectic here, at least through Mardi Gras. Then, God willing, we'll give you a call on a free week-end.

I am doing very little. It is a question of melancholy and depression. Sometimes I think that the creative urge comes from malice—a strong desire to attack one's enemies or at least those in the culture one considers

---

7. This is the first surviving letter from Percy to Foote.

to be wrong-headed and injurious—from one's own malice, envy, pride, and other capital sins. This, I am sure, was true in Dostoievski's case: that he wrote best when simply angry, angry at a rather low level too, i.e., politically angry, ideologically angry etc. What happens is that you get fired up by a relatively low and censorious emotion, hatred, moralistic self-righteousness, and you let go with the notion of striking out—THEN, if you are lucky and God loves you, you do the good things almost by inadvertence.

Which is to say only that the head of steam is low. Or my sights are too high. I keep thinking that it is always possible to do the BIG ONE, bigger than Don Quixote, Moby Dick et al.—which is the shortest path to melancholy and perdition, since as St. Theresa of the Little Flower used to say, the only road is the Little Way, viz., the only way to do great things is to choose to treat of little things well. The other path leads to grandiosity of spirit, flatulence of the creative powers and perdition in general.

But I am in low estate. I have in mind a futuristic novel[8] dealing with the decline and fall of the U.S., the country rent almost hopelessly between the rural knotheaded right and the godless alienated left, worse than the Civil War. Of that and the goodness of God, and of the merriness of living quite anonymously in the suburbs, drinking well, cooking out, attending Mass at the usual silo-and-barn, the goodness of Brunswick bowling alleys (the good white maple and plastic balls), coming home of an evening, with the twin rubies of the TV transmitter in the evening sky, having 4 drinks of good sourmash and assaulting one's wife in the armchair etc. What we Catholics call the Sacramental Life.

But it won't go, it doesn't swing, I am hung up, alas oh hopelessly hung; sitting in front of my paper at 9:05 AM and growing sleepier by the minute. Fresh out of malice, piss, the love of God, hatred of things as they are, or whatever it takes, which I don't have.

Hope you do better. At least you are speaking to the young, for whom you have both a liking and a hope.

Best,

Walker

Am going to NY.C. March 2 to serve with a Foundation. Yall? w.

---

8. This would in fact be his third published novel, *Love in the Ruins* (1971).

19 Mar 68

Many thanks for paperback Gentleman. I find the cover quite discreet, especially in consideration of some of the possibilities opening out from the doctor's ruminations on the subject nearest his heart. Do your job and let the Signet people attend to theirs; which theyll do anyhow. What do you care who buys it? Unless maybe youre worried about who wont, and theyve already bought it anyhow most likely.

Terrible news. Mother is in the hospital in Memphis dying of cancer. How long it will take they dont know. She last saw a doctor in 1933. She is now undergoing a series of 15 radium treatments, after which she will come home with us for a two-week rest, then back into the hospital for an operation to remove a tumor about the size of half a grapefruit in her vagina and the insertion of a urinary duct (or whatever it's called) to replace the infected natural one. She is 73 and that helps. So far, the infection is limited to the area of the tumor and the duct—lungs, heart, kidneys, liver, even bladder are intact. How long she's got they dont know and cant guess until later, after the radium and the operation. It's a strange thing, being in close touch with a Saint. She lies up there and this is what it all came to. She was a widow at 28 and paid her way, and mine too away past the norm, and now she's still paying her way. In her concern for never being a burden she not only has Medicare and Medicaid, she also has three civilian policies and she's giving Margaret her social security to live on and, just like always, if there was anything on God's earth I really wanted she would get it for me the day I asked her to, flat on her back and dying with nothing to look forward to but a crescendo of great pain. Gwyn is by far the best practical help; Mother sees her as she saw herself forty years ago when my father's mother was dying the same way and none of her children had half the concern for her that Mother did. Grandmother told her that, just before she died, and now Mother sees Gwyn in that role and Gwyn is playing it to the hilt. As for me, it has all come full circle in a really good way, because now at last I dont care how much she sees how much I care about her. She takes a lot of satisfaction in that— and so do I, at last.

I get home most weekends but wont be through here until mid May. I like it fine here.[9] Two classes a week on the Modern Novel: Hemingway, Fitzgerald, Faulkner, George Eliot—In Our Time, Tender is the Night, The Hamlet, Middlemarch: three weeks on each, with plenty of room to move around in while looking them over. I enjoy it, knowing it's only for three months and at least pays for Margaret's expensive but abortive education. It's good to be back in touch with young people, too; I was about to despair but now I feel better. They arent nearly as bad as they look and sound, only about as bad as you and I were thirty years ago.

I'll write again later when I get less shook. Right now almost everything seems more or less irrelevant. I'm going home Friday and will be there all next week.

Shelby

542 E Parkway S
Memphis 23 May 68

DEAR WALKER

I'm back from my Hollins stint, which I enjoyed despite my sense of guilt at taking off from work. It was good to be back in touch with young people who, hippie or no, stayed with it. They were really no smarter than I expected, but they were a good deal nicer and more likeable. I found that reassuring; nice beats smart every time, in my book. I liked them and they liked me, which made it pleasant too. I enjoyed the teaching also—learned from it: especially Hemingway, whom I respect now far more than ever before when he had all that false hair on his chest. I thought he was just putting on an act of being brave, when all the time he was brave indeed— venturing out in the world with a soul held together by cheap scotch tape and an absolutely 20/20 vision for the surface of things and the feel of them. Another of the outriders, the real heroes.

Mother came through her operation in good physical style, but her recovering is being delayed by a depression of spirit. She wanted to die, and now she has to get ready to live with a piss bag strapped to her thigh, at

---

9. Hollins College in Roanoke, Virginia. Foote taught there for one semester.

least until the cancer recurs, which it is highly likely to do although the doctors say they got it all in that one 6-hour operation, four weeks ago this week. She's still in the Baptist Hospital, with nurses round the clock.

Good interview in the Southern Review; I thought you came off fine. Also not a bad critical piece by the California academic; pretty sharp chap—must have given you the meems from point to point, especially considering how basically sympathetic he was. Those boys carry a sharp scalpel, and know how to swing it, too. God forbid you fall into their hands, though in fact it's not avoidable. There is the hook that awaits us all if we're good enough. And if we're *really* good enough, we survive it and go back to the people whom we wrote for in the first place. A grisly business, best unsuspected at the outset—else we'd perhaps not set out.

I liked Updike's COUPLES very much; better than any novel Ive read in a long time. The sex stuff is just trappings—it's a serious good book at the core, concerned with the biggest problems of all, and profoundly moral—depicting a life in which Duty and Work have been replaced by Truth and Play, as goals or precepts; shows where devotion to Truth can take you—wife-swapping etc. I enjoyed it very much, and think you would too, if you can get past the shocks and shudders that kind of thing arouses in that basically puritan soul of yours.

Me, I'm back at it here and glad to be so.

Shelby

Memphis
8 Jun 69
DEAR WALKER

It was good to see you & yourn down there again, despite the hectic windup of what must have been a long ordeal of socializing. I thought Mary Pratt made a handsome bride and took it all with splendid aplomb.[10] So did Ann. . . . We called you Monday morning, while preparing to head back by jet, and found you and Bunt were off to get some deserved rest, incommunicado of course. Hope you got it, though I imagine your reflexes havent settled down even yet. Youre probably still a victim of the same

---

10. Mary Pratt Percy married Byrne Robert Lobdell on May 31, 1969.

involuntary muscular twitches that come on after a 600-mile nonstop drive on turnpikes; you lie there, weary, ready for sleep, but you keep driving, keep seeing headlights and haywagons coming at you out of the dark in the motel room. After a certain number of parties your face gets fixed in a leery grin; mine too. It will pass at last: probably around January, God willing and barring other weddings.

You must come up here before too long and give us a chance to get down to talking about books and writing. We got started again once between drinks at your house but there was no time. The subject interests me very much; I doubt there's a more important one. Our trouble is you talk about what brings books into being and I talk about books themselves. It's a very different thing. What makes (or enables) a man to write a book is one thing; the book itself is another. Joe Christmas starts out as Jesus Christ, the notion that got Faulkner started; but before too long he's just Joe Christmas, and it's far better that way—even though he'd never have existed if he hadnt begun as Jesus, since that was what made Faulkner undertake him. You (in Covington, I mean) were talking about Faulkner *writing* the book; I was talking about the book itself—the result, which sometimes, on the face of it, has nothing apparent to do with what brought it into existence, though an informed mind can still find traces of the abandoned notion in the finished thing. What helps the writer get into the act of creation sometimes has nothing whatever to do with what he creates; and not always simply because of the huge gap between conception and execution. He creates with the help of an intellectual conception which his artistic sense then rejects, perhaps because it lacks validity as anything but a motor, or perhaps because he then sees it as actually bad, even sentimental or blandly "symbolistic." I remember in writing Tournament I set out to describe the Bristol Elk's Club as a version of Dante's universe. The three stories were hell, purgatory, and paradise; I was tremendously pleased with myself—the Delta had found its Joyce, etc. But I hadnt gone far with it before I saw that the best and hardest and most valid thing to do was describe the Bristol Elk's Club and leave Dante's work to Dante. I am quite sure that symbolism has no validity whatever unless it is sub- (or even un-) conscious; then it comes into its own, it shines through the lines; whereas if you *put* it there, it amounts to no more than clutter, chaff for the intellectuals, who are valid members of the listening public but are no more to be pandered to than the

Walker and Bunt Percy with their daughters on a Caribbean cruise in December 1955. Mary Pratt is standing; Bunt Percy is holding Ann Boyd. *Courtesy of Mary Bernice Townsend Percy.*

housewives who came looking for romance. I'm absolutely not claiming that realism is superior to symbolism (if anything, I think symbolism is superior); what I'm claiming is that a writer—while writing—had better not be conscious that either one exists. You fly by a good deal more than the seat of your pants, but you had better let the various manuals and logbooks alone while doing the actual flying; else youll come down with a thump and have to patch the machine up before you can take it off again. It's like the bearded man who never had any trouble sleeping until someone asked him whether he slept with his whiskers under or out of the covers. Result: insomnia. He had never thought of it before, and now, in trying to get to sleep, he found he could think of nothing else and he didnt know the answer. Both seemed wrong. I guess the best solution would be to shave his beard off.

Anyhow it was good to see you. We had a good time in New Orleans, too. Found a superior restaurant out on the lake—Masson's. They had crawfish and all the good things. . . . Tell Bunt we were delighted with the progress in the yard. Sam must have stopped drinking; or maybe he changed brands. It did indeed look splendid, anyhow.

Come see us and bring Ann. She and Huger (if she can put up with him) could explore this end of Memphis. Bunt and Gwyn could do whatever it is that women do—explore shops, I reckon. And you and I could settle all the creativity problems that plague writers nowadays. To our own satisfaction, that is.

Rgds:
Shelby

Memphis 28 Oct 69
DEAR WALKER
Thanks for sending the O'Connor book.[11] I enjoyed it very much, start-to-finish—as I tend to do all books written by people who take their craft

---

11. *Mystery and Manners: Occasional Prose* (1961), by Flannery O'Connor, selected and edited by Sally and Robert Fitzgerald.

seriously and have the sense to talk technique more than esthetics. She had the real clew, the solid gen, on what it's about; I just wish she'd had time to demonstrate it fully instead of in fragments. She's a minor-minor writer, not because she lacked the talent to be a major one, but simply because she died before her development had time to evolve out of the friction of just living enough years to soak up the basic joys and sorrows. That, and I think because she also didnt have time to turn her back on Christ, which is something every great Catholic writer (that I know of, I mean) has done. Joyce, Proust—and, I think, Dostoevsky, who was just about the least Christian man I ever encountered except maybe Hemingway. The Jesuitical strain, as Joyce said, can be injected the wrong way. Inject it the right way and youve killed the artist; he's guilty of idolotry and has committed the greatest sin of all—putting something ahead of his art,* avoiding the total commitment, keeping soft inside while pretending to be tough. I think Catholic writers know this, and I think it's partly why they tend to club together. Even O'Connor puts their names in, excluding all the others except the biggest, like Faulkner and Hawthorne.** (Caroline Gordon, for Lordsake.) James Jones is the only nonmember mentioned, the victim of a catty and I'm afraid highly accurate stab, passed off as a quote from someone else. It's apt, though—her definition of him as a nonwriter, I mean. Thats what he is all right. . . . I always had the feeling that O'Connor was going to be one of our big talents; I didnt know she was dying—which of course means I misunderstood her. She was a slow developer, like most good writers, and just plain didnt have the time she needed to get around to the ordinary world, which would have been her true subject after she emerged from the "grotesque" one she explored throughout the little time she had.

Dont take personal offense at any of the above; I dont consider you a Catholic writer at all, except in your spare time out of hope of heaven.

Now. What are you at and into?*** My hope is that your next work will be either very short or very long; if short, then by way of clearing the decks for a long one to follow. You truly need more room for things to interlock and set each other off; two sounds that produce not a third sound but a star, as Mr Will used to like to quote Browning as saying. Tell me how it goes, and what. I myself am getting deeper and deeper in; I wont emerge for another two years at Appomattox. This week I sank the *Alabama*: wrote me a lovely little cadenz on her final going-down. Did you know Semmes threw his sword into the sea? He did—to keep it, like the *Alabama*, he said, from "the polluting touch of the hated Yankee." He'd been badly whipped, which is always hard on a proud man, by a ship no larger or stronger than his own, except that she had 11-inch Dahlgrens, while his biggest gun was an 8-inch smoothbore, backed up by a 7-inch rifle.

You ever get around to that Mozart quintet?

All best:

Shelby

*I'd be willing to put a good steak ahead of my art three nights a week, but fortunately cant afford it.

**And Henry James of course. We all love James.

***Suggested titles for a trilogy, Mailer style:

    1) The Flaming Red Pecker.

    2) The Prurient Snatch.

    3) Clap Hands Here Comes Norman.

542 E Parkway S

Memphis 17 Nov 69

DEAR WALKER

53 today; sweet Jesus! I never thought I'd make it and am somewhat dismayed that I did. You of course have gotten accustomed to it by now, but for me it's still unsettling—like finding out your house burned down while you were crosstown at a movie or having a soda down at Marion Parlor. Where'd it go? The old Edgar Kennedy double-take.

Book sounds great, affording as it does so many chances to wing it. Maybe thats a drawback in a way, because reading it over and looking back youll always see how much more you could have made of it—so you go back and do. Knowing when to turn loose and move on is one of the big problems; "a general mess of imprecision," Eliot said, and truly. A sad trade.

I went down home last week for a preview look at Mother's gravestone, which will be dedicated 12 Dec with a Jewish graveside service. We had dinner with Roy and Sarah,[12] and I drove down to Trail Lake next morning

---

12. Roy and Sarah Percy, Walker's brother and sister-in-law.

with Roy; saw Billy[13] hard at it, and looked the place over for first time in 25 years. Wierd feeling. All tenant houses gone, all woods, all Old South, *all* gone. Wierd feeling of having been there before, except not really. The air was full of efficiency and money, but being an outsider I couldnt quite see for what—so Billy could be happy with his little wife? I suppose that is plenty but somehow couldnt hook it up. What was missing was Negroes gathering at store and drinking pop and guying each other; or even working in the fields. Strangely like one of those oversized factories that covers 20-odd acres and employs about twelve people. Couldnt get it together on new basis.

New movie making rounds you ought to see; called MEDIUM COOL. It cops out at severer turns but does good job of showing dilemma. New technique undoubtedly slick but also extremely effective; you would be interested I think. Much better than MIDNIGHT COWBOY or EASY RIDER. See it and let me know what you think.

Birthday provoked lookback; lookback provoked dismay. Sing Powers, Wilson Eatherly, Billy Joyner, Roscoe Low, Louis Nicholson, Tom Finlay, etc etc. Dead: all dead. Some didnt make 25; only I made 50, though Billy Joyner was knocking at it when he slipped off that barge in Dubuque. . . . I'm going to stop thinking about it.[14]

T. Harry Williams' biography of Huey Long a disappointment. Facts all there, but absolutely no feeling of Thirties, and strangely none of Long himself. Juiceless. Big and fat and full of stuff, though. He and Clarence Saunders were perhaps our (South's) most significant contributions. Faulkner corpus pales alongside their vitality and exuberance, their involvement with the stuff of life; votes and money, stumptalk and salesmanship; hustlers who lived life seam-side-out and never by hindsight.

I sound gloomy here. I'm not. Actually, I exult in sensual pleasures—wife, food, warmth, comfort of home, familiar chair, whiskey, wine, cigar, old pipes cured to perfection, good health. Bright metal on a sullen ground—Shakespeare.

Best birthday wishes:
Shelby

---

13. Billy Percy, Roy and Sarah's son.

14. The people named in this paragraph were Greenville High School friends.

542 E Parkway S

Memphis 19 Jan 70

DEAR PECAN PETE

There went Christmas; good riddance. Happy New Year too. . . . Ive been spending the past three weeks trying to get over the interruption, and now am finally back on pulse, crossing the Chattahoochee with Sherman and getting ready to send a bullet straight up James Birdseye McPherson's ass. A good lodgment. . . . Yank soldier coming down to Chattahoochee, where early arrivers were burning houses along the bank, told comrade: "Charley, I believe Sherman has set the river on fire." Rebel prisoner, seeing Federal host that covered the landscape: "Sherman ought to get up on a high hill and command, 'Attention! Kingdoms by the right wheel!'" George Thomas, burly Virginian, heavy set, with bulb-flat eyes and bulgy forehead, stolid and without smalltalk; newsman declared that a look at his face "made one feel as if he were gazing into the mouth of a cannon; and the cannon said nothing." Cavalry brigadier reported he found a factory manufacturing Confed uniforms at Roswell under the French flag, owner claiming immunity because he was a French national. "Such nonsense cannot deceive me," Sherman told Halleck; "I take it a neutral is no better than one of our own citizens." He sent word to the cavalryman: "Should you, under the impulse of natural anger, natural at contemplating such perfidy, hang the wretch, I approve the act beforehand." Good Nazi thinking; good Nuremburg document—along with one he sent a couple of months later to another subordinate at Calhoun, Ga.: "Cannot you send over about Fairmount and Adairsville, burn ten or twelve houses of known secessionists, kill a few at random and let them know it will be repeated every time a train is fired on from Resaca to Kingston?" After the war, he was hard put to understand why former Southern friends wouldnt speak to him on the street. He claimed he wanted to reduce bloodshed by shortening the war; and did. Red-headed Sherman. I have a scene of him taking a bath in the Chattahoochee, talking with a teamster on bank; beard bristly and grizzled, face freckled, liver spots on backs of hands, pubic hair pink in sunlight. Cant use any of it; I made it up. Wait, sweet Christ, till I get back to novels!

I am convinced the novel is as much alive, and as loaded with possibilities, as it was under Dickens and Twain, Flaubert and James, Faulkner and Hemingway. The only thing that has changed is the audience, who are never to be considered anyhow. Communication is as it may be, and is none of our concern; they either latch onto you or they dont. Joyce knew; so did Faulkner in his best days, and Twain and Dickens. Fretting about the reader is something writers do in their spare time. They do it least when they work best and hardest; else theyd write novels like algebra books, with the answers in the back. Regional obscurities add reality to a book—a paradox, but quite literally true. To stop and explain what a barrow pit is, is to wreck the story by explanation. Just call it a barrow pit and let him get it or miss it. It belongs in there, but the explanation doesnt. A man should talk as if he's being understood; as if he's talking to people who feel with him about the things he cares about. I think it's true we have a problem of communication nowadays; disorderly people perhaps cant follow an event in an orderly world; or anyhow cant care about it. But thats just a condition of the tournament, and shouldnt govern us—unless, of course, we're disoriented too. Portnoy's Complaint is simply a bad book; worse, even, than Thomas Wolfe on one of his off days. The fact that people dig it is no more of a recommendation for Roth than it is for Zane Gray or Grace Metalious if thats how you spell her name.

We plan a trip to New York in the spring; probably mid-April. Havent been up there together in about five years. Too broke buying house and getting furniture for it. I'm arranging to go by Hollins for a lecture fee to pay expenses, part of them anyhow. All I want anyhow (that costs money) is a good hotel and a series of fine restaurants; dont care a damn for theater or nightclubs. I never plan how long I'll stay; only how much I'll spend. When it's gone we come home. A good substantial $1500 investment in life as she ought to be lived—occasionally. You been up there lately? I hear youre apt to get mugged right there in N.Y.22, and the service is something disgraceful, and the air unbreatheable, and no taxi gettable. Me, I walk and seldom breathe, and I solve the service problem by tipping heavily and coming back next day. I do like New York. I feel at home there—like when I look out the window and there's the Empire State Building and I say to myself, "There's the Empire State Building." I cant do that in Memphis; I dont know the names of the buildings. And dont want to.

Two things I'm going to do when I wind up the War (meaning Vol.III): I'm going to reread Proust, start to finish, for the eighth time, and I'm going back to Greenvile on a two-month visit to re-see it. Ive been haunted lately by the ride down to Trail Lake and back. It gave me the willies, seeing the changes and not comprehending them. I didnt know what to think; still dont. It seemed to make sense, though, to everyone but me. Lost, O lost, and not even grieved by the wind. . . . You ought to see 601[15]—or rather you oughtnt. A skeleton. You can look right through the walls and see where we used to sleep and read, and the fireplaces where the fires were and where Mr Will used to light his matches, padding around in fuzzy slippers and robe that he couldnt keep the belt tied to. Running his hand through his hair and turning that green-stoned ring on his left hand. Do you realize he was then about our age? DO YOU? It shook me to think it, but it's true.

Man, it's true.

Regards all round:

Shelby

Thanks for pecans. I ate them all, raw, before the cook book came. Good.

June 12, 1970

DEAR SHELBY:

Well, you're right. This is a bad deal. It's really your fault. I told you before you bought a house to buy it in New Orleans. No reason why any writing man should want to live in Memphis. Did you read Willie Morris's joke about God saying that Memphis was about as far south as he would go when it came to helping folks in Yazoo City. (Read his piece in Harper's —a lot better than his book.)

What we ought to do for the next 25 years, since you've put away your secret desire to die a poetic death in your youth, what with your youth being gone and Roy telling me last week that you weighed 200—nothing like being slim and unlined at 54—is hit on a regular summer schedule: either you or I buy a house, or better, 2 houses, wherever you like, even Gulf Shores.

What crimps our style of course is Ann, who is a gungho in-group teen-

---

15. 601 Percy was the address of William Alexander Percy's house in Greenville, where Walker and his brothers spent their teenage years.

ager and would see me dead rather than leave her friends—for which I don't blame her. If it weren't for Ann and her attachments here, in fact, I'd be long gone. After twenty-three years here, I am more of an outsider than the first day I arrived. (It is interesting how a writer *lives* in a place. I was reading about John Fowles living in this little Covington-like seaside place in England and not knowing a soul there, being flatly ignored by the locals and ignoring them and liking it. At that I like living here better than NYC—or Memphis—or Lake Washington.)

How about compromising on New Orleans when Ann and Huggie grow up?

This summer I reached the nadir of my popularity here in Covington: testified in federal court as an expert witness (an observer of the culture) in a dispute about flying the Confederate flag at the high school. The blacks want it out. I said they were right. So I got threatened by the Klan: bomb the house etc—we slept in the attic for 2 weeks—not that I thought there was one chance in 1000, but didn't want Ann and Bunt to get blown up. Then I accused the local Catholic school of getting rid of the niggers, running a seg school with holy water thrown on it. Now the Catholics (most) are mad at me. And I do believe they're more unpleasant than the Klan.

In my book *How To Make Love in the Ruins* (or *Love in the Ruins*, which do you like better, tell me no kidding), the niggers take over in Louisiana and become ten times more bourgeois and Republican ("Knothead" in book) than the whites.

Going great guns in *Middlemarch*. Mary Ann Evans is a tiger. Poor Mr. Casaubon: pooped right out in his rose garden, sometimes I feel like him, but hornier.

Often think about Margaret Shelby[16] and wish her well.

Love to Gwyn and Huger,

W

P.S. I read Simultaneous Man and kept waiting to find out why you liked it.

---

16. Margaret had broken her leg in an automobile accident.

542 E Parkway S

Memphis 15 Jun 70

DEAR WALKER

In some haste. . . . Browning's title is "Love *Among* the Ruins"—a hell of a good poem, too, if youll give it a second reading, about a couple who meet at "the quiet-colored end of evening," a man and "a girl with eager eyes and yellow hair," at the site of a former overblown civilization (bearing certain resemblances to Long's Louisiana: "Oh heart! oh blood that freezes, blood that burns!—earth's returns for whole centuries of folly, noise and sin."). . . . Give it a reading. And while youre at it, turn on to a 53-stanza poem titled "By the Fireside," which is currently my favorite poem in the world. (Something is nudging at my memory, though—a novel, I think; British, I seem to remember—with a vague recollection of a book that came out a few years ago with that title, and with the same ironic tinge. Check and see.)

Best news Ive heard in a decade is you by God finally got around to Middlemarch, which I put with the absolute top handful of novels, alongside Proust, Dostoevsky, Constant, James, and Dickens. Bulstrode and Ladislaw (the first hippie) are minor flaws in a great work, and even they are interesting conceptions. What I get from it mainly is a sense of a tremendous brooding intellect; pure brain. God is Duty, and all that—a sluggish notion, but it serves, and that big brain, that certain hand, carries it all off and along: especially if you do a little background work on the England of that time, the eve of the Reform Bill. It does what all the great ones do: creates a world in which it happens, and puts a population in that world. I sometimes think the plain country-people are the best things in it, whether talking in the farmyards or kitchens, or routing Mr Brooke with drunken abuse. Ive read it four times now and am looking forward to a fifth. If I'd been Casaubon I wouldnt have much to do with that chick either. He had more life in his dead hand than she had in her twitchy little heart; which is not to say he wasnt the blot he was; he was.

Huger is taking off on a two-week camp toward the end of July (or maybe the middle; I dont remember offhand) and we'll see about getting down to New Orleans for some part of it. . . . I know what youre feeling with regard to Covingtonites and the Klan and your fellow Catholics, but you always did care a good deal more for the decent regard of your fellow citizens than I did (partly I guess because youve always had a better claim to it); I dont really think theyre always wrong, just mostly, and certainly not to be calculated on. My brush with the Klan in Alabama[17] left me with nothing but contempt for their cowardice. Not that cowards in general arent dangerous; they are indeed; but these cowards wont even work from ambush. You couldnt possibly have been safer—being white, I mean, and owning a gun. I tell them to their faces that they are the scum who have degraded the Confederate flag, converted it from a symbol of honor into a banner of shame, covered it with obscenities like a roadhouse men's room wall. . . . Always it's the South that catches it; gets left out. "Christ Stopped At Eboli," etc. I must say, though, the South certainly cooperates in the estrangement. I wince at southern accents on TV; even (maybe especially) Fullbright. Lyndon Johnson is the only decent public man we've produced in a generation. White, that is. . . . Hemingway once warned his brother, "Dont ever trust a man with a southern accent unless he's black."

Margaret comes out of her cast this week, after close to a solid year in traction and plaster. She seems a bit subdued; but it's nothing a few pills and shots wont cure as soon as she gets the chance to pop or shoot them. First, though, she has to undergo physical therapy to learn to walk again.

Simultaneous Man I sent as an example of something you could really have gone to town on if youd written it instead of whoever. I thought the notion of erasing a brain and then refilling it was fascinating, especially in that Cold War atmosphere.

Stay in touch. Rgds all round:

Shelby

Memphis

July 4th (1970)

DEAR WALKER

I didnt say which title I liked best because the fact is I dont much like either. Why dont you ever come up with a good solid meaningful poetic

---

17. Foote and his wife had lived briefly in Gulf Shores, Alabama, during the summer of 1964 while they considered building a permanent home there. Foote incurred the wrath of local Klansmen by sporting a Johnson sticker on his bumper and by speaking too frankly in support of integration.

title like Tournament, Follow Me Down, Love in a Dry Season, Shiloh, Jordan County, or The Brothers Karamazov? The best title you ever considered was The Fall Out—which I think ties in here, too: like Camus' The Fall, only with an Out added. He fell from Grace, and he fell Out. Also means The Fuss or The Stumble. Combines religious and atomic meanings. A great title, in fact. What in God's name have you had against it all this time? Once, I remember, you intended to use it with a hyphen, The Fall-out, which wasnt half as good. Think it over. Title-seeking is a form of hell.

As for George Eliot, Middlemarch is much the best novel she did, but they all (except Romola) have enormous virtues. Felix Holt and especially Daniel Deronda, written just before and just after Middlemarch, are wonderful books in part, but both are badly flawed by her seriousness of purpose, which leads her into spending about half of each on preaching (through dull characters) to the reader unmercifully. Adam Bede, her first novel, is great reading though, and The Mill on the Floss, her second, is as much so. If you want a pleasant surprise, go back and reread Silas Marner; packed around the melodrama is some of the best writing in the world— particularly tavern scenes, with cantankerous old characters sitting around talking about the weather, politics, and the frailty of mankind. Then when you go on to D. H. Lawrence youll see exactly where he came from—the best of him, that is. The Rainbow is an Eliot novel modernized, but good as it is it cant come up to Eliot at her best. No one (English) could, except the cream of Dickens and 50 page stretches of Conrad. . . . It only deepens for me the mystery of why (except for the exceptions that prove the rule) mankind cannot produce firstrate women artists. I put Middlemarch with Bleak House and Our Mutual Friend; I cant give anything higher praise than that. It gives me great pleasure to think that youve at last got around to it, and I just hope you enjoyed it as much as I think you must have. Let me know, when you get really through. If you want to go into it further, I have something that I think will interest you, a long study titled "Middlemarch, from Notebook to Novel; A Study of George Eliot's Creative Method," by Jerome Beatty. Dont like to foist things off, but if you want to read it (about 150 pages) let me know and I'll send it to you. It's an account of her composition of the novel, as reflected in her notebooks and the manuscript, with facsimiles of the latter. A good substantial piece of work. . . . Truth of the matter, though, is I wish youd go on to Dickens. Our Mutual

Friend will truly amaze you. A study in blackness, grime, and the low nature of the human animal. Freudian in the best sense—meaning before Freud.

Ive just wound up my Petersburg section, establishing the siege after the failure to take it headlong, and now will go on for the fall of Atlanta after John Bell Hood's bloody three-battle effort to save it. From then on, the war turns soft and gangrenous; no more battles except Nashville, a botch. Götterdämerung—Lucifer in Starlight.

All best: Happy Fourth!
Shelby

July 25, [1970]

DEAR SHELBY,

Thanks for this. It confirms me in my original impression of *Middle-march* which was that it was broken-backed: that Miss Brooke was dropped and Mary Ann started out with a whole new story, the Vincis, Garths, etc—yet she bridges it over and it works.

Just finished *Silas Marner*. It turns out I never read it—I was sure I must have had it under Miss Hawkins at GHS, but no. Chief interest: the use here of ideas she developed later, e.g., 1) how a young fellow setting out to sell a horse can get into trouble, 2) how a sweet pretty girl can turn hard-headed after marriage. You found something good in Arkansas.

Guess what: I've taken up golf, after 30 years. Played last in Greenville before war—and shot exactly what I did in 1941.

I've just about finished the novel which I may indeed call Fall Out. I can't imagine when I told you I entertained such a title since I had forgotten it. It is at any rate a very loose unserious business which will scandalize you chiefly by its structurelessness—which is however deceptive. It has a structure but it's organic—like an amoeba—or, more exactly, like the last 4 years of my life.

THROUGH now with fiction—fuck it. I hope to do something seri-ous—1) a short seminal article on the nature of the semiotic process which will be my chief claim to being remembered 100 years from now. 2) a short religious-political work damning the Right and Left in U.S. life. They're ruining us, the bastards, from left and right, what with the goddamn silly radical student-professor Left and the country-club Christian Right. The Center did not hold, as the poet said.

My grandson, John Walker Lobdell, (called by some Red Label) is well—M.P. is 22 and happy—lives 2 blocks away. Ann likes a boy named Fagan.

Best,
Walker

August 4, 1970

DEAR SHELBY:

Thanks very much for the hyperthyroidic exopthalmic St. John—who does indeed look like me after finishing book. He arrived on the day I finished this bloody business, a good omen—yes, he is my patron, how did you know?—since I had to have one what with two Southern surnames for a name, even if one of them was that of the distinguished Confederate Sec'y of State.

He is also one of my models, both in virtues and faults, having of the one a certain sardonic power (he could hurt you!) and a weakness for philosophy which didn't do him much good. His best: describing episodes like the blind man in c.9.

Yes, I'm shut of this son of a bitch at last, just got back from town and mailing off two copies to agent. When I think how good it feels, I can only think how much better you'll feel, getting shut of ten or so years rather than my four. I realize now that for four years I haven't played my stereo hi-fi—simply because I had this other on my mind and couldn't detour to the corner of the room. Which is not to say I didn't waste 90% of the time—I did—but there is nevertheless this thing of not being able to do anything else. Of course one watches the tube which is doing nothing not something like collaborating with Mozart.

I've this one home copy which you are welcome to read if you like, and which I would like to hear from you about but do not require, and in fact cannot imagine anyone wanting to and in fact all I really want now is [to be] shut of it for a while.

What is it about? Screwing and God (which all Catholic novels since Augustine have been about)—to use "Catholic" somewhat loosely since you were right the other day about me not being a Catholic writer as Flannery was. Also about the U.S.A. coming apart between left and right. Hung up on titles as you know. Possibles: The Fall Out (which you resurrected and I'd forgotten about), How To Make Love in the Ruins (its present title), The Center Did Not Hold, Dr. More (the protagonist is Dr. Thomas More, descendant of Sir Thomas More: a Catholic but a bad one, unlike his ancestor a whiskyhead and horny all the time, which is not to say Sir Thomas wasn't, he well might have been since there was a curious period in his twenties when he wore a hair shirt and lived like a monk in the charterhouse and might have married not for love but to be relieved of horniness). This novel is also funny. It will please no-one. It will infuriate Catholics, Protestants, Jews, Southerners, Northerners, liberals and conservatives, hawks and doves.

Good-by to story-telling. Just when you're fixing to get back to it. Good luck. I'm taking up golf and the philosophy of language, like all good Anglo-Saxon philosophers.

Best,

W

The title presently reads like this:

HOW TO MAKE LOVE IN THE RUINS
The Adventures of a Bad Catholic at a Time Near the End of the World

The Fall Out might be better for reasons you stated—and because a fall-out actually occurs in the novel (of noxious particles which exacerbate certain latent psychic traits of both liberals and conservatives, anxiety and sexual impotence in the one, rage and paranoia in the other, driving them to violence etc.).

Memphis 5 Aug 70

DEAR WALKER

Do by all means send me that home copy. Ive been wanting to read a good new novel for months. Send it your soonest; I'm anxious to get started. . . . Glad you liked the Kell St John. I started to get it framed for you here, but then figured the glass would break en route. I remembered your taken name from your baptism. Leroy Pope Walker, incidentally, wasnt "the distinguished Confederacy Sec'y of State." He was Secretary of War—and he wasnt distinguished. Poor aristocratic bastard got himself so wound up in red tape he couldnt move. It took Judah Benjamin to extract him from the toils. So much for Davis's attempt to give an Alabamian something in the way of representation in the Cabinet. He never tried again; poor Alabama.

I dont believe for an instant youve given up on the novel. Youre just suffering the postpartum blues. Wait; youll see. Youll go the other route for a time, and then see how much better the novel is than anything else when it comes to communicating; youll come running back posthaste. . . . How else, I say, would you work out your rage (altogether justified, I agree) at the slobs at both ends of the spectrum? It's got me half out of my gourd— the freaked-out young I mean, and the stultified old. Our trouble, it seems to me, is we live by (or claim to live by) a batch of myths that never were true to start with. A nation of halfmad teenagers from the outset. The Civil War is a bloody mess from start to finish, unredeemable even by Lee or Lincoln, and all the "glory" aura isnt worth the death of a single soldier. The cause was bad on both sides, and the worst cause won. We freed the Negro into indignity and serfdom, and turned promptly to every golden calf on the horizon. Jim Fisk won the peace, along with Harriman and Carnegie, while kidnappers were trying to steal Lincoln's body from his tomb in Springfield and Belknap (Grant's Secretary of War) was selling PX franchises for $50 each, cash on line. This is not a nation, it's a grabbag, an arena where you pay for any trace of decency with your life or by going bankrupt. Dollar diplomacy even works at home. We jail Communists today the same way we burnt witches at Salem and lynched psychopaths in Dixie. Our God isnt Christ, it's that iron Vulcan over in Birmingham.

Now youve called a pause, I strongly suggest you expose yourself to the Shakespeare of our time, and by way of persuasion I include an excerpt from him.

Regards. Send book promptly.
Shelby

An image presented to us by life brings with it, in a single moment, sensations which are in fact multiple and heterogeneous. The sight, for instance, of the binding of a book once read may weave into the characters of its title the moonlight of a distant summer night. The taste of our breakfast coffee brings with it that vague hope of fine weather which so often long ago, as with the day still intact and full before us we were drinking it out of a bowl of white porcelain, creamy and fluted and itself looking almost like vitrified milk, suddenly smiled upon us in the pale uncertainty of the dawn. An hour is not merely an hour, it is a vase full of scents and sounds and projects and climates, and what we call reality is a certain connection between these immediate sensations and the memories which envelop us simultaneously with them—a connection that is suppressed in a simple cinematographic vision, which just because it professes to confine itself to the truth in fact departs widely from it—a unique connection which the writer has to rediscover in order to link forever in his phrase the two sets of phenomena which reality joins together. He can describe a scene by describing one after another the innumerable objects which at a given moment were present at a particular place, but truth will be attained by him only when he takes two different objects, states the connection between them—a connection analogous in the world of art to the unique connection which in the world of science is provided by the law of causality—and encloses them in the necessary links of a well-wrought style; truth—and life too—can be attained by us only when, by comparing a quality common to two sensations, we succeed in extracting their common essence and in reuniting them to each other, liberated from the contingencies of time, within a metaphor. Had not nature herself—if one considered the matter from this point of view—placed me on the path of art, was she not herself a beginning of art, she who, often, had allowed me to become aware of the beauty of one thing only in another thing, of the beauty, for instance, of noon at Combray in the sound of its bells, of that of the mornings at Doncières in the hiccups of our central heating? The link may be uninteresting, the objects trivial, the style bad, but unless this process has taken place the description is worthless.

542 E Parkway S
Memphis 22 Aug 70
DEAR WALKER

I couldnt be more pleased than I am with the book. I think you hit just the right note all the way down the line. Dont worry for a minute about various groups taking offense. You know any bookreading Panthers or Kluxers? And most liberals dont consider themselves Liberals of this type. They feel about other liberals the way Jews feel about Kikes, and are happy to see them taken down. Conservatives, stolid creatures that they are, will think you are approving of their position—they see it expressed so seldom in hard covers. As for your fellow Catholics, I guess youll just have to settle for being considered immoral, like the rest of us modern writers.

Congratulations on Immermann (or Immelman. It changes.), the best devil figure since Ivan Karamazov's. I particularly liked his brimstone smell of stale deoderant. . . . And on making Gore Vidal the Grand Old Man. . . . And on the ending, with More still lustful even in a hairshirt.

Colonel Ringo's wounding was to me the funniest thing in the book—in the sense of laughing-out-loud I mean. That and his being nursed by the little nigger he'd just collared; the upended 7-Up bottle, etc. All through there is good, and gets down to what writing is about.

Gwyn said to tell you how much she liked it too.

Typescript goes into this same mail, Registered for safety. I inclose a list of nitpickings, most of which can be ignored. The only big trouble is the reappearing carbine, and I dont imagine youll need more than a couple of neat paragraphs to handle it; just watch a couple of I Spy reruns or Mission Impossibles having to do with escapes through airconditioning ducts.

Congratulations. I myself just wound up Jubal Early's Jul'64 raid on Washington. Scared Lincoln shitless.

Shelby

Mon: 23 Nov 70
DEAR WALKER

Kazin was by here last Tuesday. A nice, likeable man, very Jewish New York; much taken with you, incidentally, and with Roy. I didnt see him but for a couple of hours in the late afternoon—it was my birthday (54!) and I had things planned, including snails, strip sirloin, broccoli hollandaise, chiffonade, and then to bed. I told him what I could about the South and Art: both of which, it seemed to me, were something of a mystery to him. Maybe, though, he was just in a baffled state from a week of exposure to you-alls and Louisiana food. I envy New Yorkers' yearround exposure to music and all the new movies, but thats about it. The rest is muggings and intellectualism.

You seen Five Easy Pieces yet? Do.

I'm winding up Mobile Bay. Intended to do it in eight pages, but went bravura and ran it to twenty. This thing keeps swelling. Good, though. Next comes Bedford Forrest riding into Memphis after two uninterrupted years of Union occupation. Some hooligan!

You thought lately about getting all your nonfiction pieces together?[18] I mean the more or less "popular" things, like Man on the Train, Loss of the Creature, etc. Youd do well, I think, to get them out, give them a going-over, do a couple more, and publish them as an interim step toward whatever it is youre going to do next.

Rds, all round:

Shelby

February 3, 1971

DEAR SHELBY:

As it turns out, you were right about novel-writing. I am hooked and can't get away from it.

This is a strange business. I thought when I finished the last, I'd be able to write a book about a theory of language. I still think it would be as important as I told you. I would even say that it is revolutionary: that one hundred years from now it could well be known as the Peirce-Percy theory of meaning (Not Pierce but Peirce and so pronounced Perce-Percy). No kidding. I'm not even being vain. It just so happens that this old fellow, Charles Peirce, a U.S. philosopher very few layman ever heard of (by con-

---

18. Percy was in fact thinking about such a collection. It would appear under the title *The Message in the Bottle: How Queer Man Is, How Queer Language Is, and What One Has to Do with the Other* (1975).

trast, say, with William James, who got his idea of pragmatism from Peirce), who couldn't get along with fellow-professors and universities and ended up living out in the woods in Pennsylvania with his wife and literally went hungry—a curmudgeon Yankee philosopher—that this guy laid it out a hundred years ago, exactly what language is all about and what the behaviorists and professors have got all wrong ever since—laid it out, albeit in a very obscure idiosyncratic style. I propose to take his insight, put it in modern behavioral terms plus a few items of my own, and unhorse an entire generation of behaviorists and grammarians.

Do you know that I can work up no enthusiasm at all? My heart isn't in it. What I have done is to content myself with writing an article on the subject, which I shall submit to a periodical (probably *Psychiatry*, and which they very well may not take because it is long) and let it go at that.

Instead, come 9 A.M., I find myself casting about for a story (as Flannery said to me before she died: why don't you make up another one? and I felt somewhat put down: surely I'm doing more important things than making up stories).

Believe it or not, I am thinking about writing a proper planned-out Footean architechtonic novel.[19] It's about a man who finds himself amnesic in a hospital for the criminally insane. What he does not know, and has made himself forget, and pieces together later, is that he has killed his wife and infant son. Amnesia fascinates me. (The soap operas are right about amnesia being so attractive as a theme—as they are right about fornication being the favorite American sin.) Cf. Camus's description of modern Frenchmen: they fornicated and read the newspapers. The attraction of amnesia: with it one can explore the psychology of things, even the best of things, getting old and commonplace and used up, and the reverse phenomenon of the amnesiac's being born again into a new world. Every day at 4 PM he watches the attendant in the parking lot below his window sweep the concrete, in a certain corner, where he stoops and puts his hand into a drainhole leading to the street. A small mystery which the prisoner observes with the utmost interest and clarity of perception.

———

19. What follows is the the plot of what would eventually be Percy's fourth novel, *Lancelot* (1977).

You mentioned pornography, censorship etc. I wish I could see it as simply as you, for it is a troublesome thing to me.

Censorship is something else. I am closer to your position than ever—with certain minimal restrictions about the public display of hard-core stuff.

Why? Not because I personally condone dirty books and movies but rather because Christendom no longer can or even should call the tune. If Christians believe in the kingdom, that's their business, but they should realize that the world has by and large turned away. There is no longer such a thing as Christendom, and as Kierkegaard said, maybe it's just as well.

Best,

W

July 9, 1971

DEAR SHELBY:

You are a good drunk—peaceable, gentle, amiable and ecumenical—which speaks well for you. I am told I am a mean lowdown drunk, many sneers and insults to waiters etc.

I've made a good-bad bittersweet discovery. I found out why my large bowel has been troubling me. Drink! Spirits! I've not had a drink since falling amongst evil companions at the Boston Club and after a very bad day-after, I've not had a twinge—a serene large bowel! There goes the hot bosky bite of bourbon, what will I do with my old age? . . .

Yeah, with my family's history, I count even a sober old age as a windfall. I'll read Wittgenstein and do syntactical analysis.

Going to Martha's Vineyard next week to look for a house for next summer. Interested? Hell no, why do I ask? You're going to end like William Ellery Leonard who lived within a shrinking circle, first not being able to leave Wisconsin, then Milwaukee, then his house, then his bedroom. You're going to end up in that turret with Rattler and the Magic Mandarin and As the World Whirls. But come to the Vineyard while you still can.

The book for some reason is taking off in California. Don't know whether its the hippies who are reading the truth about themselves or the Knotheads who think they are.

Think about the Vineyard. If not that, propose something else.

Best,

Walker

Walker Percy, c. 1959, in the photograph from the jacket of *The Moviegoer*. *Courtesy of* The Clarion Ledger.

July 12, 1971

DEAR SHELBY:

Beautiful! Beautiful! Beautiful!

General Lee is beautiful and mean as hell. Looking at it and being looked at revives all the ambivalence of sonship, guilt-pride, I love you–I hope you die so I can be rid of you etc. Well, I would have fought for him.

Mary Pratt says you look like Walter Taylor[20]—plus a few pounds.

Off tomorrow for Martha's Vineyard. Don't really know what I'm doing up there. Feel uneasy about going so far. Mainly to look for a house. Figure a regular change of scene and climate might be good for everybody.

Walker

September 17, 1971

DEAR SHELBY:

Bunt says Sissman[21] is right, that I *am* a smart ass! How do you like that? Actually Sissman didn't do me too bad. But would you believe that I don't care? I mean the novel is all over with and reviews, good and bad, Jesus!

I'm on something else, much more important than making up novels. It is nothing less than the lapsometer! Or its equivalent. A BREAK-THROUGH! What I have hit on is nothing less than A THEORY OF LAN-GUAGE! WHY HUMAN BEINGS SPEAK! Though I know that this subject mystifies you through its seeming triviality, the fact is after 5000 years of Western learning and 500 years of modern science, nobody can explain how it is that people can talk and animals can't. BUT PERCY KNOWS!

Yeah, the one-eyed poet[22] came and he was funny—a good poet too. He wants to get you and me together at Vanderbilt arguing about Dostoievski-vs-Tolstoy. I told him of course maybe meaning no.

Also a totally callow young man, age 18, name of Tony Brown from Dallas, appeared one day and camped here for 24 hrs. He was on his way to

---

20. Lt. Col. Walter H. Taylor, Robert E. Lee's chief aide. Foote had sent Percy a photograph of Lee and Taylor taken by Mathew Brady after Appomattox.

21. L. E. Sissman, who had reviewed *Love in the Ruins* for the *New Yorker*.

22. The one-eyed poet was Jim Seay.

take pre-med at Duke and for some reason felt obliged to call on all writers in the South. Said he'd been to see you.

Glad to hear the war is going great guns. I keep thinking we might win it this time.

Incidentally, the interesting thing about a review like Sissman's is speculating what it was he didn't like. I accept what he said as more or less valid, also knowing that there was something else that really turned him off. It could be something as simple as the satire on Coffin Cabot, the semanticist from Harvard turned anti-Vietnam activist. The orthodoxy on Vietnam in the Northeast is as monolithic as the 13th Century papacy.

Or maybe it was the novelty of seeing a Southerner putting down on the yankees (e.g. chickenshit Ohioans) instead of Yankees putting down on Mississippians, who knows?

Best,

W

Congratulations to you and Gwyn on the 15th. Ours this year is the 25th!

Sat: 9 Oct 71

DEAR WALKER

Thats good news youre into Joe & Bros.[23] As you know by now, youre in for some of the most enjoyable hours you ever spent: particularly the first section, Tales of Jacob, where Mann's elephantine humor matches that of the original (Abraham conceiving God and snapping his fingers; Esau the hairy red man losing his birthright; Jacob hoaxed by Laban; Laban hoaxed by Jacob—and my particular favorite, the Story of Dinah, the little chinless daughter with mossy armpits). It's mostly greed and subterfuge, the original Snopes Saga, and I think Mann brings it off wonderfully. The other three volumes have their longeurs—Joseph as FDR etc—but they have this other thing, too, especially in the delineation of that pack of brothers, each of whom has his qualities to delight in. All in all, I think I enjoyed it quite as much as any long book I ever read. I hope you do, too. But do, for the good Lord's sake, let the religion alone; in which case I think youll find that it will

---

23. Thomas Mann's *Joseph and His Brothers* (1934).

return the compliment and let you alone to enjoy the stories. Twenty-four years was a long wait; I hope you find it was worth it. . . . Incidentally, I got Gwyn to read it fifteen years ago. She read it with the incredible advantage of never having read the Bible, and as a result thought it was absolutely the best thing she'd ever read. "What stories!" she kept saying. Sort of like not knowing how Hamlet is going to turn out.

We're going up to New York in a couple of weeks and lie around the Algonquin for three days. I call that living.

My stretch of good hard work continues. I tell you, that R. E. Lee is a *bear*. He wanted Grant's ass so bad he stayed in a tremble all through the last year of the war. I'm with Ben Butler now; got a plan for blowing up Fort Fisher (near Wilmington) with a steamer packed to the gunwales with 350 tons of black powder. He tried it. Nothing. Next day a Confederate cannoneer wrote home: "It was awful! It woke up everyone in the fort."

Take care. Tell all your females hello for me, plus your Red Label grandson. Next month, about this time, I'll be within eight days of 55. Unthinkable. I'm tied like Yeats to a dying animal.

All best,
Shelby

November 20, 1971
DEAR SHELBY:

Am most grateful for *Bleak House*. A lovely volume. What a gift. *Was ein Geschenk! Quel une bijou!*

Had started *Dombey & Son* but was somewhat put off by your warning about what happens after 200 p. So started *Bleak House* and liked it better. The dark corridors of the English Chancery sound so much like Kafka as to be uncanny.

Have just finished a rough draft of "Toward a Theory of Language," a monstrous 50 page article which is the companion piece of "Toward a Triadic Theory of Meaning" (out in *Psychiatry* in January). It is probably unpublishable but I had to get it out of my system.

Once this is polished off, I have a clear field. A very pleasant feeling of freedom and indolence. Anything might turn up. A short novella about an island maybe. Last night was looking at a copy of Swiss Family Robinson my daddy gave me in 1922. Still remember the excitement of them going back to shipwreck to get goats, cows, pigs, nails etc.

Walker

P.S. I like the *virginity* of this Oxford U. edition. After page 12, the pages are stuck together by the gold. Some reader your mother-in-law. On the other hand I bombed out of Proust on p. 11.

W

February 7, 1972

DEAR SHELBY:

The Miss. Quarterly on Foote[24] is a delight, mostly first-class and long overdue. You ought to be proud. I am for you, despite what you used to say about not caring what the bloody scholars say about you. They did a good job, especially Simone[25] (I had some correspondence with her, I forget about what, she seems to dig Southern writers—wouldn't you know it'd take a French critic to get onto the structure of L in a D S?—there you always baffled me of course what with all your structuring and architech-tonics, keystone chapters in the arch etc., since I recognized the value but could never go at it this way, though next time I am!).

These critics and English-department people terrify me what with their literary-type questions and me having spent the best years of my life down in Venable Chem lab at UNC and with a bunch of childish medics at Columbia. So naturally I had to laugh when Harrington pitched you one about the French phenomenologists and Robbe-Grille. As a consequence, not really because of this but because they always ask the same questions, I just stopped giving interviews and am declining all invitations to do any-thing. I'll probably wind up like Salinger up there in the Vermont woods, a sour silent hermit, but why not?

All I said in the Carr interview was the simple truth: that your literary career was begun with the inspiration you received when I passed you a

---

24. The Fall 1971 issue of the *Mississippi Quarterly*.

25. Simone Vauthier, a French scholar of American literature and a contributor to the special issue.

copy of "In Somnium: in the Manner of Poe" in sophomore study hall at GHS. As evidence of the derivative nature of your poetry from this early poem of mine I cite the large number of poetry entries from *The Pica* in Kibler's bibliography.

A fellow was trying to compile a bibliography on me the other day and inquired about The Pica—all I could remember was that I authored a gossip column called "The Man in the Moon" in which I would talk about Donald Wetherbee carrying on with Mary Jane Zeiser during recess.

I was thinking: reading this special issue must have fired you up to get back to fiction—making up stories as Flannery called it. You're liable to have a great golden age of creation—like Verdi and Dickens.

Which brings me to Bleak House—ashamed to say, I've somewhat bogged down. There's all these people. What's happened is that I get sidetracked—people make demands on me, send me books, some of which I feel obliged to read; household distractions and I get back to Dickens and have forgotten who's who. But I'm persisting. It's something to do with the nature of the times that I'm more at home with a Robbe-Grillet novel about *one* disoriented man getting off a ferry boat onto an island he can't quite remember than with this great Dickensian parade of *people*; there's the truth, the good and bad of it, and I'm sure you're right, that there's more bad than good to it.

A hectic time here. Bunt's father is here, Bunt having got him in a nursing home only to have him get gangrene of the foot. Leg amputated, going downhill, all the miseries of dying old. Maybe your scrambled eggs wouldn't be a bad way to go. But no, you do have to have time to prepare yourself, don't you?

Tell Gwyn I'm not quite as porely as when she last saw me. My gut's better and I've gained a little weight. The Xmas presents were wild man wild. I'm loving my crazy nuthatch and his narrow-ass nest. With eggs yet.

Just put down money on a house in Edgartown on Martha's Vineyard for June 15–July 31. Anyone for Chappaquidick?

Best,

W

P.S. I'm sorry your mother didn't see that.

wp

542 E Parkway S
Memphis 28 Apr 72

DEAR WALKER

Thanks for your Triadic[26] reprint. Alas, I got no more from it than you got from, say, Bleak House; but for quite different reasons. I had little trouble with the characters—Pierce, Chomsky, even Carnap—no, my problem is the simplicity of what's said; "the vocable has become imbedded in an organismic matrix," as Werner and Kaplan note. It was ever my trouble. Unless physical sensation impinges I get no sensation at all. For me, physical sensation can arise from the language itself; "Ripeness is all" is a theoretical statement that excites me because it opens out, it widens. But statements such as "A symbol must be unlike what it symbolizes" stop me dead in my tracks as soon as I reach the next period. That's it: no widening out. I sit there not even bewildered. Why is he insisting on what is obvious? He must have his reasons, I tell myself. Then I go on with it, and all I get is a series of dead stops. It was quite otherwise with "Loss of the Creature" and "Man on a Train." I suppose you think of them as popular exercises, and I suppose they are; but the others—"Symbol as Need" and "The Antinomy of the Scientific Method," for example—I read much as I once read Baby Ray, except that in Baby Ray's case I never wondered at the simplicity (though it was there) or expected a revelation (which wasnt) or indeed did anything more than take the words as they came, one at a time. I feel chilly and grown old, as Browning says.

Grown old. . . . Last Friday I was doing my annual goat dance in the living room, and I made a sudden turn on my right foot, which didnt turn. Result: a badly twisted knee and a weekend spent lying up in bed like a Turkish whore. Monday morning I checked into Campbell's Clinic. Nurse, filling out form: "Name? Address? Occupation? Age?" "Fifty-five," I said with some surprise, though I detected none in her. The doctor x-rayed me, tapped and prodded, then pronounced that I had pinched the cartilage. Now I wear a knee sleeve of steel-braced elastic. Ten days of that should do

---

26. Percy's essay, "Toward a Triadic Theory of Meaning," appeared in the February 1972 issue of *Psychiatry*.

it, along with cortisone, the doc said; but no more goat dances, under any circumstances. So it turns out I gave my farewell performance. Too bad: I had gotten really good at it. . . . This afternoon I go to have my eyes examined for new glasses. Old, indeed. I always looked forward to this, gray hair and a slim dignity, the wisdom of the ages in my face, but I hadnt foreseen the twinges. Moreover, it occurs to me I'm failing simultaneously at the top and bottom. Someday my ailments will meet in the middle and that will be it. A scrotum-tightening thought if ever there was one. I cry out, "Not me, Lord; not me!" The Lord maintains a deathly silence, as if He wasnt up there. I yell again. No answer. Maybe He's not up there after all. Maybe He died, like they say up east.

It was ever thus with all God's creatures who live long enough to approach it. Hodding Carter approached and went beyond it; bats in the belfry and all that. Strange, though, to see him let down into the ground. He was the first man ever to give me a dime for anything I wrote. Think of that, all those dimes later. Not all that many of them, all the same. At least I'm spared the pressure you heavy-money fellows undergo day in day out. My financial speculations are limited for the most part to wondering how I'm going to pay the gas bill.

Rgds:

Shelby

June 11, 1972

DEAR SHELBY,

We're back—from a week-end in—DULUTH!

What's up, Doc? Write, call, or name a meeting place.

Am stuck here for rest of summer. Would like to polish off one more linguistic article and then get down to some[thing] serious—like making up a story = a horrendous crime committed by a fellow who doesn't believe in sin (just re-read *Crime and Punishment* for edification). A long hot summer spent on the front porch with ice tea.

Best,

Walker

542 E Parkway S

Memphis 19 Jun 72

DEAR WALKER

Duluth! Who's supposed to believe that? Not me, for an instant. Nor Bunt I reckon, unless she was with you; which, come to think of it, would make the junket even wilder. Is this some more of your academic shenanigans?

But never mind that. What I had in mind to talk with you about was important matters. Art; all that. Did you know Dostoevsky was 56 when he sat down to write the Brothers? He did it in three years, which left him a year to live doing nothing but basking in new glory and going around giving readings and making speeches. Now you face something like that: not the glory, of course, or even the dying, but the getting down to biting on the nail: except in your case it's more of a spike. Youve got three books behind you, essentially preparatory work (which even Notes from Underground was) for what comes next, which I think should either be a short, highly experimental novel marking a new direction, or else the really big novel you are headed for but wont undertake because youre scared: as well you might be—it might break your back. Further along these lines (as I see it) you have to do two things. One is to exploit more of your experience and the experience of those you have known and loved all your life; a tough proposition, I know. The other is to embrace a fuller exuberance; "Take eloquence by the throat, and wring her neck." Youve learned coherence and the power that comes from spareness. Now youve got to add richness of allusion. A great style not only practices control of language, it also exploits its resources. You are somewhere short of there now, and it is absolutely necessary for you to move on. Making up a story is next to nothing. You know a thousand of them, all ready to hand. Telling it is everything: which comes long after you've settled on which story to tell. The thing heats up in the process of composing it, as you well know, and I think you ought to get back to that happiness as soon as can be. And I mean in a big way. All out.

What I wish is we could get together some time this summer for two or three days, maybe four or five; New Orleans or elsewhere (Gulf Shores?) and talk this thing out. I'm onto the swift downslope of my narrative; only about 100,000 words left to do—out of 1,300,000, which makes it seem very little indeed. Ai! It scares me pissless; first, to finish it, be without it; second, to turn to new work and get my hand in, all over again. Thats terrifying. I do know, though, I can never really stop without turning into a monster, at home and abroad, railing at friends and quaking at foes; a poor halfass unworking writer, carrying his own little corner of hell around with him wherever he goes and sharing it with everyone within reach.

Good for you for rereading C&P. While you are at it, go to the short novels and give The Eternal Husband another run-through. He writes much like you in that one.

We have no plans whatever. Which suits me fine. I like hot weather and plan to stay here and work right on through Appomattox and Durham Station, Citronelle and Galveston, then beyond them through the death of Davis in 1889, an epilog in which he watches the country get Vietnamized, what time it wasnt being raped by U.S. Grant and Jim Fisk. . . . Did you throw over the notion of Martha's Vineyard? I thought you had reserved the house and everything.

Anyhow, all best for now.

Shelby

June 23, 1972

DEAR SHELBY:

O.K., you name it. We can get away to Gulf Shores any Friday through Sunday after week-end of July 2. Bunt and I will stay at Holiday Inn. Yall could do same, or you might prefer to latch onto Bankston house. Or New Orleans, any time.

You must be prescient. Yes, I'm coming to the end of something and I don't know which way to turn. Another month and I'll have gotten rid of this last article on linguistics (even more arcane and opaque than what you read, I won't send it, but I have to write it: there it'll lie like a lion in the path for anyone who wants to understand the subject. I dare them to try any other way). Then free. A good and bad feeling, as you know. But I must question you on your two suggestions, which are somewhat elusive as they stand.

You ought to be glad to get shut of that war. Plenty folks in NY keep telling me you are crazy to have spent that much time after writing Love in a Dr S and Follow M D, and I disagree and agree, the former because they don't know what you're up to in the Narrative, the latter because you are indeed a novelist which I'm not sure I am but I'm something. What if I have to live another 20 years: I have to be about something.

Martha's Vineyard fell through because Ann decided she wanted to go to summer school. Lost the deposit but I'm not sorry: there began to be something endlessly depressing about sitting in that old house in Edgartown and looking across the harbor to Chappaquiddick. So I sit here in 100 degree heat under a ceiling fan drinking Lipton's instant and don't feel half bad.

Went to Duluth with Bunt and Ottilie (old maid friend, you remember). Flew to Minneapolis, rented a Pinto and went spinning up the tundra to Duluth, thence across state to Headwaters of Mississippi, a clear cold drinkable brook, ten feet wide. Was presented a degree Honoris Causae by the college of St. Scholastica, 1000 north Minn. girls, all dogs, not a looker in the lot. But a nice alcoholic excursion trip on Lake Superior to see the Port of Duluth—the sort of trip where an intense earnest lady takes you by the hand, looks into your eyes and says—whispers—*don't stop writing*!

Got my picture took free in NYC the week before at Pach Brothers photographers, which reached its peak in last days of Civil War and shortly afterwards—the studio was still hung with photos of Yankee generals, people like Sheridan, Halleck etc. Sure enough, my own photo came back looking like a pale abolitionist, a fiery skinny Wm Ll Garrison. Serves me right.

Make a note of my phone number, now unlisted.

Best,

Walker

6 July 72

DEAR WALKER

I'd hoped by now to tell you when we'll be going where, but I got into a stretch of work I couldnt look up from. Besides, Huger begged off going to camp this summer, which nails us pretty well down. Our hope now is to get down to New Orleans for three or four days by the end of July or early in August. We want to stay at the Saint Louis, the new hotel where Jax Brewry used to be, around the corner from Gallatoire's. Thats where we put our money, you may have noticed: on food and lodging, foregoing nightclubs and antiques—no great deprivation. Anyhow we'll surely get down there sooner or later, and we'll count on seeing you then for a night on the town. . . . I wish you could get up here for a week of leisurely talk and lounging around doing nothing. I think in all fairness you ought to admit it's time. How many times have we been to Covington? Fifteen? Twenty? Not to mention my numerous excursions in my faraway bachelor existence. Do it.

I'm truly excited about this stage of the book, a gray twilight shot through with lightning flashes, and the poor goddam ragged Confederates fighting on parched corn and Nassau bacon, and Sherman ripping up Georgia and the Carolinas with nothing but old men and boys in his path, and Jefferson Davis mumbling "We'll whip them yet" and almost believing it, and Sheridan (that bastard) going around grinding one fist in the other palm and hissing "Smash em up!" It's much of it highly unreal. Gotterdammerung; a rehearsal for later glories, such as Viet Nam, and future leaders, such as Nixon and what's his name—McGovern. Thank God I dont plan on going deeply into Reconstruction and the Gilded Age, though I do intend a postscript chapter, Lucifer in Starlight, about Davis's postwar life up to his New Orleans death in 1889. Some epilog. His dying words were "I cant take it"—meaning a dose of medicine. The hell he couldnt.

Stand fast. I want very much to see and talk with you as soon as can be. We'll get down there sooner or later. Meantime I wish you and Bunt could get up here.

Rgds:
Shelby

Sept. 14

SHELBY —

This is quite a book[27]—the modern Cannae from the losing side. Tannenberg always fascinated me—along with Verdun. The Germans cleaned the

---

27. Alexander Solzhenitsyn's *1914.*

Russkies with just a small holding force. It aint no *War and Peace*—Solzhenytszn can't quite fuse his characters with history. And the book could have done with some Foote Combat maps. But there are great moments, e.g. the burial of Captain Kabanov in the Grunflies Forest. (An odd coincidence! The action takes place in the same place as that of *The Ogre*, some 30 years apart—I read the two back to back.)

I have come to the damndest watershed in my life—done what I wanted to do in the novel, with linguistics, children gone, sitting down here in the Louisiana autumn. Everything quiet. What now? It would be a good time to die, but on the other hand I'd as soon not. It's all very spooky. Life is much stranger than art—and often more geometrical. My life breaks exactly in half: 1st half = growing up Southern and Medical; 2nd half = imposing art on 1st half. 3rd half? Sitting on Bayou and repeating over and over like old Buddenbrooks: *Kurios!*

Actually, I know what I want to do for #4. It's a good idea—but must wait for the wind to pick me up out of these 56 yr old horse latitudes.

—W—

Sept. 22, 1972

SHELBY —

They're dedicating Agee Library at St. Andrew's[28] on Saturday, Oct. 14. You're invited. Bunt and I are going up for the 13th and 14th. You and Gwyn come on up. Will drink some 2-natural and go inspect the Foote-Greene-Percy Gazebo.[29] Will get a motel room.

Best,

Walker

---

28. An Episcopal school in Sewanee, Tennessee.

29. A gazebo that Percy, Foote, and John Greene, a local handyman, had built on William Alexander Percy's property in Sewanee, Tennessee.

Oct. 6, '72

DEAR SHELBY:

Check. Sorry you can't make Sewanee. Actually I recall you were there recently. I haven't been there for over 20 years! It should be nice in the Fall, walking down to the brink.[30]

If you're headed down this way Thursday the 19th, why don't yall spend the night here. Or if not, we could meet you for a meal in N.O. Friday night. We have to be in Baton Rouge Saturday morning to see Ann (parents day at Chi Omega!).

Man, I can't write one of them saga-novels, wouldn't want to if I could, after Dostoievski and Tolstoy and Faulkner. If I did anything, it would probably be something experimental. Right now I'm in the horse latitudes, caught between thinking (linguistics) and imagining (literature), a bad place to be. A rock and a hard place. So I'll wait around. It's amazing how little one learns from this craft. All I know now I didn't know before is not to write the first sentence until the tone of voice is right. I can see you sneering.

Best,

W.

P.S. I'll tell you what we'd like to do some week-end when we've all nothing better to do. Meet at Oxford (Miss.) at Faulkner's house, take a look inside, then drive over to Shiloh and you show the high spots. It'd be a good thing to do when you polish off Kirby-Smith and write 30 to that monster. (At least I won't have to bury you in the MS).

10 Dec 72

DEAR WALKER

Suggest you give David Halberstam's THE BEST & THE BRIGHTEST a good hard three-day reading. It's somewhat over-breezy & at times highly

---

30. The location of William Alexander Percy's house in Sewanee, Tennessee, where Percy and Foote spent some of their summer vacations in their high school and college years and where Percy and his new bride spent a few months directly after their marriage. The house was called Brinkwood.

arbitrary in judgment, but it's an amazing revelation of what went on between 1960 & 1971 to rip this country apart—from the top. Power doesnt so much corrupt; that's too simple. It fragments, closes options, mesmerizes. I think you'd find it fascinating, if you could stay with it, cover to cover.

Shelby

542 E Parkway S
Memphis 26 Jan 73

DEAR WALKER

Sorry to have been so wobbly about getting down there to see you. You know I guess how much I want to come, and would have come if possible. For the past two months Ive been deep into a Lincoln thing—the two weeks down at City Point, winding up with Grant's breaking of Lee's line and his taking off after the old gray fox en route to Appomattox. I got him back to Washington yesterday (Lincoln I mean) with five days left between Sunday and his Good Friday appointment with Booth's derringer. He gets a wire that Sunday night from Grant: Lee kaput. . . . Now I go back to Lee and tell of that assbreaking march from Richmond to Appomattox—the real chapter ending. Today I put Box Four of typescript (350-odd pages, as usual) into the mail for Loomis[31] at Random. That leaves about 200 TS pages to go between now and the finish.

But about Gulf Shores: We want very much to come down. Hugs is off for camp in N.C. on July 4; will be gone six weeks. How would it be for us to plan on getting down some time in July? We could fly to Pensacola and bus over. Stay in touch on it and we'll work it out if there's no conflict at your end. What I had in mind was, say, about a four-day stay, midweek to avoid overloading you on weekends when Ann or M.P. would be over. Also, you know best on accommodations in new place; if it's possible at all, I mean. Incidentally, send me phone number when you know it—when you get in it, that is.

No news. Working tail off—some of best writing Ive ever done; all I'd

---

31. Robert Loomis, Foote's editor at Random House.

hoped for when the end loomed. If this part isnt copacetic, all the rest wont matter. But it is, man, it is!

Regards, usward to youward.

Shelby

March 1, 1973

DEAR SHELBY:

In answer to your question about Cochran house: it sold last year for $48,000. A steal. Too bad.

Our only hope of getting to Gulf Shores may be Bankston house. Tried to call Gwyn this morning at Ponchartrain but missed her. About baby. But when you see her Saturday, try to get her to intercede with and implore Mrs. B. We'll provide own linens and do what she likes. Would like it for month of June—or even later. Name her price. I have to get to the ocean soon or perish of anomie, Louisiana swamp rot or something.

I'll ask another favor. Robert Coles the psychiatrist (most famous in U.S., on Time cover last year) wants to come by and talk to you. In a couple of weeks. He's a friend of mine; you'll like him. Unlike most shrinks, sane and funny. He's writing something for New Yorker. Has read Foote. Let me know if it's O.K.

Best,

Walker

1 Mar 73

DEAR WALKER

Hope you had some luck with Johnny Sims or Marvin Pixton.[32] The Cochrane house would be a marvel if you could get it; only drawback is I'd turn green with envy, even if you only had it for a month. There's a room up top, sort of a captain's cupola, I'd love to be in through a storm. . . . Let me know, as soon as you get this, how you came out. Also tell me again how long you want the Bankston house for (if you still do) and what month you'd prefer. Gwyn will call Elly[33] then and get the info for you.

---

32. The names of two realtors in Gulf Shores, Alabama.

33. A Memphis friend of the Footes' and owner of a house in Gulf Shores.

Inclosed is a spare page that was tipped by mistake into my Dante. I trimmed it down to fit into the envelope, but it will give you some notion of what a handsome 3-vol set it is—and best of all some idea of the quality of the translation: though this happens not to be one of the better passages. . . . This is my third big experience with finding exciting translations of classics that made me get some real notion of what there was to them. The others were Shaw's Odyssey and Grant's Tacitus; and, oh yes, Lattimore's Iliad. Dante is one of the swiftest moving, sharpest writers Ive ever read—a real pistol. Parts of the Purgatory are as great poetry as I have ever read, and the Inferno has a grim humor Faulkner couldnt even approach at his best. Paradisio leaves me becalmed through long stretches of medieval science and theology; the very things I think might grab you hardest.

I still think you should let me order this $75 set for you. The sale price is $30. But there was an earlier version published by Appleton-Century-Crofts (the Crofts Classics) in paper I think. The translators name is Thomas G. Bergin, whose DANTE (Orion Press, 1965) is much the best general introduction to the subject I know—a great help in understanding the layout and construction.

All best,
Shelby

542 E Parkway S
Memphis 17 Mar 73
DEAR WALKER

Robert Coles was here on Tuesday; had been in Greenville the day and night before, with Roy and Sarah—a wonderfully likeable man, but somewhat puzzling in that I couldnt tell what he had come for, what he was after; mainly I guess because he doesnt take notes or press you for information. I approve of that, but scarcely knew what to make of it. He will be back though, and I reckon he'll know what he wants by then if he doesnt already. I did like him, very much, and so did Gwyn.

Funny thing happened from an interviewer using a tape recorder. Asked Fred Chappell about the novelist's concern with cause and effect, and Chappell said: "I dont frankly philosophically believe in it. Ive studied too much urban charading here to go with that." Anyhow thats how the transcriber took it down. Urban charading? Still, it had a sort of whimsical ring to it. . . . Turned out what he really said was "Erwin Schrödinger." I wonder how many phrases like that came out in Shakespeare from printers unable to read his handwriting? "And 'a babbled of green fields. . . ."

I ought to explain something to you about all Ive been doing in your direction this past six months or year: urging you to do a big three-main-character work, even suggesting the three: plumping hard for you to do a thorough reading of Dante, hoping it might be catching: etc. I know better than to hand out such advice to any writer, if only from my own experience of never taking it. But my concern is great: I think you have done a solid block of work in your three books so far, and it frightens me that you will do either of two bad things just now—stop writing novels entirely, or take off on some tangent (or, more properly speaking, *not* take off) that doesn't involve an extension of your talent or bring what I consider its best aspect to bear. I want you to do a BIG novel, big in every way, theme, content, length, wealth of characters, action, everything. Not many of our best writers ever did that—Faulkner, Hemingway, Fitzgerald, even Twain—and I think we are the poorer for it. If Faulkner had done what he meant to do with the Snopes Saga, instead of putting it off till he was into his comparative dotage, think what a wonder! . . . I'm not all that sure that Karamazov is a better novel than the Idiot, but I glory in Dostoyevsky's undertaking it and I damn well know his work would be infinitely the poorer if he hadnt tried for the longer flight. God knows there can be mistakes from this approach: Romola was such a one for Eliot, but she went on and tried again and achieved it with Middlemarch. . . . Anyhow that has been my concern, and it has been so great that I have been hoicking away at you like a fool, even though I knew it wouldnt work: except it might, to a slight extent. . . . I wanted to explain my lapse of manners and good sense—hoping youd thicken the texture of your work; take eloquence by the throat and wring her neck, as some Frenchman said.

All well here. War winding down fast, loose ends knotting up nicely, just as I planned from the outset. Thank God I was always aware of the dangers that lurk in iotas. It's beautiful—like the 20th act in a 20-act play. 1,500,000-plus words, of which I have only about 50,000 to go: a mere bag of shells. Me and Gibbon. Me and Proust. Me and the Complete Shakespeare.

All best:

Shelby

March 19, 1973

DEAR SHELBY AND GWYN:

Many thanks for seeing Bob Coles.[34] I hope you enjoyed him (he did you). I wouldn't have asked you if I didn't think you would.

Thanks also, especially to Gwyn I imagine, for tracking down Mrs. Bankston-Harwood and putting in a good word. I've got the cottage for June. I've decided the ocean is where I belong—plan to get a small boat and anchor out on the reef and fish and snorkel. Bunt may be lonely. So yall must come down. Since I'm not working, I'd be happy to correct proofs, recalling what a chore it was for Shelby last time. You should have hit Appomattox by then.

We are both poorly. My gut is shot and Bunt has a "frozen shoulder." Doctors can explain neither. I am older than Uncle Will when he died and feel like it. But the ocean will fix me up.

Best,
Walker

Wednesday [spring '73]

DEAR SHELBY,

Met a gal tonight who claimed acquaintance with you. A Greenwood gal become movie actress, etc—Carry Nye. She and her husband Dick Cavett[35] very nice.

But I write to say this: when you write the last sentence of the Narrative, send me a copy on a postcard and we'll meet you and Gwyn wherever you say, Vicksburg, Jackson, here, Gulf Shores, and I'll buy you a bottle of champaigne.

Just saw James Jones, Styron, and Willie Morris in Blackstone Hotel bar in NYC—Southron writers!

—W—

---

34. Psychiatrist and author Robert Coles, who was then in the process of writing a profile of Walker Percy for the *New Yorker*. The profile was eventually published as a book, *Walker Percy: An American Search* (1978).

35. Dick Cavett, the former TV talk-show host.

542 E Parkway S

Memphis 13 May 73

DEAR WALKER

Thanks for sending French edition of RUINS. It looks to me like a firstrate job—something you wont know till they retranslate it back into English, you German student you. Was interested to see the translator shifted to *among* (parmi), which I prefer: like Browning before me. . . . I just finished signing forms required for getting around the 25% French tax for the Coindreau translation of JORDAN COUNTY, which Gallimard (Proust's publisher!) will be bringing out by the end of the year. I wish Coindreau would re-do DRY SEASON, which is badly translated they tell me.

Thanks too for offering to meet me at any midpoint when I wind up Vol III. The midpoint is right here in Memphis and I'll give you all the needed warning. We have an imperial of Mouton-Rothschild (1959) resting for the occasion and want to have a dinner party for about a dozen people—probably sometime around New Year's. Will count on your being here for two-three days to help me celebrate reaching the end of my 20-year road. I may blow my brains out by way of a finale.

I look forward to finding out from you what madness came over the Book Award people, passing up Eudora for the likes of that! Jesus. And then to have the Pulitzer people come along and do right! That's in some ways even more staggering. The thing has come full circle from the days when the Book Award was a sort of protest against lousy choices by the Pulitzers.

Evacuated Richmond yesterday: Jeff Davis on the road. Lee strung out. Grant yelling, "Git em." And Sheridan doing it. And Lincoln about to get shot. First was Old John Brown; now there's J.W. Booth—two madmen, one to start it, another to wind it up. Then Davis: Lucifer in Starlight.

All best,

Shelby

June 13 [1973]

SHELBY—

Hope yall can come and as soon as possible. After 21st we may have to make a trip to Covington and check on Ann.

Jeb Magruder[36] on the tube now. He's no Jeb Stuart.

This is a great cottage—except for the kitchen which is a pisser and which I stay out of.

Best,
Walker

4th of July [1973]

DEAR SHELBY—

Specifics: why don't yall come down July 16 or 17, which is Monday or Tuesday? Give me your flight time to Pensacola and will pick you up.

Our new house ain't got a phone—but will be here in Covington till Sunday July 15.

We loved the Bankston cottage—signed up for next summer. This new one is an interesting experiment. Brand new, a tidy octagonal tree house sans trees—a Tarzan and Jane menage with trapdoor and air conditioning.

Glad your writing is going good. Mine isn't. I have the greatest novel of the century in my head[37]—or rather it has me by the throat—and am too dispirited to get going. It begins: Now in the middle of this journey of our life, I came to myself in a dark wood—etc.

Walker

P.S. An alternative beginning (the novel opens with a 45-year-old priest who has gone sour, is about to chuck the whole thing and take off with a 20-yr-old Bobby McGee type):

The morning after All Soul's Day I stood looking down at my mother's grave in the Felicity Street Cemetary in old New Orleans and I came to myself in the middle of my life and knew that I knew nothing and cared for nothing but following her. She was singing.

Freedom ain't nothing, Lord, but nothing left to lose.

Freedom was all she left to me

---

36. Percy followed the Watergate hearings closely, with mounting disgust.

37. The novel was *Lancelot* (1977).

Loving her was easy, Lord, when
   Bobby sang the blues
Loving her was good enough for me
Good enough for me and Bobby McGee.

It's a post-menopausal novel. The priest is not the main character, who is a noble murderer like Ulysses. *Ulysses*, a good title—has it been used? Shall probably have to settle for *Lancelot* or *Lancelot in Hell*. Which sounds better?

W—

542 E Parkway S
Memphis 10 Jul 73

DEAR WALKER

Glad we got squared away on the visit. We get to Pensacola airport (Eastern Flight 399) at 4.34 Tuesday afternoon, July 17. Will leave, incidentally, at 12.25 Friday afternoon: unless, that is, you get shed of us sooner through total exasperation.

Delighted with your novel subject—though not as delighted as I was at first reading of your handwriting, which led me to believe that your subject was "a 45-yr-old priest who has four sons," rather than "a 45-yr-old priest who has gone sour." Maybe youd consider converting him to conform to your doctorial calligraphy; sex stuff really sells these days I hear. Freedom's just another word for nothing left to lose, like Bobby says. Lancelot would be fine, in or out of hell, so long as you catch him midway in the journey of this life.

I'm working like a fiend, cooking Bobby Lee's goose but good. He sure looks good in those last scenes. Grant in some ways looks even better—for the first time in his life. Got overawed into goodness I expect.

See you Tuesday:

Shelby

542 E Parkway S

Memphis 16 Aug 73

DEAR WALKER

Presume youre back in the ozone belt by now. I watched the TV weather map nightly, and it seemed to me the A in R A I N was always over Gulf Shores. Those that use big raindrops as a symbol always had one sitting splat on top of that little octagonal structure where you were. Did the flounder-looking stingarees go away? Did you sail? Did you grow the long square-cut beard I recommended as a pledge for getting hard to work? I doubt it. Not the work: the beard. You lack the vanity required to grow a beard.

I spent two weeks on return laid up with a vicious head cold; watched Watergate to bitter end when Ervin banged the gavel. Sorry bunch of coves. Nixon's the one; the coviest of them all. Heard him on the tube last night. Not even pitiful: just clonk. He *deserves* paralysis. Which is what weve got for the next three years or more. . . . One thing, though. We dont want Congress running the country. We had that once, during Reconstruction, and believe me we dont need any more of that. Rum go.

Just wiped out close to half Lee's army at Sayler's Creek; two days to go to Appomattox, then the cave-in. There's a strange sort of twilight over all this part of the book, a murkiness as if the rebels were slogging along the floor of hell, stomachs all knotted with hunger and knees about unjointed from fatigue. Yanks threw down one scarecrow retreater, yelling: "Surrender! We got you!" He dropped his rifle, raised his hands. "Yes," he said, "and a hell of a git you got." There was never an army so thoroughly whipped, short of annihilation. But afterwards, when the Yanks came over to fraternize, one said to a Confederate: "Well, Johnny, I guess you fellows will go home now to stay." Reb didnt like being patronized, and said so. "You *guess*, do you? Maybe we are. But dont be giving us any of your impudence. If you do, we'll come back and lick you again."

Shelby

[postcard: postdated Sept. 8, 1973]

Glad you're in the home stretch. When you're finished, how about a short history of WWI? I just finished Solzhenytsin's *August 1914*. Good. You want it?

Shelby Foote in Memphis, Tennessee, 1961. Photograph by Franke Keating.

This may be a watershed year for both of us. I wish I knew what I'd be working on a year from now.

Walker

October 19, 1973

DEAR SHELBY:

Well, I ain't doing much, and that's a fact. Enjoy yourself while you can, while you're doing a great work about a great thing that already happened. Because it's a different cup of tea when you go back to making up stories. There's the rub: sometimes I come to myself and think: what are you, a grown aging man doing sitting around making up stories? What I've been doing is: (1) writing an Introduction to a new paperback edition of Lanterns on the Levee, (2) finishing an article in the works for years called simply A Theory of Language (I'll say no more, knowing how this turns you off: in fact, that's how the article begins: why people can't think about a theory of language, which is something like wearing gold-colored eye-glasses and trying to see gold), (3) this here novel. If I should try to tell you anything about it, it would be a lie and wouldn't sound like what it is, since what it is is in the telling as you well know. I think what's got me down is that the novel is attempting the impossible: to write about the great tradi-tional themes, sin, God, love, death etc., when in fact these themes are no longer with us, we've left them, even death, or they've left us. I've been in a long spell of accedie, anomie and aridity in which, unlike the saints who writhe under the assaults of devils, I simply get sleepy and doze off. I'm also bemused by the reality of being the oldest male Percy in history (LP[38] doesn't count, he was too normal to be a Percy); 57, so what lies ahead is virgin territory; imagine a Percy with arthritis! senility! Parkinsonism, shuf-fling along fingers rolling pills, head agoing! You were simply being a nor-mal Foote, padding about the beach cottage at 3 AM with a hangover and

---

38. LeRoy Percy, Walker's great-uncle and the father of William Alexander Percy, was a lawyer and a U.S. Senator.

you even know what lies ahead for you: 40 years of no more than the gentlest decline. I don't know whether I'm looking forward to doing a great thing like Kant and Spinoza and Verdi in the 1980s or whether I'll jump in the Bogue Falaya next week with a sugar kettle on my head[39] (lately it's been close to the latter). Yeah, my Catholicism is not very operative as Nixon would say. It consists just now and mainly in the deepest kind of hunch that it all works out, generally for the good, and everybody gets their deserts—which is frightening. But, I mean, artistically, there is no sweat. One waits. Not for the Muse, fuck her, but until one finds a new language, because that's about what it takes, the language is about dead.

This is all mostly bull. You know what my real sin is? Lazyness. Which is to say that if I were broke, had four squalling kids and a deadline, I'd be working my ass off, nicht? That's how come they call it a mortal sin. My only defense is that I was born lazy, like to look at a blank sheet of paper—while you are making your outlines.

I have a pet squirrel. The cat brought it in, newborn and uneaten. I raised him. He perches on my shoulder and does a trick: puts his hand behind his head so you can scratch his armpit.

Walker

P.S. Shakespeare had it easy: he had a language, a new language, busting out all around him, and he didn't even have to make up stories: the stories were around him too. We have to do it *all*, including the impossible or all but impossible task: make up a language as you go along. All you have to do to be a good novelist now is to be like God on the first day.

PPS Re Catholicism: I think that culturally speaking I am still a gloomy Georgia Presbyterian. It's impossible to escape one's origins altogether. I believe in the One Holy Catholic and Apostolic Church etc but it is intellectual and I often don't feel a part of the feast like merry Louisianians. Also, the conviction is growing that an end is at hand, whether the end of the U.S. or the West or the world I don't yet know, maybe all three. But as

---

39. The fate of Percy's ancestor, Charles, who came to America in the late eighteenth century.

the Mass said this morning: Christ died, Christ is risen, Christ will come again. Don't doubt it: the Great Beast of Bethlehem is coming back.

W—

542 E Parkway S

Memphis 11 Dec 73

DEAR WALKER

I killed Lincoln last week—Saturday, at noon. While I was doing it (he had his chest arched up, holding his last breath to let it out) some halfassed doctor came to the door with vols I and II under his arm, wanting me to autograph them for his son for Xmas. I was in such a state of shock, I not only let him in; I even signed the goddam books, a thing I seldom do. Then I turned back and killed him and had Stanton say, "Now he belongs to the ages." A strange feeling, though. I have another 70-odd pages to go, and I have a fear theyll be like *Hamlet* with Hamlet left out. Christ, what a man. It's been a great thing getting to know him as he was, rather than as he has come to be—a sort of TV image of himself, with a ghost alongside.

I finally saw your piece on Mr Will in the SatRev[40] and liked it very much. What a thing it would be to try really to recapture him as he was in life; except of course it couldnt be done. All we can do is take pieces of him and distribute them here and there through our books, and all of them together dont add up to more than a fraction of what he was. How could you ever combine the incidental petulance—mainly a boundless capacity for outrage—with the enormous compassion? I often think of the paradox involved in his sorrow from the conviction that his father never thought him a shadow of the man his dead brother would have been, though the fact was he was twice the man the Senator ever was. Spooks. All life is spooked, and ours is the most impossible task of all; a continuous assault upon the impossible.

Lord God, here comes Christmas. Rackafrax, from start to finish except for the turkey and stuffing and giblet gravy; that I like. There used to be

———

40. Percy's essay about Uncle Will appeared in the November 6, 1973, issue of *The Saturday Review*.

some sort of movement for putting Christ back in Christmas. Absurd. It couldnt be done. He wouldnt fit.

Saw a good movie lately I think youd like: Bang the Drum Slowly. Alas though, it hasnt been a good year for the flicks. Iceman Cometh was a trudging bore. I'm waiting for Robert Altman to build up another head of steam. McCabe & Mrs Miller was the last great film Ive seen.

No news otherwise. I'm on my treadmill and glad to be there.

Rgds,

Shelby

Dec. 20 [1973]

SHELBY—

Sitting here watching Wyatt Earp (Burt Lancaster) and Doc Holliday (Kirk Douglas) getting it on with the Clantons. A man will do anything at Xmas.

Interesting present arrived from Memphis—feels like a long bean bag.

The "Uncle Will" piece is a truncated version of the *Intro* to *L on L*[41]— should be out next month—I'll send it to you. A nice note from Gerstle Mack. He remembered that he told Uncle Will that there was no such word as "altophobia" (Gerstle was reading proofs of *L on L*) and Uncle Will flew into a rage—would not say "acrophobia"—settled for "Vertigo."

Art here buggered, blowed, and screwed. I'm certainly at the end of something and therefore hopefully at the beginning—Merry Xmas.

W.

Jan 3, 1974

DEAR SHELBY AND GWYN,

You can imagine emotion when after looking at an elongated heavy limber Xmas-wrapped gift under the tree for *10 days*, we opened it, to see first off: Keep refrigerated. Anyhow it is a noble side of bacon. Bunt and I argue

---

41. A paperback reissue of William Alexander Percy's *Lanterns on the Levee*, originally published in 1941.

about the proper thickness of a slice, she citing 15 years experience eating side meats in Doddsville. I tend to thick slices which smoke up the house but are lovely and crisp when I finish.

Holidays lousy as usual. I have to go to *parties* and talk to people about Watergate etc. Only good spots—grandchildren with Santy. Ann home off and on with boyfriend.

We are wondering whether we're going to make it to Gulf Shores for June and July. Maybe make it with bikes and ride to Jeannie's or sail.

Love,
Walker

542 E Parkway S
Memphis 22 Jan 74
DEAR WALKER

Thanks for LANTERNS; I liked the uncut introduction better. You did a good job there; moreover, something not easy—meaning I think even Mr Will would have liked it; not only the praise but the analysis as well. Very strange, looking back on a life once the pattern has emerged. What in God's name will they make of ours someday, if they take the trouble? "A general mess of imprecision," Eliot said.

Been going great guns; more than 10,000 words in the past month. Captured Jeff Davis yesterday, locked him up in Ft Monroe today. Now on to Andy Johnson, who looks to me as if he's headed for impeachment. Strike the tent! I'm midway through the final chapter, feeling as if I'm about to be orphaned or left childless; cant tell which. Who's leading whom?

I want some word youre out of the doldrums and into something fitten. Why dont you get your essays together, fill in the blanks and make a book? Man on Train, Loss of Creature, etc. I think it would make a likely volume; something to take off from.

Rgds:
Shelby

542 E Parkway S

Memphis 22 Apr 74

DEAR WALKER

I'm into the final ten-page stretch; will wind it up, God willing, by the end of this week or early next. Am due, alas, in Jackson on May 3 to speak for a fee I didnt feel free to refuse—something called the "Miss. Arts Festival, Inc." Then will come back and help Gwyn crank up for the party: Friday, May 10.

I hope this doesnt clash with any plans or commitments you and Bunt may have made. If so, tell whatever it is youre sorry. My hope is that you will be able to stay over for a couple of days at least. I'm feeling kind of spooky. . . . Twenty years! What could there be left worth writing about? Whats a rape or a lynching or a kidnapping compared to Chancellorsville or Booth coming busting out of the smoke in Lincoln's box? Where am I going to find me another hero to put alongside R. E. Lee or Bedford Forrest? . . . My life slips onto the down slope.

Or maybe not. Imagine making up facts inside one's own head! What fun, and how easy. I really do look forward to getting back to it; or anyhow I think so. Queasy, though.

Remember: Friday, May 10. Get here that day or anytime earlier. The guest room will be ready and I hope youll stay as long as can be.

All best,

Shelby

May 23 [1974]

DEAR SHELBY,

A lovely party—and it must have been great wine—I wasn't even hung over. I liked your friends, rich though they may be. Especially liked Lucy Fisher and little Carnegie-Rockefeller McFadden. To say nothing about Nell, a doll.

Just finished pulling together those selected essays you spoke of, plus an introduction, plus a long, unreadable article (but most important I'll ever write) called "A Theory of Language" which will also be published in *Southern Review*. Glad to be rid of it. Decks now clear.

Reading Blotner's Faulkner with interest. Don't mind details the reviewers deplored. Pity is, he has to leave out the most interesting stuff: F's relation to Estelle, how come Jill hated life at home, sexual relations with Joan and Jean, etc. Neccesary reticence of course but pity anyhow. Part on Phil Stone amazing.—

W—

FOUR

The "Third Half" of Life

June 12, 1974

DEAR SHELBY—

Thanks again. It's a noble work. I'm still staggered by the size of the achievement.

I am still bothered by the prominence of Lucifer.[1] It is after all a history of the Civil War, not the Confederacy, yet you've made the hero of your narrative of a *military* event the *civilian* leader of the losing side.

O.K., I'm not picking—otherwise it is *The Iliad*.

—W

Wed 3 Jul 74

DEAR WALKER

Herewith the last chapter of Volume III—the final 100 pages. Keep these as long as you like, then send them back the cheapest way. I'm curious to know whether these pages can conceivably be as good as they seem to me, and dont know anyone else whose judgment I respect enough to give a hoot whether they like them or not. Let me know in your spare time.

No news otherwise; I just wound up page proofs and am turning a

---

1. Jefferson Davis.

notion for a novel over in my mind. . . . Three Mississippi gangsters come up to Memphis and kidnap a rich Negro's child for ransom. I figure it's good for, say, $72,000 from paperbacks. Maybe more.

Rgds to Bunt et al:

Shelby

July 7, 1974

DEAR SHELBY—

Yes, it's as good as you think. It has a fine understated epic quality, a slow measured period, and a sustained noncommittal, almost laconic, tone of the narrator. I've no doubt it will survive; might even be read in the ruins.

2 demurrers, 1 about English, the other about ideology:

The paragraph on p. 1042, a very important paragraph, is seriously ambiguous. It is not clear whether the "sense of nationhood" you mention means in USA with solid South, or the USA for northern vets and SS for Southerners, or both. Finally, it appears you mean both. Sumpin wrong.

Most of the last 40 pp. goes to Davis. O.K., but it seems a departure from the almost icy neutrality of the narrator up to now (you can't tell whether he's from Ala or Ohio—maybe the latter considering his treatment of Sherman), then the rather partisan finale on Davis. Is this how you want it? (maybe this is Percy anti-Dorsey sentiment).

—W—

P.S. I'll return the galleys when Bunt finishes too.

542 E Parkway S

Memphis 11 Jul 74

DEAR WALKER

Glad you liked the last chapter. It brought the total to 1,500,000-plus words: a third of a million longer than Gibbon's Decline & Fall, which took about the same length of time to write. Funny; I thought those old boys wrote a lot faster than we do, not being much concerned about mot juste and suchlike.

The ambiguity of that "nationhood" paragraph was not only intentional, it was intended to be so in just the way it struck you, just the way you describe your reaction: "It is not clear whether the 'sense of nationhood' you mention means the USA with Solid South, or the USA for northern vets and SS for Southerners, or both. Finally it appears you mean both." Just so—a gradual dawning, a gradual realization* that it is both I mean. If of course it didnt work in its end effect, thats something else entirely; "sumpin wrong" indeed. Ambiguity is a dangerous thing to fool around with, but a useful device all the same.

As for the closeout narrowing-down on Davis, I think if you go back youll see that it balances the antebellum biography that opens Vol I, no more sympathetic and with the same narrow-focussed point of view. There, though, it was offset by the antebellum biography of Lincoln, and originally I intended to do two things I dropped at the end—one, a contrapuntal treatment of L's funeral, the train winding north and west while Davis fled southward; the other, an account of the growth of L's postwar reputation, interwoven with Davis's postwar life at Beauvoir. But once I had written Lincoln's death scene in such detail, once he had drawn that last long breath, I found I couldnt come back to him; it would be wrong for him to be anything but *gone* once the doctor put those half-dollars on his eyes— except, that is, the two closing touches: when the thieves attempt to steal his body for ransom, then when I re-quote him on the war as "philosophy to learn wisdom from," a final touch of the Lincoln music Davis couldnt match or even catch. I may have done wrong to drop my early plan for coming back to him, thereby offsetting the total concentration on Davis, but I dont think so. He's gone, man, gone—"like a turkey through the cawn," as Leadbelly says. Sometimes (and often they are the best of times) writing has to be done by instinct, and this was one of them. You get these instinctive reactions, and if you dont trust them youre not going with your talent.

Now that Ive got nothing else to do but read map proofs and block out a novel, I have been tending toward worrying about you. I want you going on a new novel, something different and big. That was why I tried to get you into Dante, who's got more to teach a writer than anyone Ive read since Proust, forty years ago. Not only about *how* to write, though he does that superbly, but also about what to write *about*. We could all of us write a Divine Comedy if we just had the confidence to undertake it, to lay it on the line, to bring everything we've learned to bear on something so intense, so huge in its implications, so alive from its first line. This new translation (Thomas G. Bergin) broke the ice for me, and I thought it might for you. The prose wont do; neither will the old Cary job; but this one will. I wish youd try it.

Anyhow all goes well with me. I'm just wondering who in hell is going to pay $60 for a three-volume set of books about a war as useless and ugly in its way as Viet Nam was. Hoo!

Rgds:

Shelby

*For the reader, as it was for them.

25 July 74

DEAR WALKER

Still reading proofs of various last-minute types—maps, etc. Should have first bound copies by late September, God willing. Will see you get one then.

I'm still sort of keyed up. Told Bob Loomis (Random editor) you liked last chapter; he said for me to request a blurb; I said no—*he* could, not me. Youll probably be hearing from him. Pay him no more attention than youve a mind to.

All goes well in general: still milling over a novel.

Rgds,

Shelby

July 27, 1974

DEAR SHELBY—

Glad indeed to give Loomis a quote.

Don't pay any heed to my misgivings about Davis. You're right—if it feels right to you, that's what's important.

Am writing this from Ochsner Hospital where I checked in for some tests. Finally got fed up with low-grade fever and malaise. It seems I might have, not TB, but hepatitis, which is good to know, but bad on my Early Times habit. Should be out by Tuesday.

Been reading Blotner's *Faulkner*. Am chiefly astounded by (1) what a repellent poseur the younger WF was and (2) what extraordinary fidelity and responsibilty he showed in supporting that big family and (3) how broke he was and (4) how rotten a time he had in Hollywood.

Best—

W.

[Summer 1974]

SHELBY—

Thought you might enjoy this item on Howard Mitcham.[2]

Working up to Dante any day now.

W—

542 E Parkway S

Memphis: 2 Aug 74

DEAR WALKER

Keep me posted on the hepatitis outcome—sounds grisly, but good to know I reckon; now they and you can set about ousting it. I remember Roy and Sarah once came down with it simultaneously; had adjoining hospital rooms. The doctor put them on "grease-free" diets: which sounded fine, except they soon found out "grease" included every good thing in the world, beginning with butter and moving on through every sauce in the cookbook. A person could wind up living on cornflakes without cream.

I reacted much as you did to the Faulkner biography on those same counts. My theory is that his notorious stiff dignity and confounding silence were later-in-life reactions to having made a fool of himself in his youth, not only by talking and striking poses but also by telling a long string of lies, all of which had to be lived down when he got together something valid on his own and no longer needed them to convince others, and above all himself, that he was indeed somebody. He sure was. I can see signs already that his

---

2. A Greenville native, a painter, and a chef, Mitcham had worked in New Orleans before opening a restaurant on Cape Cod—as announced in the clipping that Percy sent Foote.

reputation is headed into the trough that always follows adulation, but I dont think there can be any doubt about his reputation as one of our two or three real writers, alongside Twain and James. . . . Last week came an invitation from a fellow in the English Dept at Alabama wanting me to participate in a F. memorial there (Blotner, Rubin, Meriwether, Brooks, etc); I wrote back that I agreed with F that writers ought to stay home and write, and added (somewhat maliciously I admit) that I wish theyd thought to honor him while he was alive. Chap wrote back he would have done it then if he'd been on faculty at the time. Unlikelihood; but I didnt press the point by asking why he doesnt stage some such hooraw for the likes of you and me. Unlikelihood, indeed.

Tunkie Saunders[3] is still here; been here five months now, waiting for his wife to get squared away on the divorce details, new house, etc. He pays his board in wine, and once a week the bill when we go out to dinner some place or other. Poor chap's about undone—fifty-three and bereft of wife and kids. I cant get him to see it as deliverance. He sees it as dead end. Could be, especially since he sees it so. Half the ills on this earth would be solved if love could only be abolished.

It's hard to explain how extraordinarily good I feel about my book; little things in it, I mean, that others will scarcely notice or just rush by in the reading—like the expression on Jeb Stuart's face when they jogged him off in an ambulance with a bullet through his liver; or Lee with dysentery, tossed about on his cot and crying out of Grant, "If I could just get one more pull at him!" Or Forrest at Brice's Crossroads. "Hit 'em on the ee-end," he told a brigade commander. Or Mary Lincoln at L's bedside, saying: "Send for Tad. He will speak to Tad, he loves him so." . . . So many things, and all of them seem to me so extraordinarily *good*. It's quite different from any reaction I ever had to a novel, I guess because I didnt make it up. I want everybody everywhere to read it so they can learn to love their country.

Hope this finds you free of Ochsner and soon free of the ailment too.

Rgds:

Shelby

Dont forget the Ellmann *Joyce*. It's the best such job of them all.

---

3. A Memphis friend of Foote's.

542 E Parkway S

Memphis 26 Aug 74

DEAR WALKER

Ive heard nothing from you since you wrote of being laid up in the tongs of hepatitis—if that was what it was. What gives? You well yet? Back on Early Times? Resolved to end your wicked ways? Tell me.

I'm drifting, waiting; best of all, reading Proust, my seventh start-to-finish exploration, but my first in twenty years. Glorious! I say again, the Shakespeare of our time. . . . Hard to believe I just finished a work 400,000 words longer than his, which runs 1,300,000.* Quantity, yes, but quality? Aie. . . . A friend of mine, George Garrett, has taken upon himself the task of serving as drumbeater for my War, which he declares (without having read a line of Vol III) to be THE literary achievement of our century, no less. Anyhow he's operating accordingly; has friends all over the country committed to doing highly appreciative reviews, especially in Virginia, Florida, and Texas, where theyre mostly clustered. Louis Rubin, by the way, having read the galleys, has completed a 1500 word review for the New Republic and has it in mind to do a much longer one for the Sewanee Review. . . . So far so good. Loomis sent me a thermofax of your generous blurb: for which much thanks—I can use all the praise anyone can imagine, whether it's deserved or not. "Hats off, gentlemen," and all that. Robert Coles expressed an interest, and I had Random send him a set of galleys, too. A third set went to Robert Penn Warren, from whom only silence as befits his dignity. Wish he'd come down off it.

A new thing, this, for me. Always before, I was too busy with the next one to have much concern about the one about to appear in a couple of months. I guess it's the twenty-year involvement, plus the excursion outside my field, which I'm putting off getting back to. Anyhow I take a lively interest in puffs and such, even though I still wont quite do anything myself: guess thatll come later, when I get more edgy and acquisitive-minded. There's a sizeable chamber of greed inside all the hearts that ever beat.

Enough of that, though. Tell me, as I said, how it goes with you. Health-wise and literarywise as well.

All best,

Shelby

Decline & Fall runs 1,250,000. Never thought I'd turn out to be windier than Gibbon.

Sept. 9, 1974

SHELBY —

Carmen missed us. Everybody disappointed. I noticed a certain exhilaration as she approached and a sadness as she went away. That's the degree of alienation! NOXIOUS particles everywhere! Only 150 MPH winds get rid of them!

Glad to hear of drumbeats for the narrative. It just might make a lot of money — a coffee-table item for rich literate ladies and don't put them down.

Liver mending. Back *up* to my *normal* depression.

Best,

W.

542 E Parkway S

16 Oct 74

DEAR WALKER

Look what they did with your blurb. My guess is youll be seeing it all over hell and gone, come November, in full and halfpage ads: provided Random comes through with even a fraction of all the advertising they promised while I was humping my back through volumes one, two, three.

Got the first finished copy from the bindery three days ago. You should be getting yours within the next couple of weeks. It ran 1106 pages, including Index, and has something of the look and heft of the Manhattan Telephone Directory.

Ive seen some exuberant critical responses. Louis Rubin cut loose with a hurrah ("the majestic overall account that all knew would one day be written, but that had not appeared thus far") and George Garrett lost his critical balance entirely: "It is, in my best judgment and opinion, the most important American literary event of my lifetime." Pretty heavy, I'd say. (First rational explanation Ive seen for Hemingway's suicide: He saw this coming and cleared the track.)

Nothing much shaking here except a good deal of thumb twiddling.

Guess it will continue right on till Christmas. Once I have that behind me I presume I'll get back to work—if I can hold out that long. Doing lots of good reading meantime.

All best:

Shelby

542 E Parkway S

Memphis 27 Oct 74

DEAR WALKER

I was glad you called yesterday; glad to know youre well off, and glad to know Vol III reached you. I inclose a bookmark that will help you keep your bearings during your trek through the jungly last year of the War— the outline I used to write it by.

All looks well on the review front. The book will get decent attention I expect, but I cant believe much is going to come of it saleswise, as they say. Still, at $60 a clip it wont have to do too well to bring me in some money. For me, after all these years of cutting things close to the bone, "some" money will be a lot; more, in any case, than I ever had before.

I was so pleased to hear that Random had gotten advance copies out, I neglected to ask how your health is. Last I heard, you were laid up with hepatitis, deprived of Early Times, and in general discombobulated. I trust all that's behind you now, or practically so; let me know. Ive been asking and asking, these past few months, and you never say.

Dont underrate those Western doings. Hood at Franklin and Nashville is as tragic a figure as any in the war, and Forrest outdoes all the others by miles and miles; not to mention Farragut in Mobile Bay and Sherman on his smoky march.

All best, as always:

Shelby

[Fall 1974?]

SHELBY—

Here are the first four pages of an early draft of a book of essays (mostly published) coming out in spring.

I just discovered a peculiar thing—the first essay was written and published in 1954 (on language and Suzanne Langer's "Symbol as Need"). This introduction is the last, written in 1974—and the end of my effort in this area—20 years off and on—making up novels in between. Strange parallel, nicht? You fighting in war, me laying into old Homo himself. (I'm afraid I didn't win this war either.)

I know your mind goes blank when you read this stuff, but this beginning will give you the flavor.

W.

542 E Parkway S
Memphis: 7 Nov 74
DEAR WALKER

I enjoyed very much those introductory pages. Thats the way to do it: state the problem before you tackle it—despite the danger (which is there) of sounding like T. Wolfe—"O, lost!"—or brooding after the manner of Joe Heller in his current blousy maunderings: with the considerable difference that you then go on to confront if not to solve it, whereas they both are content, or discontent, just to marvel at it; joyously in Wolfe's case, gloomily in Heller's.

Language may indeed be the clew, but in my limited way I see it more in a gain of individuality. Thats whats done us in. Lawrence said, "The opposite of love isnt hatred, the opposite of love is individuality." The more we gained in individuality, the more we lost in personal satisfaction, in love. Marx and Freud, by identifying us to ourselves, have cost us more than we'll perhaps ever be able to pay. Gone is the brimful joy of the cathedral worker of the Middle Ages, working away at something he would never see finished and with which no one would ever connect his name. Instead we have this lifelong wrestling match with the over-demanding Self, which always wins and collects his due in dissatisfaction. Maybe, though, postMarx, postFreud, it will end with the bomb and a new life will arise and go down in its turn once it produces its Marx and Freud. I dont blame or even regret these two; I think what they found was the truth; only we cant stand it, even the approximation of the truth they pointed out. Jesus's truth could be lived with (and even *by*) but not Freud's, which puts too much on us, more than we can bear, and gives us no relief.

I had a strange experience last Sunday night, 10.30 to 11.30—a television series called "The World at War," narrated by Lawrence Olivier, a British tv history of World War II, an hour a week for sixteen or so weeks. Anyhow, Sunday night the hour was on the concentration camps; lots of film never shown before, especially of people being put into cattle cars and then into the chambers when cyanide pellets came dropping down instead of water from the shower heads. I watched it and watched it, the indignity of it all, and all of a sudden I began sobbing—sobbing I think at the fiendish nature of man. Some of that stuff I really didnt think one person could do to another. That was the whole horror. Not the suffering, though of course that was part of it. My grief was for the ones inflicting the indignities and the torture; in other words for myself, that I belonged to a species that was capable of such action. And all those fine looking German soldiers; it didnt seem to bother them at all. Maybe *thats* where the Hittites went. And the old Jews and the children, the terror that was on them—and, somewhere among them, for all I knew, some kinsman of mine from Old Vienna, with his long gray beard and the old old faces on some of the children in the camps and the women stripping naked in the cold before they stepped into the shower rooms, already knowing what was going to happen to them inside, and then, later, the bodies, all crowded into a sort of pyramid from having huddled together and then clawed their way to the top for air, the strongest of them. For me, it started with tears I didnt even know I was crying until the sobs came. . . .

Twenty years. Holy Mother! Twenty years since that Fordham pamphlet, "Symbol as Need." We have indeed been at it, you and I. Thank God for my narrower scope; I'll take Mars Robert every time. Him at least you can get actual hold of, at least from time to time, saying: "It is well that war is so terrible. We should grow too fond of it." And didnt we though? . . . One of the great pleasures I expect youll get from assembling those pieces will be a discovery of the pattern you had in mind without knowing it. It's always so with stories, essays, novels, poems, whatever. The pattern is there, though it only comes clear at the finish, looking back.

Random has high hopes for the book, Vol III and the three-vol set as a whole. Publication date is Nov 26. We'll see.

Congratulations, and all best:

Shelby

542 E Parkway S

Memphis: 4 Dec 74

DEAR WALKER

Ive been rereading your Delta Factor piece, and I'm beginning to see and wonder at things I scarcely noticed first time round. (You know me and the abstract. It snowblinds me, puts crimps in all my ganglia, so to speak, and turns the tips of my fingers numb.) I think youre right about the importance of language and the difference even a vestige of it makes; I think youre right too about the thing it grows from—symbolism. It's not only that an animal cant speak, he also cant discern a lifesize, absolutely accurate photograph of his own master; all he sees is a gray, black-and-white mass of squiggles, apparently; he cant make that step that makes them form a figure you would think he couldnt possibly fail to see. The same is true of very young children. Early on, they can see and recognize cartoons and be amused by them, whether still or moving; but they cant see a photograph any more than a dog can. That is, they cant pull it together, cant apply the necessary symbol that makes the lines a photograph and therefore see what it represents; not only represents, but *is*—an actual print of that person's person on the sheet of sensitized paper.

Something of this carries over into writing. Its glory is the metaphor, whether a similie or a more subtle form of comparison, an equating of two very different things whose comparison makes each of them far realer than before. "All flesh is grass" is one of the great statements, reaching well down into our very bones; even though, as you say, it is patently false in fact, it is superbly true in its application, in our response to the words themselves and the thoughts they provoke. All flesh *is* grass, and it is the aptness of the metaphor that makes it so much truer than the simple statement that all flesh is mortal. (Incidentally, I dont think you should leave out the *all*, which makes it even truer by wider application.) In other words, the metaphor is what makes it truer. Metaphor, if it is right, always makes everything truer. Proust called it finding the true way to explain or demonstrate a thing, provided it was encased in a "fine" style. Homer's similies, which go the farthest afield of any I know, often seem to me the very best, even though they are often "literary" in the worst sense. Mallarmé said it well: "Take eloquence by the throat and wring her neck." Keeping in mind Hemingway's precept that a writer's best piece of equipment is an infallible shit-detector, I think Proust (again) was entirely right when he said that we must never be afraid of going too far, "because the truth is always beyond." . . . In other words, youve done for me what I daresay you most wanted to do for all; youve opened up vistas demanding exploration by people who are not much given to such work. Or, for that matter, even by those who are.

I saw in a recent Southern Review that the Delta piece will be in the next issue. Thats good. I wish, though, that you were doing what you said you wouldnt do; that is, go through all the pieces for revision and improvement, especially with regard to tying them together, making each lead to the next, as indeed I'm sure they do already anyhow. Twenty years! Looking back I bet you feel much as I do—like a man who has somehow managed to swallow a 20-pound cannonball, and then pass it. The result, quoting Eliot this time, is "a general mess of imprecision," but highly satisfactory in any case, just from its very existence, imprecisions notwithstanding. A sad metier indeed.

Book goes well I hear. Returns are still a long way short of in, but it looks as though it will sell fairly well and I may have some prizes coming my way eventually. My trouble is Ive always had such heavy contempt for prizes, the Pulitzer for example, that I feel very strange lusting after them. I even sometimes doubt it's me; I put it down to idleness, which is no doubt accurate. Come New Years I'll be back at work and all that will have vanished like the wind.

Bear up and let me know how all goes nowadays. I'm still twiddling, as you can see from the length of this.

Shelby

542 E Parkway S
Memphis: 7 Dec 74
DEAR WALKER
For some time now Ive been meaning to send you the inclosed, on the off chance you might take off some fine summer and read straight through

Volumes I, II, III. It's a capsule outline of all three, and I hope will keep you oriented on the journey as well as give some notion of the organization, the attempts at balance I tried for in the writing. Anyhow, stick them in your copies of all three volumes and theyll be there for whoever turns to them in years to come. Art *is* long.

A real geewhiz review by Louis Rubin in last week's New Republic, and Random tells me there's an all-stops-out one by John Barkham (syndicated chap) making the rounds of some 300-odd newspapers. I havent seen it yet but they tell me he makes me out to be an American Gibbon. Several of them have done that—no doubt on clew from me in the bibliographical note; but I'd much rather be known as an American Foote. Still, I'm a long way from looking any gifthorse in the mouth. Right now I'm involved in the tearing business of waiting around to find out whether I'll be rich or poor. If it's rich, I'll have to hump to lay that burden down; never could do anything with money in the bank; have to lay it down before I can turn my mind to serious matters—get shed of it. I must say, though, it was never much of a problem: meaning much of a burden—I could always lay it down by buying a new shotgun or desklamp or leather jacket. This time, with luck, I may have a harder time; but I'll manage I'm sure. Besides, chances are it will just lie there like a brick. Who the hell wants to read anything whatever about the goddam Civil War? Not me.

Just tuck the inclosed away: maybe for Ann some day. Who knows? And give Bunt my regards.

Shelby

542 E Parkway S
Memphis 30 Dec 74
DEAR WALKER

Many thanks for the superegghead book on "Old Mellifluous," the sage of "Octonawhoopoo," as Hemingway called him. But I was puzzled by the presence in the package of the cap from a bottle of Tab in the slipcase from an insurance policy. Was there a grandchild in the room when you slipped the wrapped book into the folder? Or was it some kind of cryptic message? Tab. What means Tab? I dont get it. Tab. Hint of weightloss? Sugar crisis? Tab. In an insurance slipcase? Tab. Code, perhaps, for Theyre

All Bastards? Turnabout? Take A Break? I give up. Tab. Tabula rasa? I give up. Tap? Tab? I give up.

Many reviews, all full of praise and all of them amounting to practically nothing. Reading reviews is numbing—no amount of praise is enough, and one speck of adverse criticism is a speck too much. They call you Gibbon and you know thats silly, but if they dont call you Gibbon you get a feeling theyre holding back. No one knows as well as I how marvelous the work is, no one sees as well as I do all its hidden beauties, no one knows as well as I do how beautifully it's structured, the secret ties with the Iliad, the marvels hidden within iotas on every page, shimmering through every line. . . . I dont know yet how well it's selling; pretty well I think, but I'm waiting to hear whether the Book of the Month Club is going to take it for a dividend; they are *considering*—which probably means they wont. Wish theyd go ahead and decline it so I can scorn them. Until then I'm holding my fire. Same for prizes of all descriptions. Those grapes will set my teeth on edge. Foxy me.

Was delighted to hear youre into Ellman's Joyce. Best writer biography I ever read by far. Isnt he something, that great blind Milton of our time? A real scamp. Talk about foxy! A real maneuverer. "Deal with him, Hemingway!" And: "It seems to me the question is what Ireland can do for Me." Drunk nightly but always at his desk next morning, searching out the evil in the nest of a good word—a limberlegged dancer, embattled father, negligent but loving husband. "What can two people have to say to one another when theyve been married thirty years?"

I dont much like the notion of you being carved on, especially without even knowing it was in progress.[4] You should have done as I did: healed yourself. But then again that was forty years ago. I was seventeen at the time; younggutted and quick to heal. I remember I thought the world had come to an end. Just willed it shut, and it shut. . . . Ever since, Ive had two prime rules of behavior. Never make any sudden movements and never pick up anything heavy. Mind those two and youll be as hale as I am, which is hale indeed.

How goes the assembling of the essays? Sounds to me like fun, except I

---

4. Percy had had minor surgery for skin cancer.

cant understand your resistance to neatening them up, adzing them down, mitering all the joints and putting a glitter to them.

Anyhow there goes the old year. Happy 75 to you and yours, from me and mine:

Shelby

Memphis
26 Feb 75
DEAR WALKER

You were right: I hadnt seen the National Review piece. Thanks for sending it. I found it one of the best—that is, most understanding— reviews Ive gotten, so far. Theyve all, I mean *all*, been "good" as anyone could hope for: chocked with praise & admiration, larded with the right adjectives, etc: but few of them have been as close to seeing any one facet of what I had in mind. Another is by C. Vann Woodward in the current NY Review of Books.* He did a similar thing with still another facet. I'm hoping for more of that in the spring & summer literary & historical publications—though I know that, sooner or later, I'm going to fall into the clutches of some jaundiced, resentful "professional" of that type.

Sales are going good I think, but I dont seem to be in any real danger of being swamped by the long green; not in surplus, that is. All well in general. I just keep flubbing around, still twiddling my thumbs.

Rgds—
Shelby

*6 March edition.

542 E Parkway S
Memphis: 5 Apr 75
DEAR WALKER

Just back from New York: of which more later. Found here the new Mississippi Quarterly with Garrett's review of my Narrative and the long piece by Zeugner[5] on you. I reckon it gave you some hard moments of hot, bristly indignation. Yet I wonder if, in the end, you thought as I did that it was a really superior study, perceptive, inventive, and thorough in the best sense. I like it much better than anything Ive ever seen on your work; I think the virtues it points out are the virtues that count most, even though I disagree with his judgment that the uncertainties of the LAST GENTLEMAN make it a lesser work than the MOVIEGOER. In fact I think just the opposite for exactly the same reason; I think it was just those uncertainties that put the heat and juice in it that lifted it above the earlier work. Faulkner said once that writing a novel is like trying to knock together a chicken coop while a hurricane is raging. In GENTLEMAN you were bucking a fiercer wind. . . . Incidentally, I enjoyed the barb he sank in the New Yorker about midway through the piece.

We did as I said we would in NY: ate our heads off—Lutece, La Fayette, San Marco, Caravelle, we did them all in style and at incredible expense without regret. Finally found the one good thing to do with money: eat it, preferably with sauce Bercy and heavy drafts of Chateau Palmer or Gevry-Chambertin. You only go round once, they say, but we went round several times in just four days.

Another thing: I got myself a hotshot agent at the urging of old Calder Willingham who's made tons of money off him. Robert Rosen is his name and he's already at work on a plan for selling all three volumes of the War to public television for a series, plus individual sales of the early novels to individual producers and directors, friends of his like Altman, Richardson, and such. You cant tell, I might wind up rich.

Right now I'm sweating out the Book Award, ten days off, and the Pulitzer, a month from today. I'm supposed to be hot in the running, but I lack confidence. The judges are all academics, which puts my money on Genovese's Roll Jordan Roll. We'll see.

Meantime I'm still twiddling.

Rgds:

Shelby

---

5. John Zeugner's "Walker Percy and Gabriel Marcel: The Castaway and the Wayfarer" appeared in the Winter 1974–75 issue of the *Mississippi Quarterly*.

Reviews continue phenomenal; I never saw anything like them. A few are even almost perceptive. Praise generates a desire, indeed a need, for still more praise. "Stay me with flagons, cover me with apples!" I keep saying.

April 8, 1975

DEAR SHELBY:

And you were the one telling me literary prizes were shit for the birds. Well, shit or not, I'd expect the Narrative to cop both prizes. T. Harry did with *Huey Long* and yours is a lot more than that.

Don't know *Mississippi Quarterly* and nobody has told me about the articles about you or me, but I'll have to look it up—especially if Zeugner is hard on me, which believe it or not I never mind, providing it is true, and I take to heart. Praise always makes me feel vaguely guilty, as well as bored.

Another month and I'll be through with the academic scene which I was glad to do and gladder still to get over with. Then I'll have to decide what to do with my declining years—Jesus, in a little more than a year, I'll be 60—and you, what? 61? So what now? It is a question of desire, what one wants to do—write something better or run off with two girls to the islands. Having delivered the last word on the nature of man, I am in a quandary.

Am reading Heller's *Something Happened*, prepared to dislike it, and liking some of it very much. But you don't read anything current except that dirty old novelist Willingham. But if he's put you onto a good agent who makes you a lot of money I'll forgive him.

All I hear from my publisher is nothing about my book but endless hassles about copyrights—magazines not wanting to cut loose the copyright and give it back to me, which the law says they should.

Suppose you have to go back up there and get the prize—where and what will you eat?

Best,

Walker

542 E Parkway S
Memphis 29 Apr 75

DEAR WALKER

I'm fribbling around, having missed the Book Award; thought I had it more or less in my pocket, when all the time it was in someone else's pocket. Now there's the Pulitzer, which I likely wont get either, and the Parkman and the Bancroft and the Arts and Letters. Prizes never meant a thing to me, and if it keeps on this way theyre going to mean even less.

Here we are, about to enter your birth month. A full ripe 59. Unbelievable! Seems just yesterday we were kicking around the corridors of GHS, a couple of nonathletes. Our only distinction, aside from a smattering of verses which had better go unmentioned, was that you went to Field Meet (in Latin?) and I wound up editor of the Pica. Then UNC, and whisk! you were off to the sanitarium and I was off to the army. We survived them both, though with little credit on either side, and now we wind up on the cover of a little egghead magazine, flanking poor Flannery O'Connor. . . . Did you like that piece by Zeugner or did it get you riled? I thought it was pertinent and good—without, however, agreeing with most of his conclusions; especially his thinking better of the *Moviegoer* than he did of *Gentleman*. You are right about praise. It's more numbing and embarrassing than anything else. Condemnation strikes home a good deal harder; pricks up your ears, so to speak, and calls for reassessment—something we always manage to our satisfaction in the end. How not?

When comes an advance copy of the bottle message? I was expecting it by now. . . . I read the intro in the Southern Review. Enjoyed it very much except when I'd stop and try to figure what you were saying. Then I'd realize I didnt know what I was reading. So I'd go back and push forward again; then put on brakes when it came down on me again—the confusion I mean. Now I'm looking forward to seeing it in book form, something I can grab hold of by the covers as a help toward maintaining my balance while I read. What bothers me most, I think, is the simplicity of the concept —a high-planed simplicity just beyond my reach on tiptoe. I always need a central figure: the Man on the Train, for instance.*[6] Then I'm all right. But

---

6. Percy's early essay, "The Man on the Train: Three Existential Modes," was first published in the Fall 1956 issue of *Partisan Review*.

Shelby Foote and Walker Percy in Vicksburg, Mississippi, 1986. *Photograph by Haydée Lafaye Ellis.*

if he's not there, then neither am I; I'm nowhere. The abstract makes my legs ache and my mind wander. I can read William James, Bergson, Schopenhauer; but not Plato or, say, Jung. I get so my foos wont moos and my ho head haws.

Ive been reading a couple of obscene and outlandish novels by Frederick Exley. Basically junk, but very funny from point to point. Dont see how you can go those Heller maunderings. Man, writing is in *bad* shape; I figure it's up to me to bring it back home now that Ive settled the Civil War's hash. What I really wish is that I could conjure up the ghost of Charles Dickens. There's the boyo that would organize them! I just finished a ninth rereading of *Ulysses*—and, alas, all through each chapter I kept looking forward to the next, and then when I reached it, it was the *next* one I kept wanting to get to. Still, it's one hell of a novel. I put him close behind Proust, which is high praise indeed. . . . Of course youre cut off from all those cats. Slick old Tolstoy's more your meat; too bad. I just wish to hell I'd been able to con you into a rereading of Dante last year. If I had, youd be hard into your magnum opus by now. It fairly stood me on my ear! Especially the way it opens up the possibilities of writing. Christ, what a *writer*.

Happy 59. I'll be there only six months behind you.

Shelby

Am going up to NY on the 14th for something called the Fletcher Pratt Award. Small potatoes: but then I'm a sort of small-potatoes chap myself. Rgds.

*or even a dogfish

May 1, 1975

DEAR SHELBY:

Thanks for Zeugner article. I liked it very much. A very savvy piece. The best overall grasp of articles and fiction I've seen. I don't know how to answer his criticism about the unpleasant nunnes and priestes. What does he want, Ronald Colman as priest and Ingrid Bergman as nun? (Remember me getting mad at you for calling Father Igo[7] a drunk? You were right. I used him.)

Yeah: Percy, O'Connor and Foote. A fine trio. Two at least will never get to heaven. But it was a kick seeing magazine. The article on you by Garrett was very good and altogether deserved. He's right I think: the Narrative looks immortal: almost too good; time will tell. I think what will make it survive is control and purity and economy of the writing, which you don't even notice at first, and which I reckon Thucydides and those other chaps had. I enjoyed both articles even though you came off A+ and I about B−.

You should have won the Book Award, if you set store by such things. In

---

7. A Catholic priest in Greenville whom both Foote and Percy knew when they were teenagers.

fact, you were robbed. I wouldn't put it past them to have voted it down for its coda on Jeff Davis. Still Yankees you know. When I was judge, they wouldn't even nominate Eudora Welty's *Optimist's Daughter*. I had to "use up" my sole privilege just to get it nominated. No one voted for it. John Barth and John Williams won.

Will send you *Message in Bottle*. Out June 16. You won't like. You've already seen all you are going to like, the first four pages of questions: where are the Hittites? why is *flesh is grass* true? why do people drive around on Sundays like bloody wrecks? etc.

O.K., tell me which Dante to read and I'll read it. I need to get onto that magnum opus. Right now, I feel like the jig is up, with the West, me and most. Also tell me which Odyssey. I'm going to write a kind of Ulysses. Is Joyce really that good? The biography is, but I've never been persuaded he wasn't up some dim dark alley of his own.

We're all going to be in NYC, The Plaza, May 29 – June 4. For no reason. Except the ladies want to get at Bergdorfs and Bonwits. Sorry to miss you.

I just finished teaching a workshop in the novel at LSU. A contradiction in terms of course, yet I enjoyed meeting with the 7 students I chose.

Best,

W

542 E Parkway S

Memphis: 5 May 75

DEAR WALKER

First the Odyssey. The absolutely best translation I think is the one by T. E. Shaw (Lawrence of Arabia) published by Oxford in 1932 but since reissued in Oxford's Galaxie paperback series. I tried to get it for you here but the idiots dont have it in stock. Richmond Lattimore is also one hell of a translator; his Iliad is a kind of bible for me, though I never read his Odyssey because of my great fondness for the Shaw. I'm sure youll find both in any decent library. Which brings me to the Dante:

The translation that opened my eyes to Dante and the Comedy is by Thomas G. Bergin. It came out in three large volumes, illustrated by Leonard Baskin, in 1969; publisher, Grossman, New York. That's the one I sent you a couple of sample pages from, a couple of years ago. You might or might not be able to find it in the Library, but there's a note in front that says "The present translation was originally prepared for the Crofts Classics; the version of the Inferno appeared in that series in 1948, the Purgatory in 1953 and the Paradise in 1954. In 1955 the three parts were published together in one volume, The Divine Comedy. I should like to thank the publishers, Appleton-Century-Crofts, for allowing me to make use of the version of the Crofts Classics in the preparation of this new one. The principal difference, in fact, between this translation and that of the Crofts Classics is that I have here translated in full the passages that were summarized in the earlier edition; I have also revised a number of lines." I hope you can get the big deluxe edition, the one I wanted to send you after I got mine back in early 1973; but I dont know whether youll be able to find it. It was this one that made Dante at last readable to me. The prose one (Carlyle & Co.) didnt do the job at all, and the standard Cary translation was even worse—Victorian in the worst sense. The Bergin one is modern and hard-hitting, and Bergin himself is a true Dante scholar, thoroughly aware of all the meaning behind individual lines and passages; a real true job, one for our time and place.

Which leads me to the next matter, which is the Bergin handbook. Called "Dante," it was published by The Orion Press, New York, in 1965. Alas, it's no longer in print, and even the Orion Press has gone out of existence. But I'm sure it would be in the Tulane or LSU library. To me, it was almost as important as his translation of the Comedy itself: filled me in on Dante's background, political, religious, etc, as well as on his early works, then moves on to the Comedy itself in four wonderful chapters examining it as Narrative, Allegory, Doctrine, and Method ("Tools and Tactics"). What I kept thinking, all through my study of it, was how fortunate you would be in my shoes, being already familiar with St Augustine and Aristotle, the two who hung the moon for Dante. Before long, though, I forgot about you and Augustine and even Aristotle—Dante himself had me by the balls. What amazed me was my reaction once I put the Inferno behind me. I had thought that once he got out of hell the story would sag into banality. I couldnt have been wronger. The Purgatory was exciting beyond belief—and, though I couldnt really compass it without the theological background, I could see that the Paradise would be the best of all for someone prepared to appreciate it. That goddam Florentine was a magician! He could get more into half a line than most of my favorite poets could into a stanza, and it's the absolutely cleanest writing I have ever read—lean and lovely and utterly shitless, aboil with effects that no one even suspected until Hemingway came along, and as modern in every sense as modern can be. All it took for me was that Bergin translation; I wanted to bang my head with a hammer because of all I'd let myself miss for all those years. For you, it might not take that; you might like the prose best, I dont know; but I do know that if youll go *into* it (reading the Bergin or one of the other hotshot handbooks, which will put you in a position to read him for what he is) you are bound to have something of the reaction I had. It made me proud (whatever the remove, the distance) to belong to the same clan: Writer. Thats what he was, all right, a writer. T.S. Eliot put him with Shakespeare and said, "There is no third." I dont agree. Homer is a third. But he sure was right to put him with Shakespeare anyhow.

Do go on with it. Surely LSU will have the books and you can take them out on extended loan. All Dante ever wrote about was Love, and once you understand that, you will read him with an immediacy that outdoes Faulkner or Hopkins or anyone else on the list. . . . I got my 3-vol set from Publishers Central, a cheap remainder outfit; it's not listed in their catalog any longer, but I'll keep my eye out for it for you. If it comes down to the worst, and you really want it badly, I'll lend you mine on your solemn oath to wear white cotton gloves at all times while reading it.

So much for litry matters. Today's the first Monday in May—Pulitzer Day. It's 3.20 in the afternoon; which presumably means I didnt win it, since I havent received a wire or a phonecall. I really thought I had it sewed up—the Pulitzer at least. Shows you how stupid I can get, to think I could crack through that academic screen. Actually, I'm coming to understand it a lot better. If merit was the basis for selection, the confusion would make decision impossible. Far better to let politics decide. Then at least the judges have something concrete to go on. Anything else would be anarchy, a bruhaha; blood would flow at every meeting and theyd never arrive at any decision at all. Besides, if some professor gets it, he gets so much more than someone like me would get. He gets promotion, marvellous offers from rival faculties, even tenure. All I would get is sales and a salving of pride; both of which he would get anyhow. . . . There's some sour grapes involved here, but I dont think that invalidates the reasoning. As Bellow said in another connection: "Just because I'm a little paranoic doesnt mean theyre not out to get me."

Good for you for taking your women up to New York. We do wrong to neglect that town. Restaurants are what interest me, & Abercrombie and Fitch & Hammacher-Schlimmer, but the fact is there's everything there a man could want—on a visit, that is; for I remember staying there six months once, and about midway into the stay I suddenly realized I hadnt seen the moon or stars in all that time. While Bunt is upstairs at Bergdorf's shopping, I strongly recommend that you pay a visit to the barbershop just up from the men's department on the ground floor. It's the best shop in NY and youll come out resembling Rock Hudson.

I was sorry to learn from your letter that you and F. O'Connor wont be joining me in heaven—I presume thats what you meant when you said that two of us three wouldnt be making it.

No, Joyce isnt really that good. He's just the best we've got. Matter of fact, he and Dante are a lot alike. Fierce haters, both, great payers-off of scores and both with ice water in their veins when they wanted to scorn the wicked who had crossed them.

Am going into training for the arrival of your Message. Straighten my head out.

Rgds,
Shelby

(Dumas Malone won the Pulitzer for history, I just learned. So be it. I consider myself chastened for my presumption & unworldliness.)

542 E Parkway S
Memphis: 8 May 75
DEAR WALKER

There comes to you under separate cover—book rate, which means slow freight—my own copy of the Bergin *Dante*. Keep it as long as you like, then return it. I got to thinking you might not find it, even at Tulane or LSU, and I wanted you to have it by way of preparing for the Comedy, which should reach you in about ten days or two weeks: ample time, I figure, for you to go through the Bergin volume as prolog to the great fun youre about to have with Dante himself. As you know from previous acquaintance, he of all writers is the one you need to know most about outside his work—and not only him, but also the people who appear in the Comedy. This, to me, is by far the best introduction in that regard, telling you all you need to know about Europe, Florence, etc. before moving on to Dante himself. There are whole libraries of books on Dante, and no doubt many you will find more interesting from your own point of view, but to me this is by far the best on a basic level—a sort of minimum. It helps a lot, I think, that it is also well written and very cool in its approach.

How I came to get you the Comedy was a sort of accident. I got it just over two years ago from a "remainder" house called Publishers Central Bureau; lately it's been out of their catalog; then this morning their new catalog came and it was back in—just as I was wondering how in hell I was going to be able to find it for you. Funny business. Anyhow, I ordered it sent directly to you, post-posthaste. Theyre slow, but it should be along within a couple of weeks. . . . If I seem to be pressing you hard on this Dante business, thats because I damned well am. All through my study and reading of the Comedy, two years ago, I kept getting the strong notion that this was *your* book, the one youd get more from and feel closest to of all the books I know. Even back then, I tried hard to get you to commit yourself. You wouldnt; but now you have, and I am doing all I can, from my end, to see that you hold to your commitment, including bombarding you with all the necessary texts. Believe me (despite my nonsuccess with Saint Marcel Proust and Bleak House in your direction) youve got one hell of a happy month coming up on your calendar. Whats more, I expect enormous dividends: nothing less, in fact, than your own private excursion through Hell and Purgatory and Paradise, which I have no doubt youll see laid out before you by the time you turn the final page of his.

Shelby

May 18, 1975

DEAR SHELBY—

The Bergin arrived and I'm into it. You're right—it goes well. Both understated and lively. Delighted you found *Commedia* in Pub. Cent. Bureau [Publishers Central Bureau]. Due to your nagging I'll probably actually read it. I even have hopes of enjoying it. In all truth I never get past the *Inferno*. Ain't that something? And me having read Aquinas' *Summa Theologiae* cover to cover. Turnabout is fair play. Say when you want the 2 vol. set I have. If Dante is as good as you say, I'll will you my N.Y. ed. of H. James.

I'm glad you got the sense of *Message in the Bottle*. It is actually a very ambitious smart-ass book. I shall not require you to read "Symbol as Hermeneutic to Existentialism" which I'll admit is a barbarous title.

It will hardly be reviewed—or if reviewed by the new linguists, will be ridiculed. But like I say, they got to climb over me to get out of the box they're in.

I will call you in a few days to recommend a couple of good restaurants for me and 3 girls in NYC. What's your weight? Try jogging down Parkway to Holiday Inn for breakfast.

Best,

Walker

542 E Parkway S

Memphis 30 Jun 75

Monday morning

DEAR WALKER

Delighted to know the Dante got there. Hope now youre deep into it. Hang on for Canto 22—the cops and robbers chase around the lake of burning pitch. That just *kills* me, as they say.

Inclosed is a throwaway for Altman's new film "Nashville." Saw a prevue the other night. Really good! I like all of Altman's films, and this one is right up there with "McCabe"—maybe even better, except there's so much going on at once you dont have time to sort it out. Two great lines I remember. One is a wealthy country star welcoming guests to a party. "Welcome to our lovely home," he says. The other is said by the husband of a neurotic Loretta Lynn type; he's her manager. "Dont tell me how to run your life!" he yells at her; "I been running it for years."

I envy you the Dante reading—especially the change of pace when he sails into the Purgatory. All my reaction (concerning you, I mean) centered around the notion that this is one hell of a novel. Whats all the hooraw about a new form, now that the old forms are worn out? The Comedy is the newest form of all. I kept seeing it as a sort of cross between Faulkner and Celine—F's skill and precision, C's gropy search for the meaning of life itself amid the squalor. Only in the Paradise did I get a feeling of being out of my depth, and even there I had an overwhelming feeling of being involved in the very greatest conception of them all; the windup mystical rose, the love that moves the stars, all that.

What news on the Bottle Message? CivWar is still clicking along, they tell me. $25 a volume now. At 15% that comes to $3.75 per each; $10.25 a set! Big business. Now comes fret about taxes. No sweat; I hired the man who does Presley's and knows all the dodges available to us artist types, including deductions for haircuts.

All best:

Shelby

542 E Parkway S

Memphis 4 July 75

DEAR WALKER

Happy 4th. . . . Herewith the Bergin roadmap of Purgatory, which I fig-ure youre about ready for by now. Somewhere up ahead youll encounter one of my favorite characters—a man who climbs a dark and stony slope with a lantern strapped to his back. He walks in darkness, barking his knees and shins, so that those who follow can see their way. I havent yet decided whether he's John the Baptist or Gustave Flaubert, but in any case I honor him.

I read a good new novel this past week: RAGTIME by Doctorow, who wrote THE BOOK OF DANIEL a couple of years ago. It's really good for the first two thirds, then diminishes somewhat because he felt he had to get the story moving. Youd like it I think. Good clean sparse writing most of the time and a lively jump to the sentences unfolding. Scott Joplin set the pattern, and he does a good job following it. Houdini is one of the main characters, J.P. Morgan another, plus Henry Ford, Emma Goldman, Sig-mund Freud, Harry Thaw and Evelyn Nesbit, the Archduke Rudolf, and others.

All's well in this direction. I'm expecting a clump of royalties in August and intend to see how much of it I can spend in New Orleans shortly afterwards. Till then, stay with the Dante.

All best,
Shelby

Sat: 26 July 75

DEAR WALKER

I figure you're midway up the seven-story mountain by now, about on the fourth terrace with the slothful. For God's sake dont stop there; Aquinas identifies sloth as a form of *sadness*.

Things are progressing hereabouts. Ive found my time span: 4Sep-4Oct.1957—Little Rock to Sputnik—& we had a great big kewpie doll in the White House.

Stay with it; or get started, as the case may be.
Shelby

542 E Parkway S
Memphis 4 Oct 75

DEAR WALKER

Been doing something strange these past ten days: reading Shelley, whom I found unreadable for the past forty-odd years. It came about as an extension of my continuing fondness for Keats. I read the Aileen Ward biography (the fourth, I believe: Amy Lowell, D. Hewlitt, Bates I'd read before) then romped happily through the poems and letters and was left feeling bereft when they ran out. Happily I remembered seeing reviews of a new biography of Shelley, so I went down to the bookstore and got it. $22.50, for sweet Jesus sake! It was worth it; high praise indeed. Written by a young Englishman named Richard Holmes, it's one of the best biographies Ive ever read—up to the standard of the Ellman Joyce. . . . Ive never, as I said, been able to read Shelley—found the lyrics vapid and diffuse, badly marred by selfpity, and altogether too bloodless for my liking; found the longer poems (except Epipsychidion) exactly the opposite and far too much so, lurid and extreme. Now that Ive read this Holmes book, however, I'm tuned in to the inner workings that tie the work to the life, the forces that brought the poems to the surface of his thought. I still dont like a line of his as well as I like whole pages of Keats (or Chaucer or Shakespeare or Browning or, for that matter, John Crowe Ransom) but I do get far more from them than I ever got before, and the gain has been a real one. He's as good as anyone ever said he was, and the extent to which I cant see that is a measure of *my* shortcomings, not his.

Anyhow thats what Ive been doing: still killing time, you see, before I disappear into the dark abyss of labor on my novel, whose diagram I noodle around with between six-hour stretches of reading. Partly the delay is caused by obligations I acquired earlier: the trip down home last week to do the TV thing I promised, the trip I'll make a week from now to UNC, where I'm to be declared a distinguished alumnus, and a commitment to go to Baton Rouge on December 6 for a Civil War Roundtable speech, to be followed by a New Orleans visit. After which I'll dive into more accustomed waters: work. Thats by and large the only real happiness, as you well know. Incidentally, I do at last have a real agent. His name is Bob Rosen and he has flown into a frenzy of activity on my behalf, here and in Europe. He has flaming offers from Simon & Schuster and Athaneum for the book I'm about to start, both of whom say there's nothing they wouldnt give to have me. My inclination is to stay with Random, but under the double influence of flattery and money—especially money, if Random doesnt match it—loyalty melts as fast as snow at midday. It's a pleasant enough prospect. For too long now, all my writing life in fact, Ive been cursed with lousy agents—except perhaps MCA, till the Feds shot them down. Now Ive got one and I feel much better, knowing my interests are being looked after in areas about which I know nothing or less than nothing.

No news otherwise—if, indeed, any of the above was news. I just wanted to keep you posted on what I'm up to now that Ive given up devoting all my time trying to nudge you onto Dante. What I want now is to know what *you* are up to, perhaps in the same vein. Tell me.

Rgds:

Shelby

Oct. 9 [1975]

DEAR SHELBY—

What type of fellow are you? Are you telling me you can sit there in your castle in Memphis happily reading Shelley 5 hours a day? You are certainly a happier man than I, but I'm not really sure I envy you. Shelley 5 hrs per day?

Don't you ever want to (1) shoot your wife (2) burn your house (3) run off with 2 26-yr-old lovely Foote-admiring graduate N.C. students (incidentally, congrats on your UNC honor—Louis Rubin told me last year) (4) shoot your mother-in-law (5) move to Greece . . . ?

Christ, you sound like Ralph Waldo Emerson. Please forward the secret of your maturity to a demoralized Catholic.

From the enclosed[8] you will learn that, far from being a crackpot, I am probably the next Copernicus of the 20th Century. I think, probably both are right.

I'll tell you a commonplace about writing a book which you, of all people, already know. You write a book which you think is *the article*—and what happens? Nothing.

But, as you also know, it all comes out in the wash—20 years goes for something.

W

542 E Parkway S
Memphis 11 Oct 75

DEAR WALKER

Good for Hugh Kenner! I always thought he was the best critic left around, and now I know it. Last year he published the best survey of modern literature Ive read in a long time: A HOMEMADE WORLD, THE AMERICAN MODERNIST WRITERS (Knopf). Isnt it a strange added fact that we both got one of our few really understanding reviews in the Natl Review, of all places? Maybe we're conservatives after all—or should be. In any case we seem to have found a kind of home in that nest of reac-

---

8. An adulatory review of *The Message in the Bottle* by Hugh Kenner in the September 12, 1975, issue of the *National Review*.

tionaries. . . . Just to play it safe, I'm keeping in simultaneous touch with my Communist friends as well. An eye out for posterity: if any.

As for aching for hooraw, shooting wives and mothers-in-law, moving to Greece, and all that, let me say that if I were taking up with something hot and hollow it wouldnt be one of those hot-eyed little graduate students, it would be a real bigtime whore—Rita Hayworth, for example. I want something substantial to snuggle up to and be appreciated by—something I could learn from, too, and nothing resembling an intellectual. In fact I'd prefer an illiterate: which I figure Rita about is.

Dont underrate Shelley. He's a kind of a sort of a shithead in an ideological way, but he sure as hell burned with a gemlike flame. He could light up a poem with a line that would burn like a searchlight down into all kinds of shadowy corners of your brain.

Good for Hugh Kenner, I say again. Let me know when something else decent comes along.

Rgds:
Shelby

Incidentally, Kenner's a hell of a good *writer*. The book I mentioned—A Homemade World—is interesting just for the way he puts words on paper. . . . Going to UNC tomorrow. I'll tip my hat at Old East for you & spit in the Old Well.

542 E Parkway S
Memphis 23 Jan 76
DEAR WALKER

Theres a rather decent review of your MESSAGE, back-to-back with one of my WAR, in the current (that is, Winter 1975) "Georgia Review," in case you havent seen it. A bit querulous but in a respectful way I think you might enjoy—decent reviews being the rare things they are.

Was in Jackson again last week and had dinner in a seafood place with Eudora, whom I like more all the time. She asked about you; wondered what you are up to, fitten or unfitten.

I'm into a long synopsis-outline of my novel, trembling on the verge of the plunge, and having a great new read at Browning, who I still think has

about as much to teach a writer as anyone I know; this writer, anyhow. . . .
What a pity he's another of your blindspots. Like Kierkegard (cant even
spell it) for me.

All best:

Shelby

542 E Parkway S

Memphis 25 Sep 76

DEAR WALKER

Things are going well here I do believe. I'm into the middle chapter
(fourth of seven) of the novel-in-progress, SEPTEMBER SEPTEMBER, and
enjoying it a lot; dreadful and funny, both at once. SHILOH went into
another small printing within a month of republication, which is maybe the
best news of all. Coindreau has completed his translation of FOLLOW ME
DOWN and has begun DRY SEASON. The hope is that Gallimard and
Denoel will bring them out together next spring, with a forward by André
Malraux. So things in general are shaping up on several fronts. One bad
note is that I have to go down to Jackson, Mon–Wed of next week, for
another script conference on the Faulkner TV thing. Otherwise Ive managed to keep disentangled, busy here at my desk.

What I want now is some word of you, not excluding the new book. Has
it gone to the printer? Did you get terms that please you? Whats it called?
When's it coming out? What are your plans now? And so forth.

Ive got myself a writing schedule set up and have held to it closely so
far—a chapter every two months. If I can get a little ahead on this one,
Gwyn and I hope to get up to NY on an eating expedition in late November; also to do Xmas shopping. Other than that I intend to hang on tight
here (Aplexus expecta) down to the wire, and finish the novel by late spring
so as to get started on my big one, TWO GATES TO THE CITY, by next
summer. It will take two or three years and may run longer than Vol III of
my narrative; a sort of Civil War all its own, outdostoevskying Dostoevsky.
God willing, that is; Big Sixty is looming.

Let me hear from you.

Rgds:

Shelby

I wanted to pass along a high compliment I got word of just last week. Malcolm Franklin, Faulkner's stepson, is publishing his informal reminiscences of Faulkner this fall, and it includes references to SHILOH:

During one of these discussions Pappy turned to me and said, "Buddy, have you read Shelby Foote's *Shiloh*?" I said no, and he told me, "Well, Buddy, you should read it. It's the damndest book I have ever read and one of the best."
One day a few weeks later Pappy said, "I have something for you, Buddy," and he handed me a copy of *Shiloh*. He must have gone by or written to the Three Musketeers bookshop in Memphis (across from the Peabody Hotel) where he preferred to get such books. "This is twice the book that *The Red Badge of Courage* is," he told me, adding that Shelby wrote as if he had been there himself—"he knows what he's talking about."

So there. You can imagine how set-up I felt when I saw that. But almost at once a reaction set in. What compliment will I ever receive that will compare with it? It's all downhill from here on in.
I discount it somewhat by the knowledge that he was encouraging the boy to get him interested in the war, but he then went on to do something else I value:

Then he told me that Shelby was writing several volumes on the War, and that he was going to present me with them as they were published. He gave me volume one, *Fort Sumter to Perryville*, in 1959. But he did not live to present me with the second volume, which came out in 1963.

I think maybe I like that even better.
S.

17 Nov 76
DEAR WALKER
Thanks for that sweet medallion of Nixon. I send along a companion portrait by way of return. As you can see, this Diomed was an underhanded sort of fellow, much like Nixon, and like him got tipped on his head—

though I must say he was in there trying, right to the end, in his under-handed way.

I cant say I'm too fond of being sixty. Fact is, I dont hardly like it at all. What I cant figure is where all those years went. It was only yesterday I was editing the Pica. Now look what's come of me. Like Yeats, I resent being tied to a dying animal. About the best I can say for it is, it's better than being *un*tied.

Been thinking these past few days about your book—about the way it leaves your hero stalking toward Bethlehem after all the mayhem he committed upon those children of perdition. I think maybe everybody got what was coming to him, except poor Percival who was left to mourn. It's a good book, sharp, incisive, mean as a booger; an excellent warmup for thickening the texture of the big novel that follows your LAST GENTLEMAN to where he was about to take you.

Mine's a boomer too. I'm past the midpoint now and going great guns: SEPTEMBER SEPTEMBER[9]—whole flocks of incredibly believable people, black and white, cruel and gentle, and all absurd. I like it very much, so far, and hope to finish it by early summer.

Your fellow over-sixty elder citizen,
Shelby

542 E Parkway S
Memphis: 2 Feb 77
DEAR WALKER
Last week I finished the fifth of my seven chapters—right on schedule, which is one every two months for a total of 120,000 words in fourteen months. Over the years Ive found that I average a hundred thousand words a year, history or fiction. That is slow, but it damn well piles up down the years—providing of course you have them. As for me, I operate on the theory (faulty of course) that I'll last well beyond eighty, plunking down those chiseled hundred thousand every year. I figure that allows me two more average-length novels, two long ones, and a couple of short ones at

---

9. *September September* would be published in 1978.

the end. I hate to see the string run out but I guess it's got to come someday. I never was one of those people who cant stand to leave the party.

Hugs got busted out of Memphis University School—smoking pot on the tennis court during a recess. So I took him down and put him in a stricter school; Briarcrest, it's called, though it's by no means as swanky as its name. Education in Memphis is a nightmare, all down the line. The public schools have degenerated into nothing and the private ones arent much better, even the old ones that were here in my father's time. . . . I must say, though, Old Hugs is following in his father's footsteps. I remember, back in '35, I had to spend a week at Mr Will's when I got expelled from GHS. You and Roy were away; just Phin and I were there, and even he wasnt there during school. I read damn near every book in the Percy library in that one week.

Any more big news on LAUNCELOT? I dont know just yet, but Bob Rosen thinks SEPTEMBER SEPTEMBER is likely to be one of the big money-makers of all time. Could be.

Regards,
Shelby

February 8, 1977
DEAR SHELBY:
Glad to hear *September September* is going along apace and what's more looks commercial. Wonder of wonders, *Lancelot* is going to make money too—250 Gs this year. Now ain't that something: two Mississippi boys turning their backs on high finance to court the muse and getting their pockets stuffed with simoleons! It strikes me as nothing else but funny— and also convenient. But the only difference that I notice it makes in my life is little things, such as taking the taxi from Kennedy to NYC rather than riding the bus. Alas, I don't even go to Four Seasons and spend $10 for lunch—leave that to my publisher who did it for us last week.

Just back from week with Bunt in NY and Cornell. Promotion inter-views and stuff in NY, lecture on Chekhov and reading at Cornell in the snow and ice—O.K. Hate to admit it but the Yankee boys and girls are keener than ours, at least ours here in Louisiana.

Now what. I have two vague things in mind and must accordingly take care because once I get started on something, I notice that I see it through for better or worse and whether it takes five years. The main question: whether to go flat out, throwing caution and readership to the winds and write a dreamlike novel exploring all the fuckups, options and delights of the new consciousness—somebody has to do it, name it, frame it, the way Virgil did for the new Rome, why not me. It would be Kirkegaard translated into Huck Finn, H.C. Earwicker transposed to Louisana, pure ventures into whatever is potential now and with all novelistic canons abandoned, plot line, characters, tone, point of view etc. Start with Kafka's burrow-creature, have him stick his nose out into the sunlight, take a whiff of the new world, explore the immediate vicinity; venture out of Viking III and even after a spell peep over that first ridge.

The other possibility is a Gulliver's Travels sort of fable-satire, serious-unserious, easily read and on at least two levels: e.g., a modern version of Body Snatchers: business man with avocation of photography takes photos at his son's wedding, notices that some of the faces come out smudged, which turns out to be no slip-up: they are smudged because they've been evacuated and occupied by *them. They,* moreover—the enemy—discover that he is onto them—through some quirk of photography—and get after him. He and pretty lab assistant have to take off and live off the land on the Appalachian Trail, making HuckFinn-type forays into the little towns (e.g. Luray, Port Republic) to check on the progress of the snatchers. Will everyone in the U.S. become evacuated, etc.

You can see my dilemma. Have a little fun and with a little luck, crank out something Gulliver-good. Or go flat-out for the Big One—and possibly bore everybody (including myself) to death.

The only thing I'm sure of is that I can't do what you suggested, write a novel-type novel, the doings of Will Barrett after he leaves Santa Fe.[10] I think what you were saying was that that is what you can do. We are hoeing different rows, you know.

The other longterm project is to devise a semiotic experiment (a regular scientific article) in which I actually *demonstrate* that Peirce-Percyan semi-

---

10. In fact, Percy would return to Will Barrett in his next novel, *The Second Coming* (1980).

otic is true.[11] At present the various theorists who have read Message in Bottle simply shrug and say it ain't so (a few exceptions). A proper Galileo-Einstein hypothesis: say a semiotic study of Faulkner: if such and such a set of theorems are true and such and such an hypothesis can be induced from Faulkner's life-and-writings at stage A, then facts a, b, . . . n, will hold true at a later stage B. The problem is to pick and choose the right subject. Faulkner is probably too hard to get a holt of. Perhaps a pop field like TV or print media: given such and such a set of factors, e.g., successful sitcoms like Rhoda and Mary Tyler More and the public's inevitable weariness with them and given certain elements of the American consciousness, one might predict that in the near future Rhoda and Mary Tyler will be a certain kind of ordeal-TVfilm; girl pursued, kidnapped by madman, stranded, etc. What I dream of is something neat and elegant and so convincing of itself that one can write it in the same offhand style as Einstein's relativity article (almost a throwaway style: here it is, fellows, in case you're interested).

What happened is that, not dreaming I would actually make money on this book, I signed up last year for several Yankee lectures this year (they pay good) and so am now stuck, e.g. to Ann Arbor next month. Not being a pro at lecturing, I have to work at it and it distracts me. No more of that. No more of students either. Finished with class at Loyola. Very little talent around. If you know of any published deserving writers, I'm on board of American Academy, giving away money—it's unbelievable: they've got the money and can't find anybody to give it to but poets, Christ poets all over the place whom nobody reads but each other.

Reading about Faulkner and Meta Carpenter. As Faulkner said, Women—shit, but it's still interesting. W.F. probably the horniest little man in Mississippi. Another possible semiotic study: the relation of horniness to art in general and fiction in particular. Are novelists hornier than poets or do the artists have it best of all, Picasso the horniest and longest lived of all. Of course I've done this novelistically (fucking as the sole remaining channel of re-entry into the world from the orbit of transcendence and abstraction) but not semiotically-scientifically.

---

11. This idea would lead not to an article but to a book, *Lost in the Cosmos: The Last Self-Help Book* (1983).

Be sure to read your Book-of-the-Month Club News this month and choose wisely. The beauty of B.O.M. which I never until now appreciated: 100,000 subscribers will have to address and stamp and mail a letter with instructions in order *not* to receive Lancelot. We're approaching the Gold Age of the arts.

Best,

W

542 E Parkway S

Memphis 14 Feb 77

DEAR WALKER

I say by all means go flat-out for the big one, horrendous though it is as a commitment. I say it for several reasons. First, Ive thought these last two books—much as Ive liked and enjoyed them—were departures from your main line of endeavor; sports, that is, taking off from a situation which seemed to you indicative of a sickness in our time and interesting to explore; which you certainly did. The future one, RUINS, and now LANCELOT, a study of a crime of passion: they make a pair. But what I want, and what Ive kept saying, is an extension—especially a broadening—of the ground you worked in GENTLEMAN, which is much my favorite of all the things youve done. The reason I kept harping on a family novel was that I wanted a thickening of the texture, which I felt would come from handling a number of strands in a book with a multiple hero. I never—never—meant that you (or even I) should turn your hand to a "family novel" in the conventional way. What I meant was far more KARAMAZOV than it was FORSYTHE. Youve touched on exactly what I mean in your letter: Huck Finn and Earwicker, as ramjam experimental as you can make it.

That's first. Now for second. We're sixty. This next may be the last one. I dont lean on that too heavy, but it damned well may be true. And God knows you dont want to check out before youve shot your wad with all youve got. You owe yourself and the world that. . . . For the past six months Ive been reading FINNEGANS WAKE—the Wake itself and every technical book I could lay my hands on (there are thirty or so topnotch ones)—and by God that's the way to go; all out, for real. It measures up to Beethoven's last quartets in the way of an exit; moving forward, I mean, and giving it all youve got right down to the line, the big blackjack. It's one hell of a thing to undertake, though; the corn of wheat and all that chaffing jazz. I dont know that anyone has a right to ask it, even of himself, let alone anyone else. Yet I do hope for it, not only for you but for myself as well. When I finish SEPTEMBER, which will run about 120,000 words (Jesus, that seems short after the 1,650,000 in my War) I'm due to tackle TWO GATES TO THE CITY, which will run, I figure, about half a million words. Everything in me cries out No! dont put yourself on that hook. And by golly I may not; I may just rip off another short one for a bit of further practice and entertainment. In a year I can pause again for a rest and a lookround; whereas with TWO GATES there will be no discharge till it's done—in how many years?

We are indeed doing well on the money scene.* Ive got $84,679.70 in back royalties piled up in the vaults at Random for my Narrative alone, and a $100,000 advance for the next two, and four of my early novels coming back into print; SHILOH already, the others to follow. It's more money than I care to spend in the time that's left me, but anyhow I know I'll be able to educate my son wherever he chooses to go to college. That's something. As for you, youve fairly got money running out of your ears. But hellfire you always did have, within limits. Money is really no answer to anything we're asking; just nice as hell to have, convenient and all that. The fact is, there's almost nothing I want, and I honestly believe there are lots more things I want than you do—which then is even less than nothing.

I'm glad to hear, too, that youre about off that lecture circuit. Theoretically it puts you in touch, but I dont think it does; mainly it alienates, plus which it's downright exhausting. As for teaching, it's been my experience that it draws on much the same reserves as writing does. Which sure as hell wont do. As for young people, theyre either a bunch of shits or a bunch of bores, with a few wellspaced exceptions.

I havent seen the BoM Club news but my mother-in-law called me the other day to tell me what was in it. I sure do like that notion of all those subscribers having to send in a letter saying no. We ought to have that all over the country, not just the funnicking Club.

Alas, I dont know a soul the Academy could give money to. No poet today is worth the salt in his food, let alone cash money. There's a Texas girl (a former Greenvillian) wrote a book called COME BACK LOLLIE RAY;

she might deserve it. I cant remember her name; Doubleday published it last month, I think. It had a certain juice to it; not much, but maybe enough to justify support from the arts-and-crafters. I read it in galleys and now I cant find the goddam thing to remember her name. Beverly something. I know! Beverly Lowry. You might look into it.

I agree with you about the horniness. I thank God for every sinful lustful thought I ever had; theyre the very coin of my enterprise, and as R.E. Lee said, when asked if his fondness for the ladies continued into his postwar years, "I perceive no diminution." Faulkner is a good case in point. Ive known some of his exprotogées. Premature orgasm was his hangup, a splendid one I think, indicative of lust in its purest form. I remember Caruso's wife said of him when someone asked her about his infidelities, "I never blamed him. A woman could touch him and he'd burst all in flame." Still I dont think it's much of a way of life unless youve got a steely nature like Don Giovanni and can keep your brain uninvolved. *I* never could.

By way of goodbye let me tell you I'm just crazy about the book I'm writing. I'll send you a xerox when I wind it up in the late spring. Lots of fucking but none of it hardbreathing; just gangster stuff for the whites and lots of fretting for the blacks. The book's about half and half, black and white, and I sometimes think Ive done the best writing about Negroes anyone ever did; certainly better than any black man ever did.

One further suggestion. If youre free these days, sort of kicking the gong around as Cab Calloway used to say, why dont you come on up here and visit a while? It might be pleasant. Me, I cant go anywhere at all, my nose being to the grindstone as it is, but I'm free as any bird once that quitting-time bell rings every day around 4.30—

All best, as always,
Shelby

LANCELOT got here. I like it a lot, reading it in print. They sure did give you a handsome binding.

*Youre wrong, though, if you think we've done all that well comparatively. Roy & Jack Baskin, say—even Doyle Morrow[12]—make us look like

---

12. Roy Percy and two other prosperous Greenvillians.

used car salesmen, financially speaking. Of course, they can go bust any day. We cant; which is comforting.

20 Apr 77

DEAR WALKER

I'm into the last twenty pages of my novel, & will finish it next month. It cant possibly be as good as I think it is, but then again it just might be. I set out to get my hand back in, but I wound up doing a great deal more; I think.

Anyhow I'll send you a xerox around June 1 & we'll see if you agree. Rgds.

Shelby

[postdated April 25, 1977]

Your book sounds like a winner—mine selling well most places but NYC—shot down by a one-two from NY Times! When was the last time you saw a Southern novel on the N.Y. best-seller list? GWTW?[13] Back from Ann Arbor—OK, but no more lectures.

W.

June 22, 1977

DEAR SHELBY:

September September is real good. Read it straight through. I was floored and pleased by the happy ending. Now that's curious, I was think-ing when I finished: here you write a sunny novel, a *Meistersinger* or *Reivers* and I write a *Gotterdammerung* or *Fall of the House of Usher*.

Things I like about it: (1) the handling of the details, the plan of the kid-nap, the cash, the notes, the attention to places and streets etc., (2) the transformation of a cliché—thieves fall out over women and money—into a believable action. I see *how* thieves fall out over women. (3) Rufus getting

———

13. *Gone with the Wind.*

Shelby Foote at his desk, 1987. *Courtesy of Collection of Lucius Lampton, M.D., Magnolia, Mississippi.*

wiped out, erased, fingerprints and all at the end. The clean getaway of Podjo and Reeny is very satisfying. (4) The handling of the children—Teddy is very real (and funny)—maybe the first real black child I ever read of (except Luster). An 8 yr old child—that's hard.

I picked up a few anachronisms:

140–5 (from bottom): *trash* as verb—I never heard it till Vietnam

142–9: *hype*—even later

142: *went down* for happened (also in Chap 5 title)

183–14: *wasting* for killing, also Vietnam

278: *beaver* for women, only known to news reporters in '57
? *bummer*

232–15: *clew*—sounds affected

243: *hooraw*—too many hooraws

200–245: we lose track of Teddy for a long time

144: shouldn't Podjo be pleased by Sugar Ray losing to Carman?

297: *some private muscle*—NY-LA slang?

252: *brunt end*—indeed.

I think you got a winner—
Best,
Walker

542 E Parkway S
Memphis 29 Jun 77

DEAR WALKER

I am greatly pleased that you like the book, most of all with your reasons for liking it. I wrote it slowly, taking pleasure in the pains, with the notion of getting my hand back in after twenty years of writing history. In point of fact, as I said from the start, it wasnt really all that different: who did what, and why, and above all *how*. However, I did find a missed delight in watching those people take shape under my hand—particularly the women, Reeny and Martha. There were all too few women in the CivWar; moreover I was conscious all the way of the common charge (all too true) that American writers, particularly the best of them, have been at their weakest in depicting women. I had a strong feeling, throughout the writing, that I was

succeeding in this, and it gave me a feeling of exultation. Women! Jesus. . . .
And something else. At the time Styron's Nat Turner book came out I criticised it as a futile exercise in historical reconstruction because it was aimed at a notion instead of the truth, and I said further that I thought the Negro streak in it (perhaps its most important element) was all wrong because Styron had depended (so I'd heard) on discussions with a Harlemite, James Baldwin, for his basic attitude. I told some interviewer that I knew a hell of a lot more about Negroes than Baldwin even began to know—mainly, I said, because I was Southern. I meant it, and then when I sat down to SEPSEP I had to prove it. I think I did, but it scared hell out of me at the time. I had an added problem, you see; which was that these were bourgeois Negroes, and I never really knew a single bourgeois nigger in my life; never wanted to, because the few I met were so unutterably *dull*. Here too, though, I found them coming truly alive for me and I found that perhaps the most exciting experience of all—Eben I mean, and old Tio too, and Martha's concern with what she thought was her ugliness, and the two children, so alike and so different, and the old aristocratic-looking illiterate grandmother, even the niece-servant Dolly: I enjoyed them all the way through the writing, and I enjoy looking back on them now, finished and in their box, about to go into print—probably about to be ripped to shreds by Baldwin and others like him, who wont recognize what they see even after Ive shown them.

Anyhow, whatever else I did or didnt do, I sure as hell got my hand back in, and now I'm ready to go on. TWO GATES TO THE CITY, the big family thing Ive been planning for twenty-odd years; in preparation for which I'm just winding up my fifth or sixth rereading of Dostoyevsky's BROTHERS, by way of seeing whether I can bring off one of my own—that galloping drive, that bigness; a drive so furious that it has to be bridled with filler stuff (even the Grand Inquisitor) to keep the writer and reader from being run off with. What a writer, what a writer.

Louis Rubin is coming down on the 7th and we will drive down to Jackson next day for some kind of dual interview with Eudora at a studio there. I wish youd come up and join us: not for the interview, but for the evening after. Think it over, and come up if you can; that is if it's not too close to your leaving time. Call me here and I'll tell you where we'll be in case you can come.

You were right about the anachronisms. I changed trash and type and wasting, but held on to beaver and all the hooraws. I had meant to get you to thank Bunt for the "brunt end" for me, after all these years, but I forgot. I was glad to see you didnt forget. The wonder is you never used it yourself.

No news otherwise. I'm just fuddling round till I can clear the decks for another thirteen or fourteen month stretch of uninterrupted writing. Ive about decided to do the book in three volumes, ten years apart in time, with each volume totally independent and all three tied together at the end—late 40s, mid 50s, early 60s. I cant go later because about then I stopped looking, or anyhow caring.

All best,
Shelby

Mar. 28, 1977

DEAR SHELBY—

Simone[14] did a good job on you and "Pillar." The French really kill me—it's *all* form. Come to think of it, you would like them better than I do. Read Roland Barthes (whom I can't understand) and Levy-Strauss, the founding father of structuralism.

What's up with *Sept Sept*? *Lancelot*, despite early promise, fizzled sales-wise. I thought I was going to be rich—all I'll be, come April and taxes, is broke. So now I have to give speeches and readings and write another novel. Rats. Better luck with *Sept Sept*.

In the flush of all those Yankee dollars coming in I bought an old (140 years) house in Mandeville, great old raised cottage built by De Maurigny (Peggy's ancestor) c. 1840.

Seemed like a good idea at the time, as an investment (Mandeville is a hot item real-estate wise), but it's costing me so much to fix up, I'll probably sell at a loss.

Or—we may sell the house and move into the cottage. Depends on $. I should have stuck with medicine and gotten rich like all the doctors I know.

------

14. Simone Vauthier, the French scholar, who had written articles about both Foote and Percy.

What a profession this is. I'm working on a novel which I've just torn up and started over.

Oh, why didn't I do something respectable, become a MD, lawyer, planter, historian?

This is all going to end badly. I'm going to end up old, broke and a flasher. What do you think of the Hindoo custom of old men taking a begging bowl and hitting the road?

Best,

W—

[note from Aug 10, 1977, on back of copy of WP's high school poem]
SHELBY,

An admiring GHS classmate, Mrs. Ruby Dean, saved this over the years and sent me this xerox, keeping original for herself. I felt like sharing it.

W—

542 E Parkway S
Memphis: 2 Dec 77
DEAR WALKER

Good to hear from you. It sounded to me like you had just the amount of despair in your soul to make you truly happy. Keep up the good work, and dont stay out of touch so long again. Last time I talked with you, Ann was in labor and you told me youd let me know the outcome.[15] I heard nothing and was scared to ask, having lost a child myself some years ago. I assume all went well though and youre now a grandpa—what is it? thrice-over? Jesus.

That Simone Vauthier piece I sent you was one of ten (the only one in English) published in a special edition of DELTA gotten out by students and professors at the Université Paul Valéry at Montpellier. Who but the French would name a university after a poet? Anyhow, the whole issue was not only dedicated entirely to a study of my work but was almost entirely, too,

---

15. Ann had married John David Moores on November 29, 1975. Their first son, David Lawson Moores, was born on September 19, 1977.

an examination of JORDAN COUNTY. You never saw such diagrams, circles, triangles, pyramids, etc. I found it so fascinating I even studied up on my Chapel Hill French, which covered a period of nearly two months and which I flunked. Now I understand just how I went about putting that book together. I did a much better job than I knew, and any time I have any doubt about my immortality I just go back and limp my way through another of those articles for reassurance. The eggheads call the turn, you know; especially French eggheads, which are the pointiest kind.

SEPSEP has been taken by the BOMC as first alternate in February, but nothing really heavy has come down yet; Hollywood I mean, TV, stuff like that. It's all pending, and I stay out of it, letting Bob Rosen take the heat and ten percent. I cant really imagine anything of mine raking in big money; it's far too well worked-out for that, and the boys who have the heavy money know it. Any book of mine wont stand a glib superfluous look; it comes apart under such treatment and theyre left with a handful of chaff. Result: they know to stay clear of it or else buy it cheap and convert it into something correspondingly niggard, if they turn their hands to it at all. Mostly, they take options and then a good hard look at the work itself; whereupon they decide not to do it after all. A wise decision. My consolation is theyd come acropper in just the same way with LIGHT IN AUGUST or THE IDIOT. Or, come to think of it, LANCELOT or THE LAST GENTLEMAN. Let's face it; those pocket-sagging Capote sums aint for the likes of you and me. By way of compensation, though, we're also spared a host of Capote woes, including alcoholism and fairydom.

I have my doubts about the Hindu wisdom of hitting the road with a begging bowl. As I remember, Tolstoy tried it, there at the end, and didnt get far down the track before he was sidelined in a station master's shack, toes-up, with his shrew of a wife yelling outside the door: "Let me in! Let me hold his dear little head!"

Keep the faith.

Shelby

I enjoyed the *Esquire* self-interview very much; struck just the right note, I thought.

Rgds.

S.

[postcard, postdated Dec. 15, 1977]

Got turned on by Cezanne show in NYC—first time by a painter. Went to see Gerstle[16] and got his biography of Cezanne. You have till Jan 3 to see it. Tut here is OK too.

Ann's baby, David, is fine. Sorry I forgot to tell you. You should have one.

W.

542 E Parkway S

Memphis 24 Dec 77

DEAR WALKER

Merry Christmas; or rather, by the time you get this, congratulations for having got through it. Bah, humbug, I always say, and I say it more fervently with every year that passes.

I had exactly the opposite reaction to the Cezanne exhibit, though I was delighted to hear of yours. Cezanne is one of my three very favorite painters of all time; Vermeer and Klee are the others. I went to New York back in November, went straight from the airport to the hotel, washed up, and went running to the Museum of Modern Art. Cezanne's last years have always been to me by far his best and I couldnt wait to get there or take a chance on not getting into the place every day I was going to be there. Alas, there were about two thousand people with two thousand dripping umbrellas—half of them, I'm convinced, attending the show to get out of the rain, and the other half talking their heads off about the artist—his unfortunate relationship with his father, his late-married wife, his fixation on masturbation, his extreme touchiness about being touched, etc. Jesus; the paintings looked as if he had dipped his brush in mud; they hung there utterly dead on the walls; I never saw dead fish any deader than those paintings were—paintings, mind you, I'd have crawled on my knees halfway round the world to see, paintings I'd pored over in reproductions for twenty solid years of staggered wonder, paintings I believed held a good part of the answers to mysteries I'd been scratching my head over for decades. There

---

16. Gerstle Mack, an old Greenville acquaintance.

they were, and they were dead, mud-colored, stagnant on the walls. All I learned from the show was never to go to another one in my entire life. Tut! To hell with Tut if that's the way I have to see it, elbowed along by a herd of nitwits, some of them showing off to their girls or wives, others just showing off to themselves. Ive never disliked people so fervently in my life—not even when I saw the Mona Lisa fifteen years ago in Washington; the same setup, but it didnt bother me even a fraction as much because I didnt care a fraction as much for Leonardo as I do for Cezanne, and there he was, man—dead, dead on the wall.

You ought to talk with Phin about it. He went through a real craze over Cezanne about thirty years ago; it was he who hung the Card Players in the guest house out on Military Road. . . . I am absolutely delighted, though, that a painter finally got to you. I remember you were somewhat taken, once, with El Greco (a real bad painter) and later with Velasquez (a real good one), but they were back in your highschool days or college, and it seemed to me you got over them rather promptly. Hemingway used to say a writer could learn more from painters than from his fellow writers—he also used to say it was best to see them on an empty stomach; sharpened the perception, he claimed, and the closer you were to starvation the clearer you saw.

I'll have an early copy of SEPSEP for you soon after New Year's. Still no big financial coup, but I'm still hoping and Rosen is still humping.

Regards all round:

Shelby

Jan 5, 1978

DEAR SHELBY,

I'm glad you're going to be on the Cavett show. You'll do a good job.

I told him I didn't want to, didn't like to do talk shows, didn't do a good job.

Actually he is excellent and I like his show. We spoke about getting together when he is in New Orleans with Carrie.

If he calls me or he mentions it to you, is it all right if he and Carrie go out with us Thursday?

W.

P.S. But it would be more fun if just the 4 of us went.

W.

542 E Parkway S

Memphis: 1 Mar 78

DEAR PHINIZY[17] LECTURER

The inclosed was sent me by a fellow named Kibler at UGa. Seems the photographer managed to make you resemble Barry Goldwater. How'd he do that? In any case I thought you might like to have it for your scrapbook—a momento of your Goldwater phase; sort of like Picasso's blue period or Vermeer after he broke that water jug.

Book is cripping along, 7/800 a week on reorders, more or less marking time till it takes off. Which it might do any week now; or else it wont and that is that. Decent reviews are beginning to come in, on the heels of a lapsus, and the advertising campaign is about to get underway. We'll see. . . . No movie sale yet. Rosen says one reason is theyre scared to death of kidnapping stories out there this year, alas. Theyll come round, though, in time. God willing. . . . I'm going over to Atlanta next week to tape a Gene Moore TV thing, then come back and get myself settled down for TWO GATES TO THE CITY, wherein I propose to examine the Delta for what made it what it is and us what we are; a tall order. It might take me a good five years, if I have them. If I dont, that's all right too: it wont bother me where I'm going.

We were down home last week and Gwyn found the Luschei Wayfarer book in a store there. Interesting in a lot of ways. We ought to have some way, though, of controling just who likes us; they have so much to do with *how* we're liked. . . . I'm into a French thing. Theyve gone ape over my work. FOLLOW ME DOWN and DRY SEASON are coming out there this month in new translations (Coindreau, God bless him) and *Paris Match* is sending a photographer this week to illustrate a feature they are running on me and my work. My sun is rising in the east, and the hope is that some rays will be shed in this direction. Isnt it strange that it should work this way. What are the French to me or I to the French?—except of course most

17. Percy delivered the Phinizy Lecture at the University of Georgia that year. The occasion was organized by Percy's cousin, Phinizy Spalding. A version of the lecture appeared in the January 1979 issue of *Harper's* under the title "Southern Comfort: Thoughts on Southern Literature, Southern Politics, and the American Experience."

of my favorite writers have been French, old and new; new through Proust anyhow, and Celine.

It occurred to me the other day how strange it is that almost no one in Dostoyevsky works for a living, has a job or has to face any kind of day-to-day life. That's no concern of his, and he leaves it out. Imagine Mitya with a job. Or even Ivan or Alyosha for that matter—they need all their time to concentrate on being characters in his books.

Sooner or later we'll have to get together. I dont mean for a few hours over drinks or food; I mean a couple of days. Here or there or New Orleans: I suggest we work it out.

All best, as always:

Shelby

March 4, 1978

DEAR SHELBY:

What do you mean, what are we to the French or the French to us? A great deal to both of us and in entirely different ways—all going back to the old Cartesian split, a typical Frenchman who perpetrated a typical French disaster from which we have been suffering ever since—with of course exciting consequences—with you on one side of the split and me on the other. The French are ideologues, i.e. madmen, and yet without them we'd sink into a torpor. The mind-body split, locked-in ghost in the machine on one side, structure and world on the other, me with the former, you with the latter, like I used to make ghostly spiritual (but flyable) Lockheed Vegas and you used to make solid structural admirable perfect unflyable P-51s.

Re SepSep: hope it makes a lot of money, but don't count on it. Like Roger Strauss told me today, this is a crazy business. I collected a $2 bet with him. He was absolutely certain Lancelot would take off (that's what publishers know) and I told him he was nuts. How could it? being a dramatic monologue*—a basically uncongenial form—the reader still likes a once-upon-a-time third-person-singular story and he may be right. So what? One does what one feels like doing.

Yeah, have a go at *Two Gates*. You say 5 years, but it might take ten. You've got plenty of time. Footes live indefinitely and your mama's family too. But what about me? I've lived longer than any Percy in history and therefore have no precedent. Therefore it's all new territory. What's interesting is the apocalyptic feeling: that anyday I'll get tapped on the shoulder by the family ghost: OK, it's your turn now, pull the sugar kettle over your head and jump in the Bogue. What's nice is not doing it. What's nicer still is that *this time* the interior individual apocalypse coincides with the world apocalypse (your side of the split). If this were 1927 or 1915 or 1789 I may not stick around. But things being as they are, I think I will.

So what's wrong with Goldwater?

Yes, figure out a place where we can spend a couple of days which will be tolerable to the girls—I don't care where—N.O.? St Francisville, Vicksburg,—I can't afford NYC now.

Best,

Walker

*I know how Camus did with *The Fall*. How did Browning do with Bishop Blougram?

542 E Parkway S

Memphis 6 Apr 78

DEAR WALKER

I just finished *The Magic Mountain*, my third reading since 1934, when I first heard that the three great novels of the first quarter of this century were it and *Ulysses* and *Remembrance of Things Past*. Incidentally, I still agree with that assessment, expanded to the first *three* quarters. For some time previously, however, I had doubts about the Mann, and though I decided to reread them (along with some others) as an exercise in repreparing myself for novel writing, I didnt much look forward to Mann's *Mountain*—I figured I would hear too much of the machinery creaking, would encounter too much German "thoroughness," and certainly didnt expect to enjoy hearing Naptha and Settimbrini wrangle on and on. . . . Lord, was I wrong. For one thing, I had forgotten the humor, evident on almost every page, and for another I had thought it was all too obviously learned— which it wasnt, not even a little bit, or at least not a bit too much. . . . What a sneaky trick Mann played on you: wrote your magnum opus just as you were approaching puberty.

Before I began it, I went back and researched it a little among some of the egghead studies. I found out some interesting things. For one, he began it as a sort of sequel to *Death in Venice* and intended for it to be even shorter—a sort of satyr play, mainly humorous in a somewhat grisly way—introduce an "unassuming" young man to the fantastic horrors and absurdities of a TB sanitorium. Then he began it, and saw the possibilities of expanding it into a Bildungsroman, one of those coming-of-age things. So he did, and then saw it as a possible microcosm and began to work that in too. He didnt, though, know how it was going to end; "Something will turn up," he told himself. Something turned up, all right; the War. It turned up with such a vengeance that he stopped work on the book altogether and turned to polemics on the world situation, lest (he said) he overload the novel with the ideas that were coming at him so fast. At any rate he now had his ending, and when the war was over and he had cooled off a bit he returned to the book and worked hard at it for another four or five years—ten in all. The result is *The Magic Mountain* as we know it, and one hell of a book it is. It has strong elements I had almost forgotten; humor, for one thing, and for another a sort of tipsy tenderness nobody else has come within miles of either before his time or since. If you dont believe this last (I wouldnt have, a couple of weeks ago) try rereading the "Dance of Death" section in Chapter 4. Youll remember it as you read, but if youre like me youll be amazed at how thoroughly good it is, how well it strikes just the right note of combined comedy and sadness.

My thought (I finally get around to it) is that you should pay absolutely no attention to the fact that Mann covered this ground you know so well: far better, indeed, than he did—both as a patient and as a man with a medical background. What you do with it will of course be compared to what he did with it, but what difference will that make? Comparisons are odious only in the case of slavish imitation, which wouldnt be what you would be doing here any more than it was in the relation between *Last Gentleman* and *The Idiot* or *Ruins* and *Brave New World*—taking-off points at the worst.

Anyhow I absolutely guarantee a rereading of *The Magic Mountain* will light all kind of fires youve long kept banked. (Like Aschenbach, Hans Kastorp is on vacation). I guarantee it.

Here endeth the lesson for today. . . . Now on to more personal matters; a good deal more briefly, I hope.

I'm still fiddling with the material that will be going into TWO GATES, waiting for the moment when something tells me, "Stop. Get going." God knows when that will be. I dont much care. Amplexus expecta, and all that. For one thing, I intended to go back down home and lounge around, looking, for a week or ten days, getting back in touch and jogging the old memory. For another I'm due at the University of S.C. in mid-May; theyre holding a symposium on my War Narrative and I promised to be there, at least on the last day. That seems to me to be a good point to start from, back here and settled down. . . . I am given pause, however, by your recent experience in the ivied halls. A chunk of meat in the esophagus! Jesus; what a way to go—almost as bad as Sherwood Anderson with the martini toothpick.

SEPSEP is selling at a trickle, nothing great. It had a first printing of 15,000 and has finally achieved a small second printing, but that looks as if that may be it. Snakebit; that's me. . . . I did have a glorious double review in the Paris L'Express last week though, when translations of DRY SEASON and FOLLOW ME DOWN appeared. I'm the belated white hope of American letters, it seems, according to this two-page double-spread review. To wit: "Les amateurs comprendront qu'il s'agit d'une merveille, d'une découverte littéraire comme il ne s'en produit pas tout les ans."[18] I absolutely agree, though I cant quite understand why some of my fellow countrymen reviewers cant find the words to say so too.

That's about it, in the way of news. Let me hear something of you. . . . By the way, have I ever thanked you for never advancing the notion that there is something or other I ought to read or write? Well, I do.

Rgds all round:

Shelby

---

18. "Admiring readers will understand that what they have before them is something of a marvel, a literary discovery of the kind one does not come across every year" [editor's translation].

June 10, 1978

DEAR SHELBY—

How did it go in South Carolina? The only two times I was in Columbia were both trouble: one, visiting Sammy and Bob Horton;[19] the other, getting put in jail with Ross Allen.[20]

Nothing doing here. A long hot summer ahead and I ain't going anywhere. Don't want to. Does that happen to you? There are fewer and fewer places you want to *see*?

Have you read a young Mississippi writer named Barry Hannah? Read his latest, *Airships*.

Have you seen the enclosed? A fine-looking fellow.

W.

542 E Parkway S

Memphis 12 Jun 78

DEAR WALKER

All went well in S.C. No Horton, alas, but thank God no Sammy either. They treated me much better than they did you and Ross Allen, in part I reckon because I had sense enough not to ride around collecting kerosine warning-lights from in front of barricades. What it amounted to was four sessions, or seminars I believe they called them, two in the morning, two in the afternoon. A very strange sensation, sort of like attending a memorial service—all solid praise, except for one history graduate student, a meek little fellow who claimed I failed totally to catch the essential genius of Stonewall Jackson. Strange; I thought I did perhaps a better job on Jackson than anyone else in the book. Just goes to show you: a writer is a poor judge of his own work. . . . The general consensus was that those three volumes constitute the best, solidest single work of any American writer (not historian; *writer*) in this generation. Pretty heavy, that. I didnt mind hearing it at all, even after the third or fourth time around.

---

19. Robert Horton and his wife Sammy were old friends from Percy's Greenville years.

20. A friend from Percy's undergraduate years at the University of North Carolina.

SEPSEP was no bestseller by a long shot; went into a small second print-ing, and that looks to be about it. Ballantine is bringing it out in paper next year—we'll see what comes of that. No movie sale yet, either, though I had considered that a cinch. Hollywood it seems is scared to death of kidnap-ping stories; might set off a rash of them and get them sued or something. Idiots! All that money sitting out there in those California banks, and me sitting here wanting it, and they wont turn it loose in my direction. Idiots! It would make one hell of a movie, I maintain. Looks like I'll never know.

Thought I was altogether through with the Civil War, but here comes the National Geographic wanting me to do a 1500-word piece on Shiloh—for $3000. How in God's name am I going to turn down a chance to be paid $2 a word at least once in my life? Answer: I'm not. Gwyn and I rode over there last week—first time I'd seen it in ten or fifteen years. I enjoyed it and look forward to doing the piece. I'm going back to Greenville for a week or ten days when I get the Shiloh piece finished. My notion is to get reac-quainted with what I'm fixing to write about in TWO GATES; then come on back here and disappear into the deep abyss of labor.

Not *going* anywhere? Man, I havent been anywhere in years except under irresistible pressure from Gwyn or Random or some special aca-demics—and very few of these last when I was close to not being able to pay the light bill. They paid it and I was thankful, but I sure dont like that stuff. It makes my knees ache. . . . There's not only no place I want to see; even if I wanted to see it, I wouldnt go. William Ellery Leonard: remember him? Couldnt leave the town, then the block, then the house, then his room, and finally I guess his bed. It will be like that for us, I bet, before too long. I must say I wont mind.

Thanks for the photo of Jeffy D. A true aristocrat—grandson of an illit-erate Welsh peasant. Havent read Barry Hannah; havent read anyone but the standards, Keats-Browning & Co.

Shelby

12 Sep 78

DEAR WALKER

A long time; too long. We shouldnt ever get this much out of touch. All I remember from New Orleans, back in March, is you were into a novel that centered around a woman. That surprised me, having heard so often that all American writers have shared the inability to write about (or anyhow create truly) women or even a woman. Good for you. How does (or did) it go? Women characters' trouble is they scoot about like quicksilver under the thumb. I guess maybe the answer is, dont put them under your thumb.

Ive had glorious news from France—in the form of a dozen reviews sent me by Gallimard from the newspapers and magazines. FOLLOW ME DOWN and DRY SEASON came out in Coindreau translations over there in February, and you never saw anything like those reviews. It seems a new sun has risen on the literary horizon, no less brilliant for having been delayed nearly thirty years. FMD won the French Academy award as best translation of the year, and DRY SEASON is up for best foreign novel of the year. Not one of the reviews was anything less than ecstatic, and some of them went so far as to say that they now understand what Faulkner was getting at. Jesus! . . . Best of all though, they were without exception really intelligent reviews—meaning that they really went into things, saw what made the books tick, and even referred to books not yet translated; in other words they are not only reviewers, they are students of what they read. I never had an American review that came up to even the feeblest of these French ones. I couldnt be more pleased: in part because I always expected it would happen this way, which was another way of saying thank God for Flaubert and Proust, the two who hung the moon.

I'm still flogging the dog—fumbling round while I call myself getting hyped up for that Shiloh piece for the Natl Geographic. What I'm really doing is reading—a great go at it these past nine months or so, tuning up for my one big job, TWO GATES TO THE CITY. Ive been turning it over in my mind these 25 years or so, and I'm almost set to start. A huge affair. I plan to put into it everything I ever saw or heard down in the Delta, 1916–1946 and maybe after: planters, niggers, flappers, sheiks, the works. If I start it this winter, that will be the last the world will see of me for the next five years: provided, of course, Ive got them. I think maybe I have, and the doctor backs me up except for a touch of arterio-sclerosis which only serves to put more lines of character in my face.

In any case I'm going down home on a week or ten-day visit in a month or so, and soak up all Ive been missing these twenty-odd years Ive been away from it. Not that I really need to—it's all right here in my pointy head; but God knows what things may come flooding back in full force on the actual scene where I first learned them. It will be interesting, too, to see what-all has happened to some of the people I knew best there: not for actual use in the book, but rather to see what will become of them after the book is over; that is, to see where theyll be headed while theyre doing the things I'm going to have them do. . . . Can you honestly ever imagine having been anything but a writer? I cant, and I'll bet you cant either.

I saw in the NY Review that the Coles book[21] on your work is coming out next spring. I look forward to that.

Another tiny item of good news: Ballantine is bringing out the paper SEPSEP without a naked woman on the cover. It's to be a 600,000 printing, which should make me moderately rich. Remember, the contract Rosen negotiated gives me *all* the paperback royalties. No 50-50 split with Random. 600,000 copies (at $2.50) will bring me $203,125—if they sell, of course. In hard-cover, it barely made 15,000. I'm already moderately rich (for me, I mean) and this will put me in clover, and that aint hay. To me, I mean. Of course, for bigtime operators like you and Puzo that might not sound like much of a fortune, but for me it sounds like Fort Knox emptied out.

Gwyn's fine and sends her best. I wish there was some way we could get down there or you and Bunt get up here for a stay. As I said, it's wrong to be out of touch to this degree. Let me know what's with you nowadays. I calculate youre through the firstdraft stage on that novel—which, in your case, means getting ready to sit down and go to work in earnest. Revisions, revisions! I prefer to do them as I go along.

All best, as always:

Shelby

Just finished a book I know youd like in case you missed it—Paul Fussell's *The Great War & Modern Memory*. Won the NBA back in '76; an Oxford paperback now.

---

21. *Walker Percy: An American Search* (1978).

Sept. 18, 1978

DEAR SHELBY—

Your news from France is indeed glorious. You're in a great tradition after all. Like E.A. Poe and Faulkner. What it is is structure, which you and the French were always nuts about—which is why I do better in Italy and Germany (Gefühl!), even though I maybe owe most to the French. I remember meeting Faulkner's French translator at Tate's house in Princeton (I had read WF and had the standard Mississippian attitude toward him: dirty obscure writer—corncobbing women etc.) where I embarrassed the Tates and invited ridicule by asking the Frenchman: why bother with him? So *FMD* wins the French Academy award—and *D.S.* is up for best foreign novel. That ain't bad for a Pica[22] staffer.

I'm nearing end of first draft of this thing—which seems as always such a mess and this time might be sure enough. Though I see a few glimmers of virtue. I realize now that I've been suspending everything until I can get through it—I haven't swept my office room for two years. Now I'll have to rake it.

The best part for me occurs when I can read it through the first time—best, that is, if it works. Then, no matter what the faults, you can at least see it whole, surround it, grab aholt of it, work and knead it. I'll let you know in a month.

Ever heard of a writer in Memphis name of John Fergus Ryan. Somebody gave me some stuff of his. Yeah, how come yall live in *Memphis*?

—Best

—W—

[postcard, 1974]

Now I have to know how John Maxwell[23] got his horological torpedo abord the barge—Send p. 544.

Had enough of Gulf Shores for the next 100 years. Next summer for Patmos and Corfu.

W

---

22. The Greenville High School newspaper.

23. A Confederate spy whose primitive time bomb did considerable damage to one of the Union barges.

[postcard, Fall 1978]

—a stone, a leaf, and unfound door; of a stone a leaf, a door, and of all the forgotten foes. O Lost and by the wind grieved, ghost come back again.

It's still there, like an island in the interstates, 48 Spruce St.[24]

I never did know whether I liked him.

—W.P.

[*Editor's note: Percy sent Foote the following note from a journalist in Georgia. It was accompanied by an article she had written for the October 19, 1979, issue of the* Plains Georgia Monitor, *in which she criticized Percy's friend Robert Coles.*]

[Fall 1978]

I'm sho glad Louise got it straight about what we were doing growing up and that consequently you are no. 1 sex-writer.

W

DEAR WALKER

Your unworthy Svengali, Coles, is starred in the top one, along with his Alma Mammy.

Your buddy Shelby Foote does—in FOLLOW ME DOWN—the best explicit sex AND evokes the rural South better than everyone I ever read, and I've read everyone. (Of course Joyce Gary does love-sex better than anyone—especially in THE AMERICAN VISITOR—but he is never explicit.) Sounds as tho while you were boys, you ivory-towered while he made hay or hit the hay, but life, art & sex being what it is, it could have been vice versa.

Louise

---

24. The Thomas Wolfe house in Asheville, North Carolina.

25 Jan 79

There finally goes into this same mail the Christmas present I forgot to bring down to New Orleans with me last week. It's the funny-paper book I told you about, and it will give you, as it gave me, a chance to visit again with the Bungles and other old friends. I did have some strange and vivid memories while leafing through it—memories of childhood Sunday mornings; I could even remember the weather outside, back there when I was seven or eight, while I read certain strips; especially, for some reason, the Katzenjammers and Bringing Up Father and the Gumps. (Happy Hooligan too. And Moon Mullins.) I hope you both enjoy it half as much as I did.

I'm sorry, though, that we got to see so little of each other down there. Fact is, it's always like that, and I reckon it always will be. . . . I wanted to tell you something of what I am about to get into: a prodigious undertaking, so much so that for the first time in my life I felt a willingness, even an urge, to talk about it, if only in a tentative sort of way and of course only to you. I'm at work on a framework that I think will bear any and everything I want it to support; every good and bad thing I ever learned or saw while I was growing up in the Delta—and believe me I learned and saw a lot, much of which I have come to understand only recently. It's an undertaking as grave and big as The Civil War, though God grant it wont run much over about one third as long. Everything I have read or experienced for the past couple of years has seemed strangely designed to contribute to what I am about to begin—Dante, Joyce, and perhaps most of all the Oresteia, which I just finished studying to the dregs for about the tenth time in the past twenty years. Same thing with experiences; yesterday, for example, a friend of mine from back in the early thirties, Harold Mosby from Indianola, came by and spent the afternoon. There he was, rich and sixty-three years old, and he still was Harold Mosby, even though he's lived in California for the past thirty years. I suddenly remembered things I'd long since forgotten—corn whiskey, dances, a girl named Jean Kent Early, hosts of things. All grist for the mill.

SEPSEP is about to hit the stands in paperback, but I have given up all notions of getting rich. My main concern is to keep from getting poor; quite a different matter. Fortunately I really dont know of one damned thing in this world I really want—that money can buy I mean, except maybe ser-

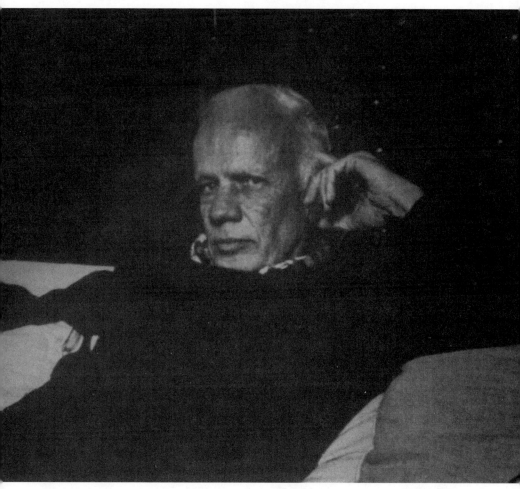

Walker Percy, almost at ease, in the late 1980s. *Courtesy of Washington County Library System.*

vants to bring me things on trays in my old age and make me comfortable by the fire.

A week or so ago I wrote to Bob Coles telling him how much I liked the full-length version of his book on you, and today I got a strangely gloomy note in reply. It meant a lot to him, he said, but "I get depressed more often than I have any excuse for—and wonder what the point of it all is. There may not be any real point, but it's nice to know that a bit of one's intentions get across, sometimes." Heavy, man. I reckon we're none of us exempt from the doldrums. Anyhow there's no more use expecting a psychiatrist to be happy than there is in expecting a G.P. to be healthy.

I'm going down home on Tuesday to fulfill a promise I made some months ago to talk to a WAP Library[25] meeting. It will be good to see it again. . . . Incidentally, I got worried about Jo Haxton's lack of readership and success; I talked with her about it while I was down there last fall, and when I got back here I called my agent, Bob Rosen, and told him I thought he would like to handle her work. She sent some to him, including a novel-in-progress. Result: he took her on, and in December got her a $40,000 advance on the new novel. She's now up on approximately Cloud 9. Money *is* nice; reassuring, too.

Middle of next month I'm due in New York for the first NBA meeting with my two fellow History judges, a couple of eastern professors. I really hate that stuff, but they had me boxed; I'd been claiming that nothing but academics were sitting judgment on historians, so when they asked me I had no valid way of saying no. So I'm doing it — despite the knowledge that one-out-of-three wont do the trick. You just wait and see what gets the prize. I'll give you two to one it will be some badly written drivel that will get its author tenure.

So much for now. I was serious, though, about meaning to get down there for something more than an overnight stay. Lord knows when it will be, or how, but I think it's wrong we see so little of each other these past ten years or so. If in the meantime you get the chance, come on up here. Or if a simultaneous occasion looms, I'll meet you half way. Say at Le Fleur's.

Regards:
Shelby

Jan. 29, 1979
DEAR SHELBY:
Got the comic book today and turned immediately to Buck Rogers. Yeah it does bring things back; Happy Hooligan and Krazy Kat being the first things I remember. I would like to do the same thing with cars: Cars I

---

25. The William Alexander Percy Library in Greenville, Mississippi.

Remember. In fact toward that end I visited Harrah's car museum in Reno a few years ago and looked up the Chrysler convertible with rumble seat and little door for golf clubs which my father owned in B'ham (and Roy and I used to ride the rumble seat over the mountain to the movies (Seargant Quirt and Captain Flagg)). A real eerie feeling looking at the dashboard and seeing how little everything was. Would also like to find model A Ford touring car Harvey Kerr and I turned over in at Lake Chicot and got chewed out good by WAP:[26] "What do you mean, you turned over?"

Sounds like you've done your backing up on the new (old) novel and have got a good running start on it. Well, good luck—I'm glad you have a stomach for it. As usual, we differ. I think beginning a new novel is like the onset of a chronic illness, something to be suffered and gotten through, if possible, in one piece. I've just finished a draft of this here one (presently entitled The Second Coming) and am glad to have gotten through to the end without a catastrophe (it dying, me dying, the world coming to an end) but that's about as far as I can go. I think I'll put it aside for a while and come back and take a look. I promised NYTimes to do a review of a new edition of Kierkegaard's Letters—a larger job than I wanted, entails going back to SK whom I hadn't visited for years—but it's a valuable thing to do.

Sorry Bob Coles sounded depressed. I hope he wasn't depressed about my response to the book. I am of course very grateful to him for what he did, in fact overwhelmed that he should even undertake such a task—and I have written him so. And he has succeeded in plowing through the articles unlike almost anybody else, and—unlike almost anybody else, actually making sense and understanding them. Yet I am somewhat embarrassed by the profiles and book. I do not altogether recognize myself. I think it is because he is projecting a good deal of himself, a kind of good-hearted Colesian decency which may apply to him but not exactly to me. I feel a good deal more malevolent, oblique, phony, ironical and, I hope, more entertaining. His WP is both a good deal more worthy and admirable but also, I hope, less dull. Then again I am having the uncomfortable feeling of having at last been stuck in my slot—as a "Christian existentialist." I hear sighs of relief all over: now that they know what I am, they don't have to

---

26. William Alexander Percy.

worry about me. It is like being kicked upstairs from coach to Athletic Director or maybe being made professor emeritus—a good deal of admiration but at the same time I've been slipped out of gear. This is not Coles' fault. It's the nature of "existentialism," a word I was never sure I understood in the first place and which now means nothing at all. So I may have to write a mean nasty novel to break out of this mold.

Then again, I am as usual somewhat guilty just at the spectacle of Bob Coles' industry, decency and out-goingness . . . none of which virtues I have. What little I accomplish seems to get accomplished through a peculiar dialectic of laziness, malice and self-centeredness. I've tried to explain this to Bob (actually the Esquire self-interview comes closer to the derisive tone I find natural rather than Coles' edifying tone) and I think he understands but he still tends to give me more credit than is warranted. You, for example, know exactly what I am talking about because you are a writer and because we have known each other forever—and because we are Southern?

Have fun at NBA. I've put in my time with them and don't feel obliged for a while. It's a real chore and you usually end up making enemies for not giving people the prize.

The meal with Will C.[27] was fun.

Best,

W

542 E Parkway S
Memphis 10 Mar 79
DEAR WALKER

Another cassette goes into this mail. I promise I wont bombard you with these things, but at least I wanted you to have these two monuments from the quartet literature, Beethoven's 14th and 15th. The latter (written first) is the one with the Heiliger Dankgesang for the middle of its five movements. The former, in C-sharp Minor, is the miracle of all chamber music, the most daring and, after a good many listenings, the most beautiful piece of music ever written. It is in seven movements, with no break between any of them,

---

27. Will Campbell, the Baptist minister, writer, editor, and civil rights worker.

but it boils down to a true four-movement quartet with certain embellishments. Like so:

1. A long fugue-introduction.
2. Actual first movement (ABA, "arch" form).
3. A bridge passage.
4. Actual second movement; theme and seven variations, plus coda.
5. Third movement: Scherzo.
6. Bridge-introduction to the finale.
7. Fourth movement—Finale. (Sonata form)

I dont know whether you have listened to much late-Beethoven these past few years, but if you havent, you will come back to it with a considerable pang of recognition—most obviously to the 15th's Adagio (the Dankgesang) but even more so to the whole 14th, beginning with the introductory fugue. It's a goddam miracle! In the variation movement, he throws away the first three or four variations, then finally gets down to work on the last three—and caps them with a coda that goes beyond anything ever dreamed of in the first half of the movement.

Did the Mozart quartet and quintet pull you to them? I hope so; it's one hell of a world youve been neglecting these past twenty years or so. All I can tell you about these two, the Beethovens, is they will give you back whatever you are willing to put into them. After about the twentieth listening, the C-sharp Minor becomes radiant in all its parts. See if it doesnt.

No news here. NBA cogitations continue; five nominees already made; we select a winner in April up in NY. I'll be glad to have that foolishness behind me. I plan to spend a week or ten days down in Greenville getting reacquainted with the thirty years I spent there, then come back to the quiet of Memphis and put all thirty of them into TWO GATES.

Rgds, as ever:

Shelby

March 13, 1979

DEAR SHELBY,

I'm awed by Q 14 and 15. Thanks. They're better tapes than I can buy. I can listen to them endlessly while typing in my little dump of an office. A great pleasure. I have a little Sony 510 stereo radio with $60 plugged in Craig speakers. Yet it is all I desire.

At this moment watch a good Pb TV 2-hr Ustinov program on Einstein. Amazing. I almost understand it. Then why should someone not make the same great leap in understanding human affairs as Einstein in physics?

All best,

W.

April 18, 1979

SHELBY—

Am sending you this[28] because otherwise you might not see it. I attach great importance to it—a truly remarkable lady, laconic, funny, tough, smart, hard-headed, no-nonsense, the very best of US, South and Catholicism.

Just finished reading (one hour ago) Troyot's *Tolstoy*. Truly credible and incredible. Do you think I do not understand completely how Tolstoy could have been so great and so phony and in the end ludicrous? What a way to go. It just occurs to me to compare his going out with Flannery's—with all her sacraments which he would have had only contempt for—and to be so sure she had the better of it—let alone which was right. Just when I'm writing what an inflated ego Tolstoy was, I read *The Death of Ivan Ilych* (last night) and am astounded by how good it is. Pore damn writers—we're lucky to die with any dignity at all.

All best,

Walker

542 E Parkway S

Memphis: 2 May 79

DEAR WALKER

Thanks for sending the O'Connor letters. She is indeed all you say, especially brave and funny and very southern in her mockery of her prejudices, which she never turns loose of for an instant all the same. I like her, though

---

28. The collected letters of Flannery O'Connor, *The Habit of Being* (1979), edited by Sally Fitzgerald.

I never read but one of her books, her first one, WISE BLOOD. In it, she struck me as a shortstory writer, heavy on the Gothic, and I never went back to her except for a couple of stories I read in magazines down the years. Just never hooked atoms, as they say. Sooner or later I'll get around to reading her; God knows I been reading some dreadful stuff of late—Styron's new novel SOPHIE'S CHOICE, for instance; some of the absolutely worst writing Ive read in years, though the story itself could have been a great one. The adjectives flutter past, trailing their modifying adverbs. Thought I'd scream, as women used to say at cardgames. If it hadnt been for reading McCarthy's SUTTREE last month, I'd have thought American literature had gone completely to hell in a bucket.

Strange: I happened to be reading "Ivan Ilich" at the same time you were. Jesus what a story. But I made the mistake of going on to "The Kreutzer Sonata," and had to continue through "Hadji Murad" (which is just about as good as Ilich) to get all that picknose Tolstoyan sex out of my mind. I was writing you urgently ten years ago to read the Troyat biography, and now I'm glad to hear you finally did. Last year I read ANNA for the first time in better than twenty years, and I emerged liking it better than ever before. I'll say one thing for him; he certainly takes rereading at his best. I guess it's the simplicity—that's what wears best down the years. I still think, though, that basically he's about as slick as owl shit, the slickest substance known to man.

Recently I saw something in Evelyn Waugh's JOURNALS I think will please and amuse you. He happened to be in New Orleans one Ash Wednesday and was delighted to see so many people going round with smudges on their foreheads. Commenting on it, he said the thing I think youll like. Catholics, he says, are "members of a great brotherhood who can rejoice and recognize the limits of rejoicing."

Wise-pitiful quote from a letter I got a couple of months ago from some crazy nigger down in Mound Bayou: "Funny how when a man going down a road his mind say no he tries to get as many to go along. Thats the reason its so hard on him when God say why?"

I'm glad to be back from all that NBA hassel, back in my own quiet life away from plots and elbows and late-night discussions about nothing whatever. I was told to be sure to tell you hello by several people, one being Jonathan Yardley.

I was pleased, however, to find those various Harvard-Yale professor types genuinely respectful of my Narrative. Damned white of them, now that it's safely in the past. Incidentally there's a long and rather fulsome piece on it in the current (Spring) issue of the Virginia Quarterly. I havent seen it yet but Ive been getting letters about it from fellow historians who say how grand (their word) it is. Same man wrote it that did the book on Walter Anderson, except he didnt wait till I was dead. Apparently he went all out; I'll let you know when Ive managed to find a copy. Louis Rubin wrote that it's top flight stuff, and Louis *knows*.

For the first time in my life I'm absolutely terrified about starting a book. TWO GATES is so huge, so all-inclusive, I'm as terrified to start it as I would be when contemplating a leap into the Atlantic off a cliff. I keep telling myself what I ought to do is another short one—something I'll be pretty sure of having time to finish. Fact is, I cant imagine anything better than collapsing in the shafts. I'm going ahead with it as soon as I get down home for a serious lookround; groundwork for putting all I ever knew about the Delta into this monster project. Ive got all my people worked out, birth dates, highlights, etc. Even got the Goddam thing organized as to length and method, but I cant start till I get down home and somehow manage to quit shaking in my boots. What's worse, Ive long had a growing feeling that there's very little down there much worth writing about; especially the people—which of course isnt true. But it *seems* true from time to time.

I was pleased to see us moving in tandem in Rubin's anthology THE LITERARY SOUTH: you first, of course, as becometh age.

Keep in touch. Let's work out a meeting sometime soon.

Regards and best, as ever:

Shelby

4 May 79

DEAR WALKER

I finally saw a copy of that spring *Va. Quarterly* I mentioned in my letter. The Civ War piece is a good one; I was pleased with it almost from end to end. To my surprise, though, the lead article (by Louis Rubin)[29] has a

---

29. "The Boll Weevil, the Iron Horse, and the End of the Line: Thoughts on the South."

middle section concerned almost exclusively with *The Last Gentleman*. Inaccurate in some details (mainly biographical) it says some splendid things about you & him & the South. Be sure to read it.

Rgds:

Shelby

2 July 79

DEAR WALKER

There's an absolute miracle in a cassette you ought to order: Schubert's C Major string quintet, Op. 163, recorded by the Guarneri Quartet with Leonard Rose on the extra cello. It's RCA, catalog number ARK 1-1154; get some dealer to order it for you. I once considered it the greatest piece in all Romantic music, & maybe still do.

All well here, comparatively speaking. Life *is* hard, though.

Rgds—

Shelby

May 21, 1979

DEAR SHELBY—

Well, I think you did a good job picking Davis' *Intellectual Life in Colonial South*—or did you do it? Anyhow the reviews were good and I aim to get local librarians to get it.

How do I get Virginia Quarterly? If you have an extra, send it.

Just read Josephine Haxton's new novel—really quite good. The girl is steady getting better and better.

You do well to be scared of starting a long novel but I doubt that you have much choice. I seem to know that it is something you are bound to do. All sympathy: I'm writing a medium-length novel[30] which is nothing but trouble. I'm convinced that times were never worse for novelists in the sense that somehow the straight narrative form is in default and so one must resort to all manner of tricks, cons, blandishments, obfuscations, curses, lies, jokes, animadversions. It is a matter of semiotic breakdown.

---

30. *The Second Coming* (1980).

What I would like to do is get this here novel in passable shape and then spend a few years figuring out *how* TV rots the brain (nobody knows).

We've just about finished *The New Kumquat*—Ann's bookstore—a really lovely little building. I'll have a cubby hole in the attic. Incidentally, how can you stand to stay holed up in your house night and day? Do you know what a pleasure it is to walk a mile to work in downtown Covington? You could get an office near Holiday Inn. Just watch your toenails. That's where it started with Howard Hughes.

Girls keep trying to haul me off someplace this summer. I defaulted on France and aim to stay put and sweat.

—W.

Aug. 29, 1979

DEAR SHELBY:

Writing this from my new office. Moved from my place in Art Assoc. to an attic room over the new Kumquat—a delectable little Cajan cottage Ann and John have built for the Bookshop-Gift shop. A single window overlooking the street, Haydn on the FM. I've just finished this here novel (at least this here go-round with it) and feel myself somewhat at loose ends. It reads pretty good—a sequel to the Last Gent—what happens to Will Barrett twenty years later . . . how he falls apart when he gets his dream house built, takes early retirement etc. It's being xeroxed now, I'll pick up copies tomorrow and will send you one for your edification.

Re Styron: I started it with great enthusiasm and developed forebodings which got worse. Something wrong here, wronger than your objection to the language, which I found not so much bad Faulkner as occasionally crappy cliche: ". . . her graceful undulant walk." He had a lot of nerve taking on the Holocaust and for this I admire him—nobody's been able to handle it, not even the survivors, maybe especially not the survivors. I suspect that it can't be handled, that is, the dead weight and mystery of the horror can't be got hold of by esthetic categories—and when you try, bad things happen, both to the writer and the subject. It would take a Dostoevski to do it, and he would by the utmost guile, indirection and circumspection. The only novelist I know to get hold of one of our little horrors of the 20th C—in this case the bombing of Dresden—was Vonnegut, and he knew that the only way you can write about such a thing is not to write about it—to write about the calves of the British prisoners "big as cannon-balls" and outer space. Styron jumps right in in good old-fashioned novel-writing style: a chapter on Stingo (bad deal, this name) trying to screw (funny, his horniness and miscues) Jewish and Southern princesses, alter-nating with Sophie's flashbacks: "Meanwhile back at Auschwitz. . . ." Hm . . . something bad wrong here. Styron is an excellent writer and doesn't mind taking chances (he'll probably get racked up for this by some Jews just as he was by some blacks over Nat), but he's not good enough to get away with this. Maybe nobody is. Also he falls prey to one of the less attractive traits of American novelists (and film-makers), what I think of as a trust in excess and gigantism to substitute for art (I think of Deerhunter and Apoc-alypse Now). Book as orgasm. Let it all hang out. Styron seems to think that a lot of fucking in a novel is better than a little fucking and that the greater the variety of fucking and cock-sucking the better. There is a mis-taken notion here that confessional frankness in excess will somehow do the job—it reminds me of the spiels of A.A. members, each trying to top the other in performance. The best thing about Styron's fucking and maybe the whole book is the humor. Styron seems to be saying to Roth and other practitioners: O.K. boys, let's see you top this. This ain't bad for a ol' Vir-ginia smalltown boy.

It's nice having an office uptown. I don't see how you can sit in that house all day. I go to the P.O. (often walk the mile and a half) and to work like a proper U.S. business man.

That Mozart-Beethoven tape you sent me is the best I've got. What do you do about wowing in a tape—I have maybe fifty tapes and half are worthless due to wowing—otherwise I much prefer tapes to records. I've been playing a lot of Mahler.

Strange, having finished this novel and having a free choice of what to do. All I know is I don't want to write another novel now, maybe ever. A novel is an incredible ordeal, which gets worse and worse, requiring all manner of alternating despairs, piss-offs, deaths and rebirths, too much for an aging infirm novelist (for Two Gates you're going to need Uncle Hugie's longevity). Right now I can't decide whether to do a little stuff with semi-otics—I still think there's a way of getting at such things as the effect on a man of watching TV five hours a day for twenty years which other conventional psycholgies don't know about—or writing a child's book "The Beast of Honey Island Swamp" or the like. Rat now, I'm resting.

Am sending your Deltas back as soon as I can remember to find a label. Best,

W

Sept. 15, 1979

DEAR SHELBY:

Many many many thanks for the word on TSC and especially for the follow-up. I needed it because I am wiped out by that book, not the book so much as finishing it and so feeling shaky, seedy, molted, unfit, with no stomach for tackling anything yet mindful of your youthful trick of polishing off a novel in the morning and starting one in the afternoon. Only three people have seen it and like it but seem a little baffled (Bunt looks dark and shakes her head and says Barret shouldn't have been so ugly to his daughter); an artist friend here likes it a lot but says it should have more sex in it; Robert Daniel is reading it after his cataract operation, going slow but says he finds it compelling, agent likes it (tho she couldn't know about the agenbites of inwit)[31] and thinks it might sell, unusual for me.

Yes, that chronology. That's the penalty I pay for not being systematic like you. I should have plotted out a calendar of birthdates, deaths, graduations, wars etc. What happened was that I started writing this not knowing this guy was Barrett, then discovered he was about in the middle, then grafted him onto Will's lifeline. I never did make a chronology, so I guess this might be a good time. I do give myself a certain leeway by having Barrett by turns feverish and disoriented when he is time-skipping with Ross Alexander, Chester Morris and John Ehrlichman—he could even be remembering things his father told him about (especially Eddy Stinson).

I think I'm taking some time with this. I told my agent to sit tight and not submit it to anybody. Before, when it went off to an agent, I felt like I had hit the publishing assembly line and had to make revisions on the run. I

---

31. The phrase "agenbite of inwit" comes from James Joyce's *Ulysses* and roughly means a pang of conscience.

don't need the money right now, so might hold off till January, since I got paid for Moviegoer film rights this year.

You're probably right about the Intermezzo—and the italics might help. This might have been a case of overkill, but I know from experience that the reader is dumb and is apt not to know what the novel is about unless you tell him so I told him. Will run this through the hopper again.

No doubt due to your jacking them up, Love in a Dry Season arrived in mail this morning and I'm already off in it, starting right off with Major Barcroft in your maestro classical-novel style. It's a goodlooking book and needs to be around. Yes, God bless us for doing what we did and even surviving.

Am removing again to a new office. This attic garret gives me the creeps. I sit looking at a tin roof, a camphor tree, a patch of sky and listening to people downstairs buying Jackie O and Scruples. We're dinosaurs. But it's great walking around town with my three-iron. Hang in, blast off on Two Gates.

W

Sat: 27 Jan 80

DEAR WALKER

I dont much like asking favors (or granting them either, for that matter) but in this case I'm asking one. I want to get Huger into Chapel Hill, and Louis Rubin thinks a letter of recommendation from you will be helpful. Inclosed is a letter I just sent the director of undergraduate admissions. His full address is:

Richard G. Cashwell

Director of Undergraduate Admissions

UNC at Chapel Hill

Chapel Hill, N.C. 27514

Part of my eagerness is due to the fact that Hugs has also applied to Pamona (in California, for God's sake) and Sarah Lawrence, which is even more horrendous—I'm terrified theyll take him, out of sheer perversity. He also has a Tulane string to his bow; alas.

Are you cocking an ear to that Mozart string trio? Aint it something?

Rgds:

Shelby

January 28, 1980

Mr. Richard G. Cashwell
Director of Undergraduate Admissions
UNC—Chapel Hill, N.C.

DEAR MR. CASHWELL:

I am writing to commend to you my young friend, Huger L. Foote, who is applying to UNC for admission as a freshman this fall.

His father, Shelby Foote, and I have been friends practically for life and attended UNC-Chapel Hill in the thirties. We both set great store by the quality of education at Chapel Hill and I would hope very much that Huger would be allowed to benefit from it.

Huger is a very bright, very attractive young man who, I believe, has done quite well in school except in math—a shortcoming which, I trust, will not disqualify him.

I truly believe that he is the sort of person you are looking for as a student and that both he and the University would profit from his enrollment.

Sincerely yours,

SHELBY:

Don't take alarm: the original of this looked okay. I hope Huggy makes it. I wasn't kidding: he is the sort of kid they ought to be looking for.

You would not believe the main source of my distress these days. I would be perfectly happy to be let alone for the rest of my life because I know what I want to think about and write about: semiotics, which is very important tho you may not think so—and which nobody knows anything about, or very little. Instead I know I will be getting heat from publishers to come up there and help publicize this book—which is horrifying, twice as difficult as writing a book, and I feel guilty about turning them down since they've got their money riding on it etc. And getting heat from academics: "I really don't mean to hound you but I can't understand why you can't come since Lewis Simpson and John Barth etc are going to be there"—and again I feel guilty because they are probably right: I ought to be there. Weh ist mir: why does it fall to my lot to be afflicted by these absurd horrors, which are in fact comical when you come to think of it. I need you to tell me that it is perfectly all right to tell them all to go shove it and do what I want to do. Well, anyhow the Mozart is a consolation.

best,

wp

3 Feb 80

DEAR WALKER

I'm somewhat into the thing that's fretting you, the importunities of academics and publishers, and I dont like it either. The publishers are the easiest to handle; they simply know that certain writers dont do that, and they honor the decision. Academics are much harder; they have nothing to lose, not even your regard, and they act accordingly. The fact is, there's money in us, money and reputation and, above all, tenure. They have something much heavier than "publish or perish" to deal with; they have to make their marks in other ways as well, as organizers and prime movers of symposiums; theyre out there fighting the good fight for culture and academia, above all not making the mistake their predecessors made in ignoring Faulkner before the Nobel lightning struck. You of course know all this, but I maintain it's up to us to play or not play that game, though it's true certains things can make a fairly irresistible claim. In my case it's Mississippi, and what makes it so irresistible is my guilt for having peeled off on the eve of the civil rights struggle instead of staying to fight for the good of both whites and blacks. I'll go almost anywhere I can believe I'm needed in Mississippi, in almost any capacity. Otherwise I dont have much of a problem: I just tell the inviters I dont do that. I even have a disarming way of saying it: that I'd be absolutely delighted to come, that I know I'd enjoy myself enormously etc. but that I disapprove in my soul of the participation by writers, on the grounds that writers ought to stay home and write. It always works. They reply that they not only understand, they highly approve, though theyre quick to add that they are bitterly disappointed; which they are. Lately Ive found another kind of answer, one that seems to work about as well even though it verges on bad manners. I say I think that academic matters should be left to academics, as indeed they should, since academics do a much better job of giving their fellows what they want right down the line. I'm right and they know it. . . . My point is, you are wrong in agreeing with them from the outset that you "ought to be there." You should not be there on any grounds whatever; not even the making of money for them (publishers *or* academies). They are making more money than I am anyhow, and if I cant make it for myself, how the hell am I going to make it for them except by puffing their reputation?—which is never the basis for their appeal and therefore doesnt even need refuting. Sometimes, on the other hand, enough money is involved in the honorarium to justify breaking the rule. Ive done that to pay some bills, and found the relief most welcome. But outside of that I dont see much excuse for participating— unless, on second thought, you want to use it the way Bill Dickey does to get some groupie academic ass, which I suspect is pretty lousy ass in the first place: hungry-eyed little 19-year-olds with nothing under their hats but frizzly hair and ivory and you have to put a pillow under their twats to achieve a proper angle of penetration. Aint life grizzly?

There is, of course, another danger involved—one that can be demonstrated by the career (?) of J. D. Salinger. He got such a bad case of the horrors (plus other things I suspect) that he disappeared entirely, not only as a speaker but as a writer. I agree with old Maugham: "Writers are very unhappy people, and should be left alone." . . . Another ploy, and a good one, is to tell the inviters youve taken a solemn oath not to appear anywhere in the calendar year 1980, but you hope theyll asked you again next year; which you can deal with in much the same way when *it* comes around—if youre still here, that is.

Semiotics is an utter mystery to me and is likely to remain so. I can scarcely even comprehend the definition in the dictionary, let alone what's behind it. I'm much more interested in the way people behave psychologically than I am in what underlies that behavior. Also I dont much like looking into things that I'm not sure have an answer—like whether God has withdrawn behind the stars. Chaucer and Shakespeare and Donne and Browning and John Crowe Ransom are my kind of writers; plus Proust— always Proust, who just may be the top knocker of them all aside from Shakespeare. Yeats for example is a really good writer but it's despite his special interests, which have to be ignored before you can really get down to the beauty of what he's saying. Some of them can only be admired when they are what they would call "misunderstood." To understand Yeats is to go along with a lot of hogwash and moonshine. "Byzantium" for instance is a very great poem if youll only refrain from understanding what he's saying, and the same thing is even more true of the earlier "Sailing to Byzantium." A goddam mechanical bird, of all things!

In closing, I want to thank you for recommending Hugs. You struck just the right tone. I consider him as good as in. . . . Incidentally, it pleases me greatly to think of him up there, much as we were fifty years ago, a poor damned lost soul in search of his bearings. Theyll come bearing down on him soon enough anyhow. God forbid Pamona and S. Lawrence! Speak of your fates worse than death—

Rgds,
Shelby

In at least one ethical respect, with regard to this symposium thing, I'm in far worse shape than you are. My problem is I actually enjoy such things, at least in part—& that really *is* sinful.

Sept. 3, 1980
DEAR SHELBY—
Now there's a fellow with taste—even though he makes me sound like the light reading he does during the heavy historical stuff.

I've been reading a batch of letters written by Uncle Will to Gerstle Mack, over 100 letters spanning 1918 (right after war) to 1941, a few months before his death. Makes you see how much fell in on him in such a short time, death of parents in 1929, the Depression, mother's death, having to lawyer, bad health (do you remember how often he got the "flu" and took to his bed for days?). Yet we seemed to cheer him up (he wouldn't have lied to Gerstle): e.g.: (1930): "The little Percy boys are interesting little animals."

Other memorable quotes: "God, Christmas was awful as usual."

"Walker and Shelby are at Brinkwood living a monastic life."

It's amazing how he carried on despite all. It's also surprising how much he traveled even after we arrived. Apparently he would call in an aunt to take charge, Aunt Ellen—"a pleasant totally inefficient woman"—or park us in Sewanee—and take off—to Tahiti, Samoa, Rio.

Am feeling somewhat poorly and at loose ends, not working. Have decided to start a new life: gave up sleeping pills and now thinking of giving up booze (I feel liverish, a touch of liver)—a decision I'll live to regret.

Best,

W—

P.S. What school did H get into?[32]

W

6 Sep 80

DEAR WALKER

Glad to get you spotted: Ive been confused all summer as to your whereabouts. Back in June I remember you said you were heading for three places, Clarabell Island, Canada, and North Carolina: but I didnt know in what order or for how long each. A couple of times I called Covington, and when there was no answer I figured you were in one or another of those three places. But which? God knew.

The big thing of course was to say hurrah for the bestseller list. What a glorious thing, week in and week out, and the sheckles raining down. I believed from my first look at the typescript that it was headed there, but you never really know until you see it listed and it never means much unless it stays there for a while, which it sure as hell has done. I think it's great—carrying as it does, I mean, it's own particular satisfaction of knowing youre not only egghead-read but are reaching out Dickens-fashion to that great mass of faceless reactors you dont know and never will know and dont even want to know; I call that satisfaction. And as for the money, you can maybe even renovate another house. Or get a Porche, or a pair of alligator shoes.

I just reread LITTLE DORRIT, which is maybe Dickens' best novel, along with BLEAK HOUSE and OUR MUTUAL FRIEND. Strange business: Arthur Clenham is a Kafka character—a Percy character, too; he's Will Barrett but even further gone in despair. Little Dorrit herself is Allison or anyhow serves that function in a world that is one huge prison. You

---

32. Huger enrolled in Sarah Lawrence College.

ought to read it, not just for pleasure (and there sure as hell is that, on every page) but for instruction. He really knew how to do it. He's with Shakespeare.

Must be a fascinating business reading Mr Will's letters to Gerstle and seeing yourself from that angle and seeing him too, alive again as you read. I remember him often; specific incidental things—turning that green ring on his finger, an unlit Chesterfield in his mouth and leaning down to light a match by striking it in exactly the same place inside the fireplace. I sometimes speculate (impossibly) on whether he should have gotten the hell out of Greenville, which he was always saying he loved yet really hated—I mean deep down. Of course he wouldnt, couldnt, but I sometimes wish to hell he had: despite all I'd have lost and you and Roy and Phin would have lost. And my God, to think how much younger he was when he died than we are now! Incredible.

Biographical note (incredible too): Gwyn's and my 24th wedding anniversary was yesterday. I sure never did think I'd be sleeping with any fifty-year-old woman. . . . As for me, I'm teenage supple and sharp as a briar—especially being into that six-month period every summer and fall during which youre a year older than I am.

Gwyn just located that Panthea Broughton collection of pieces on your work.[33] I cant get at it until she finishes it, but I was pleased to see it has a study by Simone Vauthier in it. That's one sharp lady, by far the best critic Ive ever read on my own work, and I look forward to reading what she has to say about yours. That Texas couple (Sugg and White) who did the piece on my War Narrative in the Va Quarterly last spring are winding up a booklength study of my work for a volume in the Twayne series. I look forward to that, too—finding out what it all amounts to, you might say. A bunch of foolishness, really. The overpowering fact that comes crowding in on me is that I have well over two million words between covers. Staggering to contemplate; it's enough to make you want to get under a rug and hide from having perpetrated that huge an outrage on the world. I remember, away back in TOURNAMENT, I said that Bart, looking back on his life, had the feeling of somehow having managed to swallow a cannonball. I feel a little that way.

----

33. *The Art of Walker Percy: Stratagems of Being* (1979).

I'm still blocked and blocking on TWO GATES. The Goddamn thing is going to be so all-inclusive I'm terrified to really buckle down to it. My hope is to catch, to freeze in motion, the whole bloody Mississippi delta—as of 1948, with analeptic reaches back to 1868 and proleptic jumps to the 1960's. A real son of a bitch to tackle, and for the first time in my life I'm scared pissless at the prospect, not because I'm afraid I cant do it, but because I damned well know I can. It's going to be murder, everything working on three levels to bring a whole region and way of life to task for the evils woven into its fabric from the outset.

Did I tell you how much I enjoyed Toole's CONFEDERACY[34]? I did indeed, and Gwyn did even more. My main reaction (as I guess it was everyone's) was a deep regret that he didnt survive to push all that talent in the direction he was headed. If he'd ever have gotten all that hilarity under control he'd have done some wonderful work on down the years. Too bad.

I think it's great youre lying around not working. You have earned all the rest you think you need or will enjoy. Did it ever occur to you to try your hand at, say, three short novels or long stories tied together to make a book that makes three points? I think youd enjoy the form if you gave it a try, though I daresay you dont think so in contemplation.

Keep steady under all that deluge of good-fortune. Perhaps the most dangerous place on earth is just under the mouth of a horn of plenty.

Rgds, as ever:

Shelby

September 10, 1980

DEAR SHELBY:

The only thing to do with Two Gates is get going and let 'er rip. Where I'd be hung up in a book like that is the very beginning. I refer you to your own admiration of the beginning of Don Juan—or The Brothers Karamazov. Those work eminently. Frankly I never thought the opening of War and Peace worked—a monstrous bore in fact, cocktail party conversation!

I'm blocked too. What I want to do is a sequel to Message in Bottle

---

34. John Kennedy Toole's *A Confederacy of Dunces* (1980), which Percy had worked hard to bring to publication.

which is quite tentative, answers none or few of the questions posed in the first chapter.[35] Not that I can answer them now, but I can adumbrate the answers. It is a little ambitious. The title and subtitle are

NOVUM ORGANUM
or
    Glimmerings of the New Science,
    Especially that Branch of the Science which
    Pertains to the Self, to Your Self, and most
    Especially What to do with Yourself
    Since Most Likely You do not Presently Know,
    Since the Present-Day Science, the Old science
    Cannot tell You, has no Way of Knowing,
    Cannot in Fact Utter a single word about Yourself
    Considered as an Individual Self,
    Even Though It, the Old Science, can tell you a
    Great Deal about everything else.
or
    How to Explain Some Heretofore Unexplainable
    Things.

The plan of the book is simple. Three parts. First part, list some of the familiar oddities and anomalies of modern times, e.g., the rise of boredom and suicide amid the good life, the longing of people for UFOs and trivial magic, the eroticization of society, T.V. junkies, why people applaud frantically on the Carson show when their hometowns are mentioned, the frantic efforts of primatologists to teach chimps to talk, desire for bad news (doesn't everyone remember Pearl Harbor? why?), Darwin sitting alone at his fireside in Kent, a shrinking violet, and dismantling (as he saw it) Christendom.

These apparently disparate and disconnected little antinomies are related with a straight face and in a way that everybody recognizes.

Part II: a setting forth of the Novum Organum, which is semiotic theory (my Helen Keller triangle and tetrad).

---

35. The outline sketched by Percy is the plan for *Lost in the Cosmos: The Last Self-Help Book* (1983).

Shelby Foote and Walker Percy (front row, third and second from right respectively) at the 1989 meeting of the Fellowship of Southern Writers. *Courtesy of Fielding Freed/News Free Press.*

I can already see you making faces, but this part can be done without jargon and technicalities, in an understandable way.

Part III: The disparate left-overs and oddities are now reprised and like members of a ballet, array themselves gracefully and in perfect order along the model, like a quadrille.

As you can see, this is not an entirely serious book, and yet it is serious. What it is getting at is of course my old hobby-horse that science is extraordinarily stupid about people as people and the consequences of this stupidity (combined with an instinctual confidence in science) is going to do us all in if we don't do something about it.

Hence the Novum Organum.

What I like about it is that it gives me the chance to do something of moment and at the same time have a good time getting my own licks in and both offending people and getting them to laugh.

The problem of course is stylistic: the tone of the very first sentence and the look of the first page. The choice lies between being aphoristic (like Pascal and Wittgenstein) or play it dead cool and laid back like Machiavelli who gets his best effects through the coolness. Everything depends on the first roll of the dice. So far, craps.

I feel like a hyena circling a wounded rhino. There she sits, lying there, she's yours but how to get at her without losing your guts on that horn (ah, easy to do with this kind of book!), how to get through the rhino hide. She has a weak spot of course, it's a matter of finding it.

Well, you're nice to send Browne. How do you get to reading suchlike? I'd never do him. No, I don't remember ever reading him. Recall, while you were reading goodies like Urne Burial, I was doing quantitative gravimetric chemical analysis.

Though I am 64, it was only the other day that it happened: the clerk in the health-food store, said shyly: seniors get a discount, if it so happens — he trailed off. It does not so happen, I said indignantly and took my vitamins. You qualify. Seniors are 63 up.

Re Uncle Will: You're right. If he'd lit out after his parents died, or if, earlier, he'd been kept on at Sewanee, he might have been happier and lively — tho I hardly see him as hale. But the interesting question is: what would have happened to us. We'd have been brought up in good style in Athens. But would you and I have taken up with writing? I doubt it, but can't be sure. Can you date the onset of your bibliophilia before WAP? or before you noticed me writing In Somnium: In the Manner of Poe — a much under-rated poem.

Toole's book is in many ways a botch but is he ever loaded, you're right. And Burma Jones is the best black in US lit since Nigger Jim. No doubt about it.

Get on with Two Gates. Being blocked, I am convinced, means that you're blocking yourself which is a dirty trick to play on yourself since the one thing we need above all else is the perfect freedom to get hold of the beast, which is hard enough without grappling with yourself like Dr. Strangelove. Bob Giroux has nice low-keyed advice when I tell him that nothing I write seems good enough, therefore I back up and start over after a line or two: "Well now, why don't you just keep writing."

It is strange: I feel as though I were just starting out and had a good twenty years of writing whereupon something good will come to pass, when in truth I'll probably be rolling pills and nodding at the nurses long before. But I recall when you said you'd never make thirty-five.

All best,
Walker

3 Nov 80
DEAR WALKER

I figure it's Carter, by a squeaker. Without the debate & the last-minute hostage furore, he would have won handily; but even so, despite distractions, I cant believe the choice wont be seen as a simple one in the end.

Anyhow, I wanted to go on record. Right?

Shelby

April 30, 1981
DEAR SHELBY—

I thought you might like to see when you served as an usher for a distinguished crew.[36]

W.

11 May 81

My God, the memories youve stirred up—& the ghosts!

Mary Jane Carney, Alice Finlay, Fannye Joe Hirsch, Emmie L. Rusk, Dorothy Trout, Walterrine Price—not to mention Paul Signa & Charles Mulvihill:[37] where are they now, I'd like to know.

Mais où sont les neiges d'antan?

At any rate, come May 28 youre secure.[38]

Shelby

6/21/81
DEAR SHELBY—

Well, I don't see anything wrong with Dr. Fung's(!)(x) analysis of romantic love—right on the money. I mean how would you analyze it? All he leaves out is cunt.

———

36. Enclosed with a copy of Percy's high school commencement announcement, in which Foote is listed as an usher.

37. Names of members of the Greenville High School class of 1933.

38. Percy's sixty-fifth birthday.

You're looking very distinguished here amongst the Episcopal types—if slightly decadent.(y)

We're stuck here all summer moving into the cajun cottage.[39] So I'll be needing October at Gulf Shores. I intended to spend the 3 weeks lounging in the sailboat by day and reading the new translation of the reportedly worthwhile novel by M. Proust which until now, I understand, has not been adequately remembered.

Best—
Walker

(x) How could a Fung from Memphis State be wrong?

(y) I enjoyed sitting on the porch at Rebel's Rest and drinking with 2 bishops.

Nov 5, 1981

DEAR SHELBY—

Roy sent me the enclosed. Be grateful for two things—that you didn't end up at Mt. Avery and that Viennese Boiled Beef made it under the same cover as Salt Steak.

Played Bach's 2nd and 4th Sonatas today. Was frankly surprised to like it—not at all bored like in some Bach partitas.

Moving and arranging books. It's strenuous and fun. A working library for the first time.

Best
Walker

P.S. Tell Gwyn to get on with flossing.

11/21/81

DEAR SHELBY:

I'll probably do the same—after looking over your letters and letting you do the same—lend or give them to UNC. Right now, I may have run

---

39. The small house that Percy built on his property so that his daughter Ann's family could move into the large house.

into a snag with them. After getting all this junk out of the attic, it turns out that I have quite a collection of MSs, first draft of *Moviegoer*, early versions and so on. What I am asking them to do is to insure me against the loss or theft of the more valuable items. This will entail getting an appraisal. I don't know whether they will be willing to do this, but I don't think it unreasonable. Do you know what collections of papers of writers sell for, say, to places like the Huntington Library? Big bucks. Ideally, what I want to happen is to have a law restoring a tax write-off for such donations—give it all to UNC. But until such time, I want to be protected against some con artist who walks off with *Moviegoer*, sells it to Stuart Wright for a tidy sum. Won't have it. Sabres out! Thanks for "A View of History"—a pretty book.

My library looks good—surprisingly well-used and beat-up. (I think of all the books as new, remember buying them). Most valued: WAP's OED and Loeb classics. I'll get to Dante.

Hope you're forging ahead with *Two Gates*. I can't generate any enthusiasm for a novel just now, but you always had a narrative bent. Get it on the road.

All Best,

W

August 22, 1982

DEAR SHELBY—

Enjoying tape very much. You sound much more real than T.S. Eliot reading. Appomattox is a real good underwritten job—the best in fact. I seem to recall Freeman throbbing into emotion.

Have fun with the Governor.[40] He's a nice fellow and it's a good deal. But once in Bilbo's bed is enough for me.

See you on the Flyer,

Best,

Walker

---

40. Governor William Winter of Mississippi hosted an evening dinner in honor of Foote. Like Percy, who had been feted on a similar occasion, Foote spent the night in the governor's mansion in the bed of former governor Theodore G. Bilbo.

Oct. 10, 1982

SHELBY:

Have ordered the Anderson *Dante*. The Singleton 6. Vol. not in print, so I ordered Singleton one-vol Companion. Will let you know if I need the 6. No word yet from Amtrak.[41] Another week and we'll sue them.

Best

Walker

14 Oct 82

DEAR WALKER

Inclosed is a subject made to your hand—another of those absolute demonstrations of Kierkegaard's claim that anxiety is a response to freedom. Gwyn spotted it in the New Yorker, one of those that came while we were caroming around central California and Bunt was getting rocks in her eyes from picnicing in the open air.

I am delighted youve gone ahead with the Dante. You will like the Anderson book I think, very useful on the altogether necessary background material, biographical and literary, and a full summation of all the best Dante scholarship up to the present. I reckon by now youre well into the Purgatory, maybe even the Paradiso, and will agree that it gets far better as it goes along. I envy you your preparation,* which will open for you all those doors still shut for me except the chinks provided by footnotes. . . . I didnt understand, though, your saying the Singleton is out of print at Princeton. I dont think so. I have seen, however, that they are doing it in paperback, each of the 2-vol pairs in one volume. Inferno is already out, I believe, and maybe the Purgatorio; is the first of these the one you ordered? . . . In any case, let me know what you want from here, and I'll be glad to send it along.

Stay hot after those Amtrak people. I'm looking to you, as my travel

---

41. In September, the Percys and Footes had set out on a train trip from Chicago to San Francisco, but in Ogden, Utah, Amtrak workers went on strike at midnight, and passengers were told to board buses. Percy refused to leave the train until the next morning, when he and the rest of his party were taken to Salt Lake City, where they caught a plane to San Francisco. Percy was still waiting for his refund in October.

agent, to pin those goddam inconveniencers to the mat. We'll make Ogden the gold-spike town in more ways than one. Already I'm planning my retirement to Palm Beach on the proceeds. (Incidentally, we settled our silver suit against the insurance people. It turned out rather hefty and we are feeling financial as all getout.)**

Been having a great go at Montaigne—a result of my birthday present from Gwyn in S.F., the Nonesuch Florio translation. Here's a quote on the folly of sex, in particular on M's contempt for the swagger and bluster of his own penis: "Nature should have been pleased to make this age miserable, without making it also ridiculous. I hate to see one for an inch of wretched vigor, which inflames him but thrice a week, take on and swagger as fiercely as if he had some great and lawful day's work in his belly: a puff of winde: And admire his itching, so quick and nimble, all in a moment to be so lubberly squat and benummed. . . . Trust it not, though you see it second that indefatigable, full, constant and swelling heate that is in you: for truly it will leave you at the best, and when you shall most stand in neede of it."

I'll sign off with that. As who wouldnt?

Rgds:

Shelby

*Aquinas.
**Bought a Sony color TV.

Oct. 24, 1982

DEAR SHELBY—

Well, I got my refund for plane ticket from Amtrak. Sorry about yours. I can only suppose this must be the reason—quote from Mr. Sinclair's letter (Amtrak customer relations) to Journey House: "—and since Mr. S. Foote expressed willingness to avail himself of the alternative transportation, it seems appropriate to refund him bus fare accordingly."

Fly United.

Just back from a fruitless trip to Washington—invited to be on board of trustees of Gallaudet (college for deaf founded by Lincoln)—turned out to be all sign language—refused.

Walker

29 Oct 82

DEAR WALKER

I protest. Just because you went non-violent & took up the fetal position when confronted by authority, while I by contrast was scurrying around with our bags in the rain, bribing redcaps & gathering information from all over that end of Ogden, I see no valid reason why you should be more richly rewarded & (what is worse) be looked up to by the women as rather the hero of the occasion. It's true I was somewhat demoralized, but didnt that suit the occasion? I ask you that, & rest my case.

Shelby

4 Apr 83

DEAR WALKER

I congratulate you and modern medicine on the survival of the cosmic Carl.[42] That at least wont happen again; his appendix I presume is gone for good. It might be a good idea, though, to write and warn him to watch his diet, get the proper exercise, and in general observe a healthy regimen. No doubt he's doing this on his own, however, after the recent scare.

Last week I wound up sorting those letters, 1948–1981, a neat thirty-three years. The main theme, the thread that ran through their collective body was: Read Proust. Now in this first of a subsequent series (1983–19??) I repeat the injunction: Read Proust. . . . Incidentally, I was amazed to observe how didactic I was over the years—I dont see how you managed the grace to put up with it all that time. I'm putting you up for sainthood next time I'm alone with John Paul II.

Comes by this same mail a new cassette, one that fills a regrettable blank: Sibelius. On it are the Violin Concerto, maybe the last great piece of romantic music, and two symphonies, the Third and the Sixth, the least-played of the seven but both of them particular favorites of mine: especially the Third, which we used to play at 601, I believe in a Koussevitsky recording—I remember we thought some of it sounded as if the orchestra

---

42. Astronomer Carl Sagan, the object of considerable spoofing in Percy's *Lost in the Cosmos*.

was a gigantic guitar. It will be fun for you I think to get back in touch with him. He's really great, a much greater composer I am sure than R. Strauss ever dreamed of being. . . . I have it in mind to do you a Debussy one—not the usual shimmering stuff but a different Debussy, the one of those three sonatas he wrote at the end while dying of cancer. Theyre incredible.

No news. We're back home getting settled in, preliminary to heading back to Auburn to pick up Booker,[43] who is reported to be doing well indeed. Theyre rebuilding the other rear leg in an operation tomorrow, and in three weeks we're due to go back and pick him up. . . . The new Márquez, Chronicle of a Death Foretold, is by far the best thing he's done since 100 Years. Get and read it; youll enjoy it.

All best, all round, as ever:

Shelby

Friday: 27 May 83

DEAR WALKER

I want to tell you, first off, how much I like Cosmos. It makes clear—and mainly by demonstration, which as you know I much prefer in any choice between show and tell—a great deal of what you have been saying all along. What's more, it does this in high good humor; the savageness is always below the surface yet always present. All the same I truly enjoyed the last half of your "theoretical intermezzo," probably because it got down to writers at that point. . . . Enough of shop though.

Into this same mail goes a Debussy cassette—something Ive been meaning to send you for some time, mainly because of what youll find on Side One: the three sonatas which were the last three things he wrote. The first, for cello, is altogether the most interesting in all kinds of ways; the second, for flute, viola, and harp, is the most attractive and immediately appealing; the third, for violin, falls somewhat below the other two (he was dying when he wrote it) but still has wonderful things in it, especially the finale, which is a kind of fantasia. The central narrator in all three is the Fool—

---

43. Foote's Akita, which had undergone knee surgery.

Pantaloon. In the cello, for instance, he attempts a serenade in which he employs the cello as a guitar, a mandoline, even a tambourine. His feelings are deep, he suffers, but he is a fool and has no judgment; poor damned Harlequine. Give all three a series of good listenings, if youve never heard them before, and I think youll come to enjoy them as much as I do. Debussy is really something. . . . On the other side are three orchestral pieces, all good to hear if you havent heard them in a long time: Impressionism, much like what the painters were doing around that time.

I'm thriving, converted at last to a touch of exercise—a mile and a half a day in under thirty minutes. Ive had no trouble at all since Ive been home, and dont anticipate any. Incidentally, Ive lost eight pounds, watching my diet and doing the stipulated hikes. Thank God for my Walkman and all those cassettes I have been making for the past two or three years; I really step out when it's Mozart laying down the beat.

All best, with the book and whatever else looms.

Shelby

P.S. Jacket photo makes you resemble Foxy Granpa, which, come to think of it, you are.

June 25, 1983

DEAR SHELBY—

Herein: samples of Greenville now and then.[44] The knight feels toward Miss G about like me—Bad legs.

Please note in Pica who won poetry prize and how catty Alice Finlay was toward Margaret Kirk. Why I was chasing Margaret who was a nut instead of Alice who was something, I can't say—I hadn't realized how Don Wetherby dominated everything.

We're enjoying summer doing nothing by pool.

Best,

Walker

---

44. Photographs and other materials pertaining to Greenville High School class-mates and friends. The "knight" probably refers to the sculpture of the brooding medieval warrior in the Percy lot at the Greenville cemetery.

P.S. Can't find fault with your list of Michelet and Loclos,[45] but what about Freud's *Interpretation of Dreams*, a literary if not neccesarily a scientific masterpiece? Newton's *Principia* (after all, he dominated over 300 years of scientific thought), Aquinas's *Summa*? Kierkegaard's *Selected Works*? (You did include a scientist & philosopher, Lucretius.)

WP

---

45. Foote, for his own amusement, was drawing up a list of the ninety-nine all-time best books.

FIVE

Last Things

10 Aug 83

DEAR WALKER

Mozart's C Minor Mass goes into this same mail and should reach you at the same time. I envy you your early hearings of it, though the fact is I enjoy it more every time I hear it—hear all kinds of things I never heard before. I inclose the text: not because you arent thoroughly familiar with the Mass, but because this one is incomplete: the text is truncated to include only what is set to music, the Kyrie, the Gloria, and the Sanctus, all complete; the Credo only goes through the Et incarnatus est, and the Agnus Dei and Dona nobis pacem are missing altogether. . . . Youre likely to have some trouble with the late-18th Century notion of church music, but no more than you have with Bach and Handel, both of whom were influences, Handel in the Gloria and Bach in the Quoniam, where the counterpoint for three voices is damned near incredible. Some say that in the Qui tollis they can hear the whips and smell the vinegar; I dont go that far, but I sure do like it and feel its power. What may give you the most trouble (and what I like about the best) is the Incarnatus est, a soprano aria; she soars like a bird for nearly nine minutes, outdoing herself as she goes along.

Because there was room on the tape, I started off with Ave, verum corpus, a motet Mozart wrote when he had less than six months to live. It's less than four minutes long, but absolutely marvelous once you get to know it. The text for it is on the back of the first sheet of the Mass "libretto."

Hope you located Kate Stone.[1] She ought to come in handy for what you have in mind. I was greatly pleased to hear that you are furthering the adventures of Tom More;[2] Ive always considered him the character most like you—not autobiographically, but by nature—and it will be fun to reencounter him up there around St Francisville, stumbling upon old letters and journals and such. No telling what might happen. . . . Gwyn was so pleased with the notion that she sat down at once and read straight through the RUINS, laughing all the way.

Stay on the trail of that Santa Fe notion, including the Amtrack travel to get there. I think October is wonderful out there, a good time too to do a little roaming about that part of the country, even Taos and DHL's ashes site.

All best all round:
Shelby

Memphis 3 Mar 84
DEAR WALKER
I presume youre back from Chicago and your Mellon gathering. I like the notion of your picking up all those salutes. They become you, and no doubt add appreciably to sales, which in at least one sense is what work is all about. Gather rosebuds while ye may.

I like that, as I say, but the best news by far is that youve sailed into Proust. Despite the twenty-year gap when I was engaged almost exclusively with my War, 1954–74, I have read Things Past eight times from start to finish—six times before the War, twice afterward. In fact, whenever I feel I have earned it (completing a novel, say, or moving into a new house) I immediately reward myself by taking off six weeks and reading Proust again

---

1. Percy was looking for the diary of a nineteenth-century Louisiana woman named Kate Stone. The diary was published by the Louisiana State University Press as *Brokenburn: The Journal of Kate Stone, 1861–1868* (1972), edited by John Q. Anderson.

2. Tom More, protagonist of *Love in the Ruins*, reappears in what would be Percy's last novel, *The Thanatos Syndrome* (1987).

from start to finish, always with a heightened admiration and widened wonder at his talent and his skills in demonstrating it. In addition I have read at
least thirty books on Proust, biographies, critical studies in general, and individual studies of particular aspects of his work. None of them, it seems to
me, do any justice at all to his primary skill, which is his unalterable concern
with moving that *story* forward; he had it to a degree that matches Dickens'
and Dostoeysky's, which everybody recognizes (though not nearly enough
where Dostoevsky is concerned) but without seeing it in Proust. I guess by
now youre into the Budding Grove, so let me take my example from that—
the opening sixty pages, which I outline as follows: (pp.465–524)

1. Swann, Cottard: a contrast.
2. Berma—the Art theme.
3. Françoise's cooking skills.
4. Norpois's view of literature as a profession. (Yahoo.)
5. Swann-Odette—the marriage.
6. Norpois on Bergotte; Marcel's "few lines."
7. A social lesson: why Norpois would not mention him to Mme Swann.
8. Berma review—the critics.
9. Parents' view of Norpois and the Swanns.
10. Françoise and the Café Anglais.

To a superficial eye, he might seem to be letting his pencil take him wherever it will, depending on his charm to hold the reader. Nothing could be
farther from the truth. Even 10, a humorous fillip that winds up the 8–9
epilogue, has its place in the big design, though such things are hard to see
after a single reading; for who can keep a whole 3000-page novel in his
mind even after he has just finished it? Later, though, you come to see the
always-present pattern, the reemergence of themes and habits of behavior.
For instance, 2, 3, 4, 6, 8 broaden the Art theme, which will only find full
expression in the closing pages of the book, and are as much a part of the
"plot" as, say, 5—not to mention a host of idle remarks dropped along the
way, which later turn out to have enormous implications for Marcel and,
through Marcel, the reader. For these and other reasons it does what all the
great books do, and does it superbly: that is, enlarges life. Do for God's sake
stay with it to the finish. Dont be put off by any foolish notion that it seems
"loose" or undisciplined. It's altogether the tightest, best-constructed and most

disciplined novel I ever read. Youll think so too, if you stay with it, and most of all if youll reread it as soon as that first reading has had time to sink in.

All best,

Shelby

Memphis: 30 Aug 84

DEAR WALKER

These will repay any amount of attention you will give them—particularly the last movement (variations) of that last one, Op. 111. Youve heard them before, plenty I'm sure, but getting all the way into them is something else indeed. Crank up your machine.

I'm reading a book that would absolutely fascinate you, unless that is youve already read it—Sartre's last work: THE FAMILY IDIOT, FLAUBERT 1821–57. It's volume I of two, and there's a companion handbook by a woman named Hazel E. Barnes. What he does is he takes Flaubert as a framework for a study of Art and Man, all-out, with emphasis on language—what it *is* and how we *absorb* it. . . . If somehow youve given it the go-by, thinking it is random criticism or something he wrote because he couldnt stop writing even while dying, take a look at it. You may be, as I am, amazed—though certainly not as much, because you know I'm not much for abstract things in general.

Anyhow, enjoy the Sonatas.

Rgds to Bunt, as ever:

Shelby

I'm due at Ochsner in late Sep. or early Oct.—annual treadmill stint. You going to be at home then? I'll be calling you when things get more definite.

15 Feb 85

DEAR WALKER

This[3] is the kind of thing that makes you despair of education, especially the Southern variety, & makes you know too why Quentin Compson

---

3. The following letter.

protests so loudly, "I dont hate it! I dont hate it!"[4] Incidentally, what's a media specialist anyhow?

Looks like we're going to miss connection on the Paris trip. You & Bunt are tied up for April & Gwyn is going out to visit her son Johnny in California in mid May. Too bad.

Speaking of music (as we were on the phone the other day), go back to that Mozart D Major String Quintet, K.593. Ive heard it more than a hundred times in the past twenty-five years, & it gets absolutely more wonderful every single time.

Regards to Bunt, & take care.

Shelby

January 8, 1985

Random House, Inc.
201 E. 50th Street
New York, N.Y. 10022

DEAR SIRS:

We would like to point out a concern that we have about the book, *The Civil War* by Shelby Foote, published by Random House. Why is there no mention about the Battle of Gettysburg in this book? Enclosed is a copy of a page from an encyclopedia stating that this was the greatest battle ever fought on the American continent. We find the absence of even the mention of this information rather shocking. Can you enlighten us as to the reason for this omission?

Thank you for any information you can give us regarding this book.

Sincerely,

Mary Mann

Media Specialist

MM/ph

Enclosure

---

4. From William Faulkner's *Absalom, Absalom!*

4 Mar 85

DEAR WALKER

Back from Vail? Hope you had sense enough to stay off those slopes.

Blood Meridian, Cormac McCarthy's new novel, is unrelenting violence from start to finish—Peckenpaugh raised to the N*th*—& has some of the best writing Ive read for decades. Youre likely to despise it, but I urge you to give it a try. The 1850 wild & wooly West, with a killer-protagonist five years younger than Billy the Kid when Garrett cut him down. Wild existentialism, American-style.

Shelby

Vol. I of Civ War just went into 15th printing; Vol. II, 12th; Vol. III, 8th. Not bad I say.

Sat: 23 Mar 85

DEAR WALKER

We're just back from New York—the last of several 20th Century Fund confabulations. I enjoyed them; always enjoy NY anyhow; but am glad theyre finally over and I can revert to my stay-at-home persona, not to mention a rest for my pocketbook, which suffered considerable strain beyond the allowable expenses. We'd go up for two days and stay five, eating our heads off in incredibly expensive bistros. You only go round once, they say, but at that rate I wont make it even once—plateloads of practically undiluted chloresterol. Back to Lean Cuisine!

I got home there was a note from the U. Press of Miss. thanking me for the blurb I sent them after reading your *Conversations* in page proof. Seetha Srinivason (!) pronounced it "fine," and added (rather ominously I thought) that they "plan to use it with few, if any, changes." I'll bill you later for this service, but I warn you now that I come rather high for out-of-hours work such as this. The fact that you once did one for me, free, has nothing do with my practices in this regard. The law of diminishing utility obtains in reverse; the fewer I do, the more I charge for each; and I do about one a decade, tops.

Despite the above stay-at-home resolution, we're even now tuning up for the three-week Paris visit; leaving April 20 and returning May 11. It's a blooming outrage that you and Bunt arent coming along. We'd have a great time in the City of Light, especially with Hugs[5] as cicerone; he knows all the cheap low places; what's more I have great connections with the Institut d'Anglais of the Université Paris, which when combined with meetings with French editors and translators makes the whole damned thing deductible—I think. Gwyn answers the phone and puts receipts in her pocketbook, and I claim that makes her deductible too, as a hardworking secretary, something no writer should be without, not to mention certain other invaluable services which are equally indispensable. . . . We are staying, as before, at the Hotel Pont Royal, a wonderful location on the left bank, with all kinds of activity going on around it and Gallimard only half a block away. Change your mind and I'll book you a room overlooking the Rue du Bac.

Keep flossing.

Shelby

23 Apr 85

DEAR WALKER

I'm not sure I approve of all these West-European carryings-on, but the city itself presents occasional vistas not unlike some in my beloved Petersburg, which I badly miss while resting between spurts of work on my novel; *L'Idiot* I'll call it.

Homesickly,

Fyodor D.

20 May 85

DEAR WALKER

After talking with you just now, I looked up "corgi"[6] in the dictionary, & found the definition rather startling. It's derived from the Welsh words:

---

5. Foote's son, Huger, lived and worked in Paris for two years after finishing college.

6. Percy had recently acquired a corgi named Sweet Thang.

COR, meaning "dwarf," & GI, meaning "dog." So it turns out youve got yourself a dwarfdog. Goodness—

All best, anyhow.

Shelby

Sunday 15 Dec 85

DEAR WALKER

Thanks for the NYTimes clipping. Yes, theyre coming round by ones and twos; presently theyll come around by handfuls, and when I'm gone just watch them flock. I tell you it's no small sport to have written something as great and as lasting as that (great I might be wrong about; lasting I'm certain of) and to watch it go unrecognized for what it truly is. Historians wont read it because it lacks footnotes, and liberal arts professors wont read it because it's history; I fall between two stools and mainly find my following composed of "buffs," a sorry lot who know little or nothing of either history or literature. Yet any one in either camp could pick up any one of the three volumes, open it at random, and read any two consecutive pages; he'd know right then what he'd got hold of. Yet he wont do that till enough random eggheads have preached its gospel; then he'll look into it and he'll know. By that time I'll be safe in paradise, or anyhow up among the stars like Chaucer's Troilus:

And down from thennes faste he gan avise
This litel spot of erthe that with the see
Embraced is, and fully gan despise
This wrecched world, and held al vanite
To respect of the pleyne felicite
That is in heavene above. And at the laste
Ther he was slayn his loking down he caste,
And in himself he lough right at the wo
Of hem that wepen for his deth so faste,
And dampned al our werk, that folwen so
The blinde lust the whiche that may not laste,
And sholden al our herte on hevene caste.

My clipped and rejoined colon is mending fast; I'm back to my two-mile walks in all but the bitterest weather. I'm especially enjoying the regaining of six or seven of the ten pounds I lost at Ochsner; eat anything I want, including Snickers and Baby Ruths, not to mention spaghetti with meat sauce, strip sirloins, and lemon pie. . . . I have found an excellent urologist here, Mark S. Soloway, who has done a blood test ("perfectly normal") and a transrectal ultrasound, which "indicates that the prostatic tumor is confined to the prostate itself." All this, combined with the Ochsner negative finds in the lymph node examination, indicates that either external beam radiation or prostatectomy (both of which may have side effects that differ from person to person) will let me live out my normal span, at any rate until something comes along that they dont have a cure for. By that time I'll be glad to hit the road to glory anyhow.

The Trappist cheeses arrived in good condition. Thank Bunt. Theyll come in extrahandy because this year is our turn to feed the family. For the past two Christmases, one (Gwyn) or both of us has or have been in Paris. Not this year though; we're too poor. I count that a sort of blessing, since I dont like transatlantic flying anyhow, though I sure as hell do like Paris once I get there. The City of Light.

Been reading Burckhardt. He says Luther saved the Papacy in Italy by uniting it against his Reformation. Good reading (The Civilization of the Renaissance in Italy) but not up to Parkman, whom I urged on you before. Get around to him—youll like it.

All best, all round:
Shelby

28 Feb 86

WALKER—

Here's the old man[7] peeling off: 48 years married, & couldnt face 49. . . . Lack of character, no doubt.

—Shelby

(STRONG RESEMBLANCE TO SOMEONE I KNOW, EXCEPT HIS BEARD AND CLOTHES.)

———

7. The photograph on the opposite side of this postcard shows Ivan Tolstoy setting off with his rucksack, having renounced the world and embraced "the simple life."

14 Apr 86

DEAR WALKER

Thanks for clipping of our coevals, but what happened to Frank Sinatra? He and I are not only the same age, we have maintained exactly the same weight on down the years; only difference was I kept my hair and didnt get to marry Ava Gardner. Alas. I refer of course to the loss of Ava, not my hair, which, unlike you, I still have in abundance.

As for Judy Canova, she was your girl, not mine. My girl—the subject of my lust, that is—was Betty Boop: not Helen Kane, the voice behind, but Betty Boop herself, the cartoon character with spitcurls and a head that was wider than her shoulders. I did in fact have a momentary conniption over Alice Faye, but that applied only to one scene in one picture and was therefore barely fleeting—not at all the steady unrelenting thing I felt for my handdrawn Betty. Your Judy wasnt even in the same league; her head, for example, wasnt nearly as wide as her shoulders; but her ass sure was, if I remember correctly. You ought to be ashamed of yourself. After all, youd committed yourself to Merle Oberon, and then, the minute her back was turned, you switched to that country clodhopper. No wonder, though: Merle always had too much class for you, and I strongly suspect you knew from the start you never really had a chance with her, especially when you learned that Sir Michael Korda had joined the pack. And that's another advantage to my choice: no one I ever knew or heard of had any real deepdown use for Betty Boop, a paper doll I could truly call my own.

I'm still limping round on my trucked-over foot, a full month after the encounter. Doctor tells me the only treatment is to keep it elevated so that the bad blood will run down out of it. My prayers are all to Gravity. . . . It should be in decent shape within another month—including the wear and tear of slogging around the Vicksburg lines in June if that's agreeable all round. I have to be here on June 22; otherwise I'm uncommitted. Check with your friends and let me know what dates are convenient and we'll start planning. . . . The Burns[8] brothers (Huey Long) will be here this week and Ive promised to ride over to Shiloh with them and do my "talking head" bit for their cameraman. I dont much go for that stuff but in this case they persuaded me with money, a powerful persuader indeed in my current financial state, especially with the house in bad need of painting and Hugs trying to make it in New York with apartment rent being what it is up there.

News came in about that Strawberry Festival rundown they staged in Ponchatoula. I was hoping you didnt attend, and apparently you didnt. Otherwise that old gal would surely have got you on the run if not the sit.

Best to Bunt. Regards all round in fact:
Shelby

April 29, 1986
DEAR SHELBY—
Yall are booked into Anchuca[9] June 13 and 14. As maestro I guess you're assigned to the master bedroom—we the slave quarters. We don't have to make the Candelite tour or July party.

If you can't make this, lemme know.

Enclosed is bookmark I found in Vicksburg section—It must have been around Sept. '63.

Do you think Joe Johnson was right or wrong in holding off?
WP

Sept 20, 1986
DEAR SHELBY—
I deeply appreciate your taking time with that peculiar novel[10]—and pinpointing what's wrong. Well, you're right. Every time Fr. Smith opens his mouth he, I, is in trouble. What I do is cut, cut, cut. Thanks to you, I'll

---

8. Ken Burns, director of the PBS documentary *The Civil War*, and his brother Rick.

9. The Anchuca Inn in Vicksburg, Mississippi.

10. *The Thanatos Syndrome* (1987).

probably cut him again. You can't get away with a Fr. Zossima these days and probably shouldn't.

My larger concern was with the tone and coherence of the book. Okay, I gather from you and Gwyn that the humor and irony comes across. But I worried about the heaviness of the idea—the warning about the Nazi and the pre-Nazi "humanist" scientists. Since you did not object too much to Fr. S's "confessions," I reckon you didn't mind. Some folks will.

About Thanksgiving 1996: what happened was that the fundamentalists objected to the secular humanism of Thursday. ∴ Sunday.[11] See?

Re the MacArthur folks: I don't pretend to know what they're up to.

The last MacD award I heard about was to the magician Randi who goes around exposing frauds like Vic Geller and so-called faith-healers. Don't ask me—all I say is, if it comes through, let's go to Firenze and Venezia for a year. We know a small hotel off the Grand Canal.

Thanks again for reading MS. I'll send you a bound galley—throw out that typescript.

Best,

Walker

P.S. Bunt says she's keeping your letter about that 56 yr old woman to show to Gwyn after we pass—and she's 65 year old—and she probably will—

W

Memphis 24 Sep 86

DEAR WALKER

I see now why you had Tom More call Fr Smith's confession an "incoherent tirade." You were heading off the critics by beating them to the punch, using words you figured theyd use when they sat down to do their thing on you and your book. Jesus, man, those cats got little or nothing to do with anything whatever, as you well know and in fact must have known since you read your first reviews all those 25 years ago. Apparently the rancid meat in this particular coconut was the good father's youthful admira-

---

11. The fundamentalists in the novel have moved Thanksgiving Day from Thursday to Sunday.

tion of the brownshirt Blut-und-Ehre boys. But after all, why not? And why not follow through with the later application? Everything depends on where in time you take the judgment seat. Even today, long after the dust has settled and all is known, I never hesitate to tell anyone, Jew or Gentile, that some of the bravest men I know of, in all the annals of war, were the Germans at Stalingrad—fighting in 30-below-zero cold, wearing scraps of women's dresses and whatever rags they could lay hands on. By that time they all disliked Hitler as much as anyone did on our side, but that was really beside the point. They were fighting for unit pride and they fought as long as they could lift their rifles to their shoulders—like the Confederates on the road to Appomattox, who incidentally were said by their chief adversary to be fighting in defense of slavery. . . . I say you should write what you want to write, about anyone anywhere. Besides, it's not you talking, or even Dr Tom; it's Father Smith. And as for the later application—that dreadful things can come from do-gooding singleness of purpose—who's going to argue with that? True Believers have ever been the source of dreadful things—including a host of your Popes and thousands of their followers. . . . When I asked why TM labeled the confession a tirade, I was honestly puzzled. I saw nothing tiradish about it; it never crossed my mind that the confession said anything objectionable whatever—just that it was a very important segment of the novel, maybe even its keystone. Not that I dont think the preceding speech, the account of the daydream, needs rewriting; I do indeed, but only for stylistic reasons.

I'm clear at last about the Thanksgiving Sunday. Great. I just wish I'd understood it as it stood, and I wish too that there were a good many other such things in the book, satirical things that helped so much to liven RUINS.

By the way, this typescript has no Part III, but since Part IV is twice as long as the other two and the epilog, I assume it will be broken in two. I look forward to the galleys, which will show how it's shaken down. . . . I dont envy you your custom of rewriting. It's a nightmare. I can never cut anything; every place I try to cut anything of mine, it bleeds. Adding is if anything even worse—except commas and maybe semicolons. (Incidentally, I feel like sending you a packet or two of commas. Theyd come in handy in a place or two.)

No news from here. I'm expecting author's copies of my softback *War* any day now. Next time I write Random I'll tell them to send you a set by way of thanks for the Iliad blurb. It's the least they could do. You can pass it on to Bunt for sale at the Kumquat, half-off. Damned thing is going to cost $15.95 a volume, $50 boxed—which means theyre charging $2.15 for the goddam cardboard box. An outrage. Pretty soon there wont be anyone buying books for the simple reason that no one will be able to afford them except a few Rockefellers.

Lace up your Nickeys and strap on your Parkman,[12] and keep flossing.

As ever,

Shelby

11/24/86

SHELBY—

Reverse is copy of a letter passed to me by a worker in R.R.'s 1984 campaign.

W

THE WHITE HOUSE

WASHINGTON

June 17, 1984

Mr. John Hinckley
St. Elizabeth's Hospital
Washington, D.C. 20069

DEAR JOHN:

Nancy and I hope you are making good progress in your recovery from the mental problems that made you try to assassinate me. The staff of St. Elizabeth's tell me you are doing just fine and will be released soon.

I have decided to seek a second term in office and I hope I can count on your support and the support of your fine parents in my re-election campaign.

---

12. Foote here uses Bunt Percy's favorite malapropism for Nikes and Walkman.

I hold no grudge against you, John, and I do hope that if there is anything you need there at the hospital, you will let Nancy and me know.

By the way, did you know that Walter Mondale, Gary Hart and Jesse Jackson have been fucking Jodie Foster?

Sincerely,

Ronald Reagan

RR/sdj

Feb 28, 1987

DEAR SHELBY—

Thanks for the preface to the new *Tournament*. It is fun to read—brought back a lot of memories. Like I remember when you got the check from SatEvePost. I was living in the garage with Lige[13] and you came in waving the check. What I didn't remember was that *Tournament* was not published till 1949. I'm looking at it, inscribed to me and Bunt "near Covington, September 1949—with the quatrain from the *Rubayat*: "They say the Lion and the Lizard [?] keep." I've been reading into it. Bart blowing head off that poor tenant farmer and wondering if it was right: *You don't know. And never will know. Never.* Bart was quite a man. And I believe you when you say it was there you defined my ground and set my sights.

I am doing something in April I never thought I'd do: hawk a book, go to bookstore, read, act nice, sign. And I don't know why except Roger Straus twisted my arm. I feel like Bart: is this right?

Otherwise, all well. I'm heading out now with Jack & David,[14] 8 & 9, to watch the local Mardi Gras parade roll down Covington's main street.

How're your arteries? Mine are fine, except my memory is worse than Reagan's. People's names? Forget it.

Best—

Walker

---

13. Elijah Collier, who had worked for Walker's father in Birmingham and, later, for William Alexander Percy in Greenville.

14. Percy's grandsons, the sons of Ann Boyd Percy Moores and her husband, John Moores.

August 4, 1987

DEAR SHELBY:

I thought you might want to see the present state of a superb edifice. If anything, improved with age.[15]

We walked down to the brink with Capt. Kline[16]—strangely enough it was his last day at Brinkwood. I seemed to recall an inscription. Nothing visible. We began brushing away the dirt of the doorstep and here it is: more unmistakable than in the photo: July 4, 1938.

Capt. Kline reported that Alice Hodgson claimed to have taken part in the building. I don't recall. What I recall is you and John Greene giving me a hand.

Sorry we didn't get to see you in Memphis. Give best to Huger. Nancy Lemann tells me she is going to see him shortly in NYC.

You might tell me something if you can. Is either of Faulkner's brothers, John and Murry alive? and if so where? Olivier Provosty here has a friend who was in WW II with one of them and wants to make touch.

All best,

Walker

Memphis 8 Aug 87

DEAR WALKER

Thanks for the Brinkwood photos. My God, my God: fifty years come next July 4. We ought to meet there for a decent observance—rededicate ourselves and perhaps construct an annex, dependent, that is, on at least one of Johnny Greene's two boys' survival. They did the work; you and I were at best stone-carters and hander-uppers. One major job you handled yourself, and that was the green-staining of the shingle roof; I remember you had green hands for the next ten days and green under your fingernails for a month. Alas, however, when I was there last all signs of the stain were

---

15. A stone "tea house" that Percy, Foote, and a handyman named John Greene had built on Uncle Will's property, Brinkwood, in Sewanee, Tennessee.

16. Captain Kline was a subsequent owner of Brinkwood, and Alice Hodgson, the daughter of a professor at the University of the South, was one of Percy's Sewanee friends in the late 1930s.

gone. The hardest job we had was lugging that damned couch down from the house; it weighed a ton and the man at the rear (me) had to endure the pain of banging the sharp edge of its bottom against his insteps. Fortunately, I cant remember lugging it back up the path*—that must have been a nightmare. . . . In any case, if we meet for the fiftieth anniversary, I suggest we toast it with Two Naturals—knocking it back Russian-style past our taste buds to avoid cauterization.

You did right to avoid Memphis last weekend, as you no doubt found when you stopped at Exit 18. St Jude golf tournament, the Rameses exhibit, Xiu-Oua the panda, and the tenth gathering of Elvis fans to commemorate his passing: all that's too much for one city to absord. I havent been out of the house since all those things began coming together, and neither have most other natives.

No news from this direction except the heat, which is hardly news at all. Every year we say there's never been such a summer before. Then in mid or late August, when the cool spell comes, we always say we've never experienced *that* phenomenon before.

Did you ever read that Floating Island chapter from *Gulliver's Travels?* I have another suggestion which you probably wont take either: Euripides' *The Bacchae.* He's my least favorite of the big three Greek dramatists, but this one is something else. It ties right in with the current evangelical craze, with a strong tilt toward the Dionysians. Really something. Here's a quote —nothing to do with the subject, just something I like:

"What is wisdom? What gift of the gods
is held in honor like this:
to hold your hand victorious
over the heads of those you hate?
Honor is precious forever."

That's the Arrowsmith translation, in the Chicago Press edition. I think you would be interested. Young man has his head cut off by his mother when he goes out to investigate the carryings-on; she comes home carrying it and singing a joyous song—"Look what *I* got!"

Incidentally, Mr Will should get full architectural credit for the teahouse. It was he, you remember, who had the front and side walls lowered so you can see out while sitting down, lowered it about one foot I think, much to the improvement of our design.

Regards to you and all your ladies:

Shelby

*Fact is, I think we left it down there; just brought the leather cushion back up to the house.

Oct 9, 1988

DEAR SHELBY—

Many thanks for the Gordon biography.[17] I've been skipping around in it. Poor Caroline—she had a very hard time. But she was a very dear person—took a lot more time with me than I would. I was glad to see at the very end she received the Eucharist and apparently died in peace.

I can't imagine why all those writers behaved so strangely. Ain't you glad we are normal?

Just finished baby-sitting Jack & David for a week-end while Ann & John went to N.C. Pooped.

Best,

Walker

Dec 24, 1988

DEAR SHELBY—

Here's a Xmas greeting from a Yankee friend in Winchester—Phil Sherridan beating up on Jubal Early to save the Union.

Been reading Chekhov again, I don't particularly care for the plays, but I do believe he has no equal in the short story. Here's old Grigory Petrovich in "In the Ravine":

—and the old man got into the racing droshky, pulling his big cap down to his ears; and, looking at him, no one would have said he was fifty-six.

---

17. *Close Connections: Caroline Gordon and the Southern Renaissance* (1987), by Ann Waldron.

. . . . he hated the peasants and disdained them, and if he saw some peasants waiting at the gate, he would shout angrily:

"Why are you standing there? Move on."

or if it were a beggar, he would cry: "God will provide!"

Now that's hard to top. I don't know how it can be so pitiful and funny. I
have to laugh out loud.

Be glad when holidays are over. Have a merry—

Walker

27 Dec 88

DEAR WALKER

There went Christmas; good riddance. We took our turn at having the
family over—some thirty-odd of them. Smoked turkey and country ham,
plus lots of fixings. Nice, in its way, but too much sugar for a dime.

Thanks for your Yankee friend's postcard of Little Phil arriving at a gal-
lop aboard Rienzi to put the whomp on Jube Early. My dislike of Phil
Sheridan grew stronger with every passing year of writing about him.
Stumpy little fellow, hated southerners and went around banging his right
fist into the palm of his left hand, all the time saying, "Smash 'em up!
Smash 'em up!" I kept hoping somebody would smash *him* up, but no one
did—in the East, that is; at Chickamauga he ran like a scalded dog, all the
way to Chattanooga.

Chekhov. My God, my God, what a writer! How he does it is a mystery
you cant solve by analyzing it—he just does it; does it out of being
Chekhov. You can say of other great writers, even Tolstoy and Dostoevky,
that if they hadnt come along, someone else would have filled their places.
Not him; he landed running and never looked back, a highly individual
man with his own particular fond absurdity that enabled him to see it in
others when he wrote about them. . . . There's a long story he wrote in '96
called "My Life," the longest I think of all his prose pieces except *The
Shooting Party*. He wrote it in reaction to his one-time admiration for the
Tolstoyan "simple life" and the dignity of manual labor. It's one of his few
first-person things and the narrator is a hippie eighty years before there ever
was one around to clutter up the horizon. It's an amazing performance. He
does as thorough a job on the intelligencia as he did elsewhere ("Peasants,"

"In the Ravine") on the working class and peasants. I have a good translation of it here that I can lend you if you cant find it there. Let me know—a paperback published by Norton, *Chekhov: Seven Short Novels*. Get the Cumquat[18] to stock it anyhow. . . . Also bear in mind, if you havent read it yet, that late story called "The Bishop." He was researching dying while he wrote it; that is, he was dying himself, and Lord, Lord, what a job he did. It takes the mystery out of dying, makes it almost an ordinary occurrence, and in the course of doing it, makes dying more of a mystery than ever. It's truly a beautiful thing, from start to finish.

Gwyn was delighted with her sweatered cat. . . . Tell Bunt she fairly jumped with joy.

Rgds, as ever:

Shelby

5/26/89

What's this about a model airplane in your study? Nothing against your models, but is it the Sopwith Camel I gave you?

WP

June 8, 1989

DEAR SHELBY—

Not such good news here. I've been having some abdominal and back pain for past few weeks. Thought it was my periodic diverticulitis. Went to hospital last week for exam. Colon was normal, but there were masses around the aorta and along spine. Don't yet know what it is, but presumably it's metastases from prostate carncinoma[19] or pancreatic CA. Will keep you informed. Due for bone scan and more endoscopy next few days.

Best

Walker

---

18. The Kumquat, Ann Percy Moores's bookstore in Covington, Louisiana.

19. Percy had undergone an operation for prostate cancer on March 10, 1988, but the cancer had already metastasized to surrounding tissue and lymph nodes. Despite various follow-up treatments, the cancer continued to spread.

June 12, 1989

DEAR SHELBY:

Thanks for "The Bishop." It's all you say. Nothing short of miraculous.

Father Sisoi is the best: It was hard to tell from what he said where his home was, whether there was anything or anyone he loved, whether he believed in God. He did not know himself why he had become a monk, but he had never thought about it. . . .

The Bishop is in poor shape, dying in fact.

"What sort of bishop am I?" the Bishop went on in a very faint voice. (Father Sisoi is the only one he can talk to.) "I should have been a village priest or a deacon or just a simple monk. All this is choking me—choking me . . ."

"What? Oh. Lord Jesus Christ! There, go to sleep now, Your Eminence. What's up with you? What's it all about, eh? Well, good night!"

This isn't bad, is it? What's so good about it is that it doesn't matter in the least that Chekhov was, apparently, an unbeliever.

Best,

W

Sat July 29/89

DEAR SHELBY—

No, we're headed for Mayo's tomorrow—on the strength of a new drug combo (something called interferon and 5FU) said to be promising in some cancers.

The worst thing is the travelling and hospitals. Flying around the U.S. is awful and hospitals are no place for anyone, let alone a sick man.

I'll tell you what I've discovered. Dying, if that's what it comes to, is no big thing since I'm ready for it, and prepared for it by the Catholic faith which I believe. What is a pain is not even the pain but the nuisance. It is a tremendous bother (and expense) to everyone. Worst of all is the indignity. Who wants to go to pot before strangers, be an object of head-shaking for friends, a lot of trouble to kin? I know the answer to this of course: false pride—who are you to be too proud to go the way of all flesh—or as you would write on the chart at Bellevue: "—the patient went rapidly downhill and made his exitus."

Seriously, and now that I think of it, in this age of unbelief I am astounded at how few people facing certain indignity in chronic illness make an end to it. Few if any. I am not permitted to.

Like I say, it's too damn much trouble, the running around looking for a cure. I'm content to sit here and try to finish *Contra Gentiles*, a somewhat smart-ass collection of occasional pieces, including one which should interest you—"Three New Signs, all more important than and different from the 59,018 Signs of Charles Sanders Peirce."[20] You want a copy?

Will inform you of the efficacy of the newest drug.

Best—

Walker

8/18/89

DEAR SHELBY—

Surely you jest. Is you lost in the bush boy, indeed. Agenbite of inwit, yes. Shem, yes. I must assume that you are asking, however indirectly, for my three new signs, which, believe it or not, was not included in CSP's 59,018 signs. It only remains to know whether you want the long or short version.[21]

—WP

Editor's note: On October 24, 1990, at St. Ignatius Church in New York City, more than 1,200 people came to hear seven of Percy's friends commemorate the man whose absence was felt, as Wilfred Sheed put it, "like a cold draft." Shelby Foote spoke next to last, delivering what he considered his last letter to his best and oldest friend:

---

20. Charles Sanders Peirce, the Harvard philosopher who is often credited with being the father of semiotics, the study of signs.

21. Percy was alluding again to his last work-in-progress, *Contra Gentiles*, in which he planned to return to the mystery of human language from a more overtly religious perspective. He never completed the book. Percy died in his home, surrounded by family and friends, on May 10, 1990. Shelby Foote was present, having driven down from Memphis with his wife Gwyn on May 3. Of those last days, Foote noted in his diary: "Sad time, but good time, too."

The English essayist E. H. Carr said at the close of his early-thirties critical biography of Dostoyevsky: "A hundred years hence, when Dostoyevsky's psychology will seem as much of a historical curiosity as his theology seems to us now, the true proportions of his work will emerge; and posterity, removed from the controversies of the early twentieth century, will once more be able to regard it as an artistic whole."

Similarly, I would state my hope that Walker Percy will be seen in time for what he was in simple and solemn fact—a novelist, not merely an explicator of various philosophers and divines, existentialist or otherwise. He was no more indebted to them or even influenced by them, than was Proust, say, to or by Schopenhauer and Bergson. Proust absorbed them, and so did Walker absorb his preceptors. Like Flannery O'Connor, he found William Faulkner what Henry James called Maupassant, "a lion in the path." He solved his leonine problem much as Dante did on the outskirts of hell: he took a different path, around him. Their subject, his and Faulkner's—and all the rest of ours, for that matter—was the same: "the human heart in conflict with itself."

Index

SF = Shelby Foote
WP = Walker Percy

Aeschylus, 62, 103, 107, 248
"American War, The" (WP), 113n
"Antinomy of the Scientific Method,
    The" (WP), 161
Arms You Bear, The (SF), 23, 24, 43.
    See also Love in a Dry Season

Barth, John, 208, 262
Beethoven, Ludwig van, 96, 225,
    252–53, 259
Bergin, Thomas G., 214; Divine Com-
    edy translation, 171, 190, 208–9;
    Dante, 171, 209, 210, 211–12
Browning, Robert, 46, 52, 136, 143,
    161, 216, 218–19, 239, 243, 264

Camus, Albert, 153; The Fall, 239
Capote, Truman, 234
Céline, Louis Ferdinand, 214, 238
Cerf, Bennett, 98n, 118
Cézanne, Paul, 235–36
Chambrun, Jacques, 14, 15
Charterhouse, The (WP; unpublished),
    7, 31–33, 36–37, 80n, 95n
Chaucer, Geoffrey, 216, 264, 288
Chekov, Anton, 222, 299–301, 302
"Child by Fever" (SF), 12, 14, 16, 17,
    24; content and writing of, 16, 17,
    21–22

Christ, 44–45, 82, 197
Civil War, The: A Narrative (SF), 1,
    220, 248, 285; content and writing
    of, 98n, 99, 100, 101, 107, 109, 110,
    111, 114–15, 122, 136, 139, 146,
    151, 157, 163–64, 166, 169–70,
    172, 174, 176, 177, 183, 184; publi-
    cation of, 125, 188, 190, 194, 198,
    295; WP's reaction to, 187, 188,
    190, 193, 194, 207; reception of,
    193, 194, 195, 199, 200, 201, 202,
    204, 214, 218, 226, 256, 286, 288;
    in competition book prizes, 203,
    204, 205, 210
Coindreau, Maurice Edgar, 174, 219,
    237, 244
Coles, Robert, 170, 171, 173, 193,
    247, 249–50, 251–52; Walker
    Percy: An American Search, 173,
    245, 249, 251–52
Collier, Elijah, 126n, 296
Conrad, Joseph, 32, 145
Contra Gentiles (WP; unfinished), 303
Crane, Stephen, 72; The Red Badge of
    Courage, 103

Daniel, Robert, 62, 108, 260
Dante, 133, 248; Divine Comedy, 61,
    105, 171, 208–9, 211–12, 213–14,

Dante, *(continued)*
275; SF recommends to WP, 171,
172, 189–90, 207, 208–9, 211–12,
213–14, 215, 216; SF praises, 171,
189–90, 207, 209–10, 211,
213–14; WP intends to read, 191,
208, 212–13, 274, 275
Darwin, Charles, 269
Da Vinci, Leonardo, 236
Davis, Jefferson, 107, 109, 111, 149,
164, 187, 188, 208, 243; at end of
war, 166, 174, 183, 189, 190
Debussy, Claude, 278–79
Descartes, René, 238
Dickens, Charles, 32, 35, 139, 140,
158, 266; SF prasises, 143, 145, 206,
267; *Bleak House*, 145, 158, 160,
212, 266; SF recommends to WP,
145–46, 158, 266–67; *Our Mutual
Friend*, 145–46, 266; *Dombey and
Son*, 158; WP bogs down reading,
160, 212; *Little Dorrit*, 266
Dostoyevsky, Fyodor, 28, 32, 40, 87,
129, 156, 162, 163, 168, 231, 238,
258, 300; SF recommends to WP, 4,
163; SF's high opinion of, 19, 30, 62,
64, 143; as nonbeliever, 20, 59, 62,
136; *Crime and Punishment*, 29, 162;
The Brothers Karamazov, 47, 64, 78,
163, 172, 225, 231, 269; *The Idiot*,
63, 172, 234, 240; *The Possessed*,
120; *Notes from the Underground*,
163; *The Eternal Husband*, 164
Down Slope, The (SF; unproduced
screenplay), 99, 100, 102, 107

Eliot, George (Mary Ann Evans), 131,
142; *Middlemarch*, 131, 142, 143,
144, 146, 172; SF's mixed opinion
of, 145; *Silas Marner*, 145, 146;
Romola, 145, 172
Eliot, T. S., 210, 274; SF quotes on difficulty of writing, 80, 137, 183, 199;
Four Quartets, 80
Ellmann, Richard: *James Joyce*, 192,
201, 208, 215

Faulkner, William, 32, 38, 55, 69, 108,
118, 131, 133, 136, 139, 140, 154,
168, 210, 214, 219, 224, 227, 244,
258, 263, 297; SF's high opinion
of, 4, 30, 171, 192; *Notes on a
Horsethief*, 41; *The Sound and the
Fury*, 75; SF critical of, 96–97, 172;
The Hamlet, 131; Blotner biography
of, 185, 191; praises *Shiloh*, 220;
Light in August, 234; *Absalom,
Absalom!*, 285n
Fitzgerald, F. Scott, 29, 86, 103, 131,
172; fall of, 27–28, 30, 94; *The
Crack-Up*, 28, 30; SF's admiration
for, 28, 30, 31; *Tender Is the Night*,
28, 30, 31, 131; *The Great Gatsby*, 30
Flaubert, Gustave, 139, 214, 244, 284;
SF recommends to WP, 7, 16, 35, 37;
The Sentimental Education, 37, 40;
Madame Bovary, 96
Follow Me Down (SF), 7, 12n, 20, 21,
24, 41, 165, 247; content and writing of, 12–14; publication of, 19, 38,
48; WP's reaction to, 23, 84; reception of, 23–24, 52, 58, 62, 237, 244,
246; French translation of, 219, 241,
244, 246
Foote, Gwyn Rainer (third wife of SF),
113, 122, 123, 125, 127, 130, 135,
157, 158, 160, 167, 170, 171, 173,
219, 237, 243, 267, 268, 273, 275,
276, 285, 287, 289, 293, 301, 303;
marriage to SF, 110; reads WP's
novels, 126, 151, 282, 293
Foote, Huger Lee, II (son of SF), 127,
135, 141, 143, 165, 169, 222, 261,
262, 265, 266n, 287, 292; birth of,
125n
Foote, Margaret Shelby (daughter of
SF), 28, 41, 42, 45, 46, 71, 87, 92,
93, 95, 102, 131; birth of, 7, 28n;
health of, 44, 56, 69, 142n, 144
Foote, Marguerite "Peggy" Dessommes
(second wife of SF), 15n, 17, 19, 28,
29, 45, 48, 54, 58, 70, 71, 92, 95n;
marriage to SF, 7, 42; divorce from
SF, 86n
Foote, Tess Lavery (first wife of SF),
5–6
Forrest, Nathan Bedford, 99, 107, 152,
184, 192, 195

"Freedom Kick, The" (SF), 119
Freud, Sigmund, 118, 146, 196–97; *The Interpretation of Dreams*, 280

Garrett, George, 193, 194, 202
Gibbon, Edward, 172, 194, 200, 201; *The Decline and Fall of the Roman Empire*, 188, 194
Gordon, Caroline, 7, 80n, 88, 95n, 136, 246, 299; *None Shall Look Back*, 103
Gramercy Winner, The (WP; unpublished), 47, 95
Grant, Ulysses S., 99, 107, 149, 158, 192; SF critical of, 119, 164; SF compares with Lee, 119, 176; at end of war, 169, 174, 176
Greene, Graham, 47, 58, 59, 60, 62; *The End of the Affair*, 59, 60, 64
Greene, John, 167n, 297n

Handel, George Frideric, 280
Hannah, Barry, 242, 243; *Airships*, 242
Hawthorne, Nathaniel, 136; *The House of the Seven Gables*, 30; *The Scarlet Letter*, 30
Heller, Joseph, 196, 206; *Something Happened*, 204
Hemingway, Ernest, 25, 41n, 65, 112, 118, 131, 136, 139, 144, 172, 194, 199, 200, 201, 210, 236; SF's respect for, 28, 30, 131; *The Sun Also Rises*, 71; *In Our Time*, 131
Homer, 107, 199, 208, 210; *The Illiad*, 52, 107–8, 112–13, 171, 187; *The Odyssey*, 53, 171
Hood, John Bell, 146, 195
Hopkins, Gerard Manley, 62, 210

Jackson, Thomas J. "Stonewall," 19–20, 122, 242
James, Henry, 78, 118, 139, 213; *The Wings of the Dove*, 29, 77; SF's high opinion of, 30, 40, 76–77, 137, 143, 192; SF recommends to WP, 76–77, 78, 80, 82
James, William, 153, 206
Joel, George, 46, 56, 65

Jordan County: A Landscape in Narrative (SF), 12n; content and writing of, 47–48, 95; publication of, 95, 97; reception of, 119, 234; French translation of, 174. *See also* "Child by Fever"; "Freedom Kick, The"
Joyce, James, 133, 136, 140, 248; *Ulysses*, 3–4, 206–7, 208, 239, 260n; SF's high opinion of, 7, 207, 211; WP's mixed feelings about, 208; *Finnegans Wake*, 225–26

Kafka, Franz, 32, 55, 158, 223, 266
Kauffmann, Stanley, 122n
Keats, John, 49, 87, 124, 243; SF's high opinion of, 49, 52, 104, 215, 216; SF holds up as example to WP, 84, 96; "Ode to a Nightingale," 84; SF compares with Lawrence, 86; *Endymion*, 87, 104; "To Autumn," 96, 104; "The Eve of St. Agnes," 104; "Hyperion," 104
Kierkegaard, Søren, 97, 126, 154, 219, 223, 251, 275; *Selected Writings*, 280
Kubrick, Stanley, 100n, 107

Lancelot (WP), 1, 222, 225, 234; WP dedicates to SF, 78n; early idea for, 153n, 175–76; writing of, 179, 221; SF's reaction to, 221, 227; reception of, 222, 225, 228, 232, 238; publication of, 227
Last Gentleman, The (WP), 203, 234, 240, 257, 258; writing of, 124n; SF's reaction to, 126, 203, 205, 225; publication of, 130
Lawrence, D. H., 55, 81, 86, 122, 196, 282; *The Plumed Serpent*, 44, 45, 55; "The Man Who Died," 44, 56; SF recommends to WP, 44–45; SF's high opinion of, 44–45, 55, 86, 145; *The Rainbow*, 45, 54, 56, 145; *Aaron's Rod*, 45, 56; *Kangaroo*, 45, 56; *The Lost Girl*, 45, 56; *Women in Love*, 45, 56; "The Fox," 55; "The Virgin and the Gypsy," 56; *The Later Writings*, 86
Lee, Robert E., 99, 107, 114, 149, 156,

Lee, Robert E., *(continued)*
    184, 197, 227; SF compares with
    Grant, 119, 176; SF on doggedness
    of, 158, 192; at end of war, 169,
    174, 176, 177
Lincoln, Abraham, 42, 107, 109, 149,
    151; SF writes about assassination
    of, 169, 173, 181, 184, 189
Lobdell, John Walker (grandson of
    WP), 147
Lobdell, Robert Byrne (son-in-law of
    WP), 132
Loomis, Robert, 169n, 190, 193
"Loss of the Creature, The" (WP), 152,
    161, 183
*Lost in the Cosmos: The Last Self-Help
    Book* (WP), 224n, 269–70, 277n,
    278
Love in a Dry Season (SF), 7, 57, 85,
    164–65, 261; content and writing
    of, 22–23, 26–27, 29, 30–31, 35,
    37–39, 43, 54–55; publication
    of, 45, 46, 52, 53; reception of,
    58, 70, 72, 237, 244, 246; French
    translation of, 174, 219, 241, 244,
    246. See also *Arms You Bear, The*
Love in the Ruins (WP), 225, 240, 282,
    294; early idea for, 129; efforts to
    arrive at title for, 142, 143, 144–45,
    146, 148; content and writing of,
    142, 146, 147–48; SF's reaction to,
    151; Gwyn Foote's reaction to, 151,
    282; reception of, 156, 157; French
    edition of, 174

McCarthy, Cormac: *Blood Meridian*,
    286; *Suttree*, 255
McCullers, Carson, 43
Mack, Gerstle, 182, 235, 265; *Paul
    Cézanne*, 235
Mahler, Gustav, 259
Mailer, Norman, 58, 137
Mann, Thomas, 157; SF recommends
    to WP, 4, 157–58, 239–40; *The
    Magic Mountain*, 63, 239–40;
    Joseph and His Brothers, 157–58
"Man on the Train, The: Three Exis-
    tential Modes" (WP), 110n, 111,
    120, 152, 161, 183, 205n

*Message in the Bottle, The: How Queer
    Man Is, How Queer Language Is,
    and What One Has to Do with the
    Other* (WP), 208, 211, 213, 214,
    268; preparation of, 152n, 183,
    201–2; SF's reaction to, 205–6, 213;
    reception of, 217n, 218, 224
Moores, David Lawson (grandson of
    WP), 233n, 235, 296, 299
Moores, Jack (grandson of WP), 296,
    299
Moores, John David (son-in-law of
    WP), 233n, 255, 296n, 299
Morris, Willie, 141, 173
Moviegoer, The (WP), 1, 8, 110n,
    117n, 122n, 261, 274; SF's reaction
    to, 117, 120–21, 122, 126, 203, 205
Mozart, Wolfgang Amadeus, 58, 259,
    262; SF's high opinion of, 30, 64, 70,
    96, 279, 285; SF recommends to WP,
    30, 137, 253, 261, 281–82, 285;
    Don Giovanni, 64, 103

Nixon, Richard M., 166, 177, 220

O'Connor, Flannery, 80n, 135–36,
    148, 153, 160, 205, 207, 211, 254;
    SF's mixed opinion of, 135–36,
    254–55; *Wise Blood*, 255

Pascal, Blaise, 20, 270
Peirce, Charles Sanders, 152–53,
    223–24, 303
Percy, Ann Boyd (daughter of WP),
    127, 132, 135, 140–41, 147, 165,
    168, 169, 174, 183, 200, 296n, 299;
    birth of, 98n; deafness of, 98n, 99n,
    105–7, 115n; marriage of, 233n;
    bookstore of, 258, 301n
Percy, Billups Phinizy "Phin" (brother
    of WP), 5, 18, 20, 46, 75, 222, 236,
    267; becomes friends with SF, 2, 3;
    marriage of, 98
Percy, Billy (son of Roy Percy), 138
Percy, Charles (ancestor of WP), 180
Percy, Jaye Dobbs (wife of Phin Percy),
    98
Percy, LeRoy (great-uncle of WP),
    179n, 181

Percy, LeRoy (great-grandfather of
   WP), 103n
Percy, LeRoy Pratt (father of WP), 2–3,
   18, 251
Percy, Leroy "Roy" Pratt, Jr. (brother
   of WP), 5, 6, 46, 49, 103, 115, 141,
   151, 171, 191, 222, 227, 251, 267,
   273; becomes friends with SF, 2, 3;
   wife and son of, 137–38
Percy, Mary Bernice "Bunt" Townsend
   (wife of WP), 11n, 41n, 45, 56, 58,
   71, 73, 98n, 110, 113, 114, 132,
   141, 156, 160, 163, 164, 165, 167,
   173, 183, 188, 211, 222, 232, 260,
   275, 289, 293, 295, 296, 301; marriage to WP, 6–7; SF urges WP to
   bring on visit, 97, 103, 127, 135, 166
Percy, Mary Pratt (daughter of WP),
   62, 71, 87, 127, 147, 156, 169; birth
   and adoption of, 11n; marriage of,
   132n
Percy, Martha Susan (mother of WP),
   2–3
Percy, Sarah Farish (wife of Roy Percy),
   49, 137, 171, 191
Percy, William Alexander "Will"
   (cousin and adoptive father of WP),
   2, 6, 7, 110, 121n, 126, 136, 141n,
   173, 179n, 222, 251, 298; Lanterns
   on the Levee, 2, 179, 182n, 183;
   character and career of, 2, 181, 265,
   267, 271; and Brinkwood, 11, 167,
   168n, 297; WP writes piece on, 181,
   182
Plato, 109, 118, 206
Poe, Edgar Allan, 30, 246; The Narrative of Arthur Gordon Pym, 30
Proust, Marcel, 2, 20, 21, 77, 107,
   136, 172, 174, 198, 199, 273; SF
   recommends to WP, 4, 7, 19, 62,
   104, 149–50, 212, 277, 282–84;
   WP's dislike of, 4, 81, 104, 114, 159,
   212, 282; SF's high opinion of, 19,
   30, 38, 40, 62, 81, 96, 143, 149–50,
   189, 193, 207, 238, 244, 264,
   282–84; Swann's Way, 62, 104–5;
   SF re-reads, 140, 193, 282–83;
   Remembrance of Things Past, 239,
   282

Ransom, John Crowe, 216, 264
Rosen, Robert, 203, 216, 222, 234,
   236, 237, 245, 250
Roth, Philip, 140, 259; Portnoy's Com-
   plaint, 140
Rubin, Louis, 192, 193, 194, 200, 217,
   231, 256, 261; The Literary South,
   256; "The Boll Weevil, the Iron
   Horse, and the End of the Line:
   Thoughts on the South," 256–57

Second Coming, The (WP), 223n, 266;
   writing of, 246, 251, 257, 258, 260
September September (SF), 230–31,
   232; early idea for, 188, 216; content
   and writing of, 219, 221, 222, 226,
   227, 228; publication of, 221n; high
   hopes for sales of, 222, 236, 238,
   245; WP's reaction to, 228–30;
   reception of, 234, 237, 241, 243,
   248
Shakespeare, William, 21, 25n, 35, 38,
   138, 180; Measure for Measure, 29;
   SF invokes name of, 52, 60, 69, 149,
   172; SF's high opinion of, 70, 96,
   210, 216, 264, 267
Shelley, Percy Bysshe, 215–16, 217, 218
Sherman, William Tecumseh, 139, 166,
   188, 195
Shiloh (SF), 7, 12, 24, 57, 59, 103,
   114; publication of, 15, 43, 45, 52,
   56, 62–63, 65, 70, 72, 75, 77; writing of, 43, 45, 46, 48–49; SF dedicates to WP, 46, 78; high hopes for
   reception and sales of, 52, 58, 65,
   68, 75, 85–86; WP's reaction to, 70,
   80, 84; reception of, 89, 90, 92, 219,
   226; Faulkner's opinion of, 220
Sibelius, Jean, 277–78
"Southern Comfort: Thoughts on
   Southern Literature, Southern Politics, and the American Experience"
   (WP), 237n
Spalding, Phinizy (cousin of WP), 237n
Stendahl (Marie-Henri Beyle), 55, 72
"Stoicism in the South" (WP), 108n
Stuart, Jeb, 175, 192
Styron, William, 120, 173, 231, 255,
   258–59

Symbol and Existence (WP; unpublished), 95n
"Symbol as Hermeneutic to Existentialism" (WP), 213
"Symbol as Need" (WP), 95n, 161, 197

Tate, Allen, 7, 80, 88, 246; "Ode to the Confederate Dead," 103
Thanatos Syndrome, The (WP), 282n, 292–94
"Theory of Language, A" (WP), 179, 184
Thomas Aquinas, Saint, 215; *Summa Theologica*, 213, 280
Tolstoy, Leo, 31, 72, 168, 234, 289, 300; *The Cossacks*, 29; SF critical of, 55, 104; WP's high opinion of, 55, 156, 254; *Anna Karenina*, 104, 255; *War and Peace*, 167, 269; "The Death of Ivan Ilyich," 254, 255
Toole, John Kennedy, 268, 271
Tournament (SF), 4, 7, 23, 24, 26, 57, 84–85, 267, 296; writing of, 15n, 17; reception of, 18, 52
"Toward a Triadic Theory of Meaning" (WP), 158, 161
Twain, Mark, 30, 112, 139, 140, 172, 192

Two Gates to the City (SF; unpublished), 259; intended as SF's big novel, 43, 45, 54, 57, 219, 226, 231, 244, 248; plan of, 45, 53, 54, 57; SF's initial optimism regarding, 54, 57, 60, 65, 68, 79; content and writing of, 63, 64, 65, 69, 71–72, 75, 78–79; SF abandons, 98n; SF intends to resume work on, 219, 226, 231, 237, 238, 241, 243, 244, 251, 253, 256; SF acknowledges being blocked on, 268; WP encourages SF to get started on, 261, 268, 271, 274

Vauthier, Simone, 159, 232, 233, 267
Vermeer, Jan, 96, 235, 237
Vonnegut, Kurt, 258–59

Welty, Eudora, 174, 208, 218, 231; *The Optimist's Daughter*, 208
Willingham, Calder, 64, 68, 69, 203, 204; *Geraldine Bradshaw*, 64
Wolfe, Thomas, 32, 35, 196, 247; *Of Time and the River*, 63

Yeats, William Butler, 158, 221, 264–65